American Slavery: The Question of Resistance

A Wadsworth Series:
Explorations in the Black Experience

General Editors

John H. Bracey, Jr., Northern Illinois University
August Meier, Kent State University
Elliott Rudwick, Kent State University

American Slavery: The Question of Resistance
Free Blacks in America, 1800–1860
Blacks in the Abolitionist Movement
The Rise of the Ghetto
Black Matriarchy: Myth or Reality?
Black Workers and Organized Labor
The Black Sociologists: The First Half Century
Conflict and Competition: Studies in the Recent Black Protest
Movement

The anthologies in this series present significant scholarly work on particular aspects of the black experience in the United States. The volumes are of two types. Some have a "problems" orientation, presenting varying and conflicting interpretations of a controversial subject. Others are purely "thematic," simply presenting representative examples of the best scholarship on a topic. Together they provide guidelines into significant areas of research and writing in the field of Afro-American studies. The complete contents of all the books in the series are listed at the end of this volume.

American Slavery: The Question of Resistance

Edited by

John H. Bracey, Jr.
Northern Illinois University

August Meier
Kent State University

Elliott Rudwick
Kent State University

Wadsworth Publishing
Company, Inc.
Belmont, California

Acknowledgments

The authors wish to express their appreciation to Mrs. Barbara Hostetler, Mrs. Patricia Kufta, and Miss Eileen Petric at Kent State University for helping in the preparation of this manuscript, and to Miss Linda Burroughs and Mrs. Helen Peoples of the Kent State University Library. They are especially indebted to James G. Coke, former Director of the Kent State University Center for Urban Regionalism.

July 1970   *JHB*
AM
ER

L. C. Cat. Card No.: 79–154810
ISBN–0–534–00017–7
Printed in the United States of America

1 2 3 4 5 6 7 8 9 10—75 74 73 72 71

To the memory of
two fallen warriors:
Fred Hampton and Mark Clark

JHB

Contents

Introduction

One of the more controversial of the many historical problems raised by the recent upsurge of interest in Afro-American history or black studies is the nature of chattel slavery in the United States. Partisans have taken positions on all sides in attempts to show that slavery was terroristic or paternalistic; that slavery in the United States was more terroristic or paternalistic than slavery in other parts of the New World; that blacks were submissive or resisted actively; that blacks in the United States were more or less submissive than others in the New World; that submissiveness was or was not internalized in the personalities of the individual slaves.

This volume focuses on the specific problem of the nature and extent of the resistance of blacks to slavery in the United States. The first section presents the positions of the major schools of thought on the subject of black resistance. The excerpts from the early essay by Ulrich B. Phillips, the leading historian of slavery from the slaveholders' point of view, contain his well-known contentions that slavery was a paternalistic institution necessary for the education and civilization of racially inferior barbaric Africans. Slavery, in Phillips' eyes, was as much a system of racial control as it was a system of economic exploitation. In Phillips' words, slavery was a "paternalistic despotism," a despotism in some cases harsh and oppressive, but in the majority of the cases benevolent; a despotism resented and resisted by some, but borne with light-heartedness, submissiveness, and affection by most of the blacks. Phillips' view dominated historical writing on the subject until World War II.[1]

Nevertheless, the views of Phillips and his school did not go unchallenged. From the very beginning, black scholars such as Carter G. Woodson, W. E. B. Du Bois, C. L. R. James, and Benjamin Brawley repudiated this view of slavery, but they were ignored by the overwhelming majority of white historians. In the 1930s two white historians, Herbert Aptheker and Harvey Wish, did the first detailed work on the history of slave resistance in the United States. In 1937 appeared their pioneering articles: Herbert Aptheker's "American Negro Slave Revolts" in *Science & Society* and Harvey Wish's "American Slave Insurrections Before 1861" in the *Journal of Negro History*, reprinted here. Wish, confronting Phillips without naming him, contends that "the romantic portrayal of ante-bellum society on the southern plantation, which depicts the rollicking black against a kindly patriarchal background, has tended to obscure the large element of slave unrest which occasionally shook the whole fabric of the planter's kingdom." Documenting his contentions with a lengthy listing of slave ship mutinies, colonial slave revolts and conspiracies, and the ante-bellum revolts of such figures as Gabriel Prosser, Denmark Vesey, and Nat Turner, Wish concludes:

No doubt many Negroes made the required adjustments to slavery, but the romantic picture of careless abandon and contentment fails to be convincing. The struggle of the Negro for his liberty, beginning with those dark days on the slave ship, was far from sporadic in nature, but an ever-recurrent battle waged everywhere with desperate courage against the bonds of his master.

Two years later Joseph C. Carroll published *Slave Insurrections in the United States, 1800–1860.* In 1943, Herbert Aptheker published *American Negro Slave Revolts,* the most comprehensive work on the subject yet produced.

In 1942, the *Journal of Negro History* published a lengthy article rebutting Phillips from a different point of view. This was Raymond and Alice Bauer's "Day to Day Resistance to Slavery." The Bauers contend that "our investigation has made it apparent that the Negroes not only were very discontented, but that they developed effective protest techniques in the form of indirect retaliation for their enslavement." The article goes on to describe six basic forms of day to day resistance: work slowdown; destruction of property, including livestock; malingering; feigning illness and pregnancy; self-injury; suicide and infanticide. The Bauers conclude then that slaves were not happy and content, but "frequently rebellious" and "almost always sullen," and that any inefficiencies exhibited by slaves were due to conscious intent rather than to racial inferiority.

In 1956 Kenneth Stampp's *The Peculiar Institution* explicitly challenged Phillips' conclusions concerning slave contentment and racial inferiority. The section reprinted here from the chapter, "A Troublesome Property," synthesizes the scholarship on revolts and resistance, and presents a view of slavery quite contrary to that of Phillips.

However, despite the varying conclusions, all of Phillips' critics challenged him within the framework which he created. Where Phillips alleged docility, racial inferiority, and paternalism, the critics responded with unrest and revolt, racial equality, and terrorism.

Section Two presents the problem at a different level of complexity, or at least in different terms. Using modern concepts of social psychology and a "concentration camp" analogy, Stanley Elkins' *Slavery: A Problem in American Institutional and Intellectual Life* contended in 1959 that Phillips was essentially correct concerning the lack of slave resistance. Where Phillips attributed this to the innate racial traits of blacks and to the benevolent nature of the system, Elkins contended that the slaves' lack of resistance was due to the extremely oppressive nature of the system, which compelled the internalization of submissive traits on the part of the slaves. Thus Elkins saw the childlike, dependent Sambo as the dominant personality type among black slaves. The master had absolute power, and "absolute power for him meant absolute dependency for the slave—the dependency not of the developing child but of the perpetual child."

Elkins' view was contested by a number of scholars but it was provocative enough to wield tremendous influence among other students of slavery. From the many critiques of Elkins, the two in this volume were selected for their specific focus on the different aspects of Elkins' argument. Earl Thorpe systematically examines the concentration camp analogy and contends that the substantial differences between concentration camps and slave plantations render the analogy useless as an analytical tool. Eugene Genovese's review article criticizes Elkins for his failure to see that Sambo was not a unique American product, but existed in all slave societies in the New World, and for pressing his arguments so far as to be unable to explain the large variety of responses which blacks made to chattel slavery.

Section Three consists of opposing interpretations not only of the extent but even of the existence of the Denmark Vesey plot of 1822. Herbert Aptheker in *American Negro Slave Revolts* presents the standard account. Richard C. Wade, using some additional sources, maintains that there is no conclusive proof that a conspiracy to revolt existed, and that imaginations tempered by fear and insecurity were at work among both blacks and whites. But Robert Starobin, using the same evidence as Wade, argues that the conspiracy did indeed exist. Starobin, it should be noted, makes several additional points; among other things he presents material supporting the thesis of the anthropologist Melville J. Herskovits about the importance of African survivals as a cause of several insurrections in the Americas.[2]

The final section contains three approaches to the problem of black resistance that break with both the Phillips-Stampp debate and the Elkins hypothesis. Gerry Mullin, in a detailed analysis of Gabriel's Revolt of 1800, examines the class base and ideologies of the rebellion's leaders and concludes that they came from a highly assimilated slave elite, who faced a declining status in plantation society as it was constituted at the turn of the century. His conclusions thus stand in contrast to the evidence presented in Starobin's article on the Vesey conspiracy, which suggests that rebel leaders were drawn from a broad base of slaves and that identification with Africa and African cultural survivals played an important role. Both men, however, agree in stressing that the leaders possessed a coherent revolutionary ideology.

George M. Fredrickson and Christopher Lasch, in a "think piece," attempt to make several conceptual and analytical distinctions that will clarify some of the earlier theoretical problems and open up new possibilities for the study of slavery as a social system. Their distinctions between "cruelty" and "coercion" and between "resistance" and "noncooperation" and their use of sociological studies of total institutions to explain various "personal strategies of accommodation" are examples.

The concluding selection, from Orlando Patterson's *The Sociology of Slavery,* 1967, in relating the causes of Jamaican slave revolts, makes both implicit and explicit comparisons with slavery in the United States. Patterson's views are that slavery in the United States was less harsh than in the West Indies and Brazil, and that overt slave resistance in the United States was both less frequent and of smaller dimension. We seem to be back to Phillips' conclusions again, but at a more sophisticated level of historical theory and method. Fredrickson and Lasch see slavery as paternalistic, with blacks, not racially inferior, making a variety of personal and group responses based on their assessment of the power realities. Patterson sees United States slavery as less harsh than other New World slavery, and he sees slaves in the United States unable to strike out effectively at the system for a number of reasons.

The pieces in this volume raise most of the basic questions and offer some answers. Obviously, the last words on black resistance to slavery in the United States have yet to be written. Moreover, space limitations have prevented our exploring here all the ramifications of the subject as it is now understood. For additional new perspectives on the slave revolts the interested student should consult the suggestions for further reading at the end of the volume.

Notes

---

[1] Works by students of Phillips which reflect his viewpoint include H. A. Trexler, *Slavery in Missouri, 1804–1865* (1914); R. H. Taylor, *Slaveholding in North Carolina* (1926); R. B. Flanders, *Plantation Slavery in Georgia* (1933); C. S. Sydnor, *Slavery in Mississippi* (1933); J. W. Coleman, *Slavery Times in Kentucky* (1940).

[2] See Melville J. Herskovits, *The Myth of the Negro Past* (New York: 1944), Chapter 4.

The Classic Debate: Accommodation vs. Resistance

1

Racial Problems, Adjustments and Disturbances

Ulrich B. Phillips

The Negroes

The negro population on the whole was willing, first and last, to do farm labor and to submit to control. This fact was largely responsible for the very important part which the negroes played in the life of the South. In all the regions successively made available for staple production there were landholders, actual or prospective, anxious to secure labor. The plantation system was a well-known device already at hand for the profitable employment of crude labor, and negroes, whether African or American born, were constantly available in large numbers and furnished very often the only labor supply to be had. Under these conditions, almost inevitably, negro labor was imported from abroad and transported within the South to all districts where there was prospect of large profits from its employment. These negroes when brought in from Africa were heathen savages accustomed only to precarious tribal existence in the jungles. To be fitted for life in civilized, Christian, industrial society, they had to be drilled, educated in a measure, and controlled. Had they possessed the disposition of the Indians this would have been impossible. Their pliability saved them here, gave them homes, and enabled them to increase and cover great fertile tracts of the earth and share in its plenty.

Origin of the American Slavery System

The status of the first cargoes of negroes imported into English America was indefinite, and for years remained so. They were understood to be servants under

From Ulrich Phillips, "Racial Problems, Adjustments and Disturbances," in *The South in the Building of the Nation* (Richmond: Southern Publication Society, 13 vols., 1909–1913), Vol. VI. Reprinted in Ulrich B. Phillips, *The Slave Economy of the Old South: Selected Essays in Economic and Social History,* ed. Eugene D. Genovese (Baton Rouge: Louisiana State University Press, 1968), pp. 26–34, 50–60.

control of private masters; but a definite and universal relationship was only evolved by gradual process. One item after another was added to the regulations; that the negroes should be servants for life, and not for a term of years; that the basis of their status should be race and not religion; that the legal device for securing control to the master should be a fiction of the ownership of the slave's person instead of a fiction of a contract; that children should inherit the status of their mothers and become the property of their mothers' owners; that the chattel thus created by the fiction of the law should be transferable by sale, bequest or inheritance like other chattels; that slaveowners if they so desired might emancipate their slaves under regulations framed for safeguarding the public welfare; that a special system of police and judicature should be applied to the slave and other negro population; that mulattoes, quadroons or other persons of mixed blood within stated degrees should be deemed negroes in the eyes of the law and held to slavery as if full-blooded Africans, and so on. Many of these provisions originated in the custom of the master class and were later made authoritative by legislation. Regulation of some sort for the negroes was imperative, and according to the general American practice regard was given in many cases to the needs of the immediate present rather than to those of the distant future. A system once developed in a commonwealth and appearing to work well was easily borrowed by neighboring colonies or states. In fact the legislation of Virginia was copied with more or less modification by all the governments from Delaware to Mississippi and Arkansas.

Character of Legislative Regulations

Life was rough in most parts of the South, except perhaps for the planters' womenfolk and the townspeople. The general task at hand was the conquest of a wilderness, largely by the use of involuntary labor. The population was sparse, and while a rude plenty prevailed and there was little suffering among the negroes, there was need for fairly stringent regulation to secure control by the whites. In addition, where the plantations were closely grouped in dense black belts, there was need of offsetting the smallness of the proportion of whites by keeping the blacks in a more complete subjection. There was steady occasion for guarding against the absconding of slaves into the swamps or to the Indian tribes or to the free states, and there were occasional rumors of plots for insurrection. The consideration of these things led to the enactment of laws for curfew, patrol, and fugitive rendition, and of laws for restricting assemblage, for restricting the travel of slaves except in the company of whites, and for prohibiting the teaching of slaves to read. Abundant laws for most or all of these purposes were enacted by each of the slaveholding colonies and states. And a new restriction upon the negroes, whether slave or free, would be promptly enacted in case a new possible instance were discovered where an added disability upon them would tend to safeguard the established order. It became a fixed custom in most states to legislate in prevention of possible emergencies, with a consciousness that if the law should prove inconvenient to the community it would be allowed to lie unenforced until the occurrence of the contemplated emergency should call it into life. In fact most provisions of the repressive legislation were dead letters at all times. The actual regime was one of government not by laws but by men. In fact each slave was under a paternalistic despotism, a despotism in the majority of cases benevolent but in some cases harsh and oppressive, a despotism resented and resisted by some upon whom it was imposed but borne with light-heartedness, submission, and affection by a huge number of the blacks.

Actual Adjustments Not Shaped by the Law but by Private Expediency

There was legislation also safeguarding the slaves against oppression and injury, but this likewise played little part in actual affairs. It was the master's interest, comfort, principles, and desire for good repute which mainly shaped the relations of master and slave. The principal other factor in the matter was the slave's own character and attitude. If extremely submissive he might be oppressed; if rebellious he might be flogged or shackled; if an incorrigible runaway, or a chronic troublemaker, or hopelessly indolent or stupid he might be sold to a trader; if disposed to render reasonable service for reasonable sustenance he was likely to be treated with consideration; if faithful and affectionate, as very many were, he was fairly sure to receive indulgence even to the point where it hurt the master's income; and if sick, crippled or superannuated, he would be given medical treatment and support for the rest of his life. Although the laws provided that slaves must not be taught to read, many of them were so taught by their masters or mistresses. Although the laws required that slaves should be kept directly under the control of the masters or their agents, very many of them were hired to themselves and perhaps did not put in an appearance from week's end to week's end, unless to pay their hire out of their earnings. Although there was no legal sanction for marriages among the slaves, weddings were usually celebrated by religious exercises and the rights of husbands and wives were secured to them at least as effectively as the negroes usually desired. The fundamental law of slavery provided that a slave could not own property; but under any master of average consideration any slave disposed to be thrifty could lay up what he acquired by gift or earnings to enjoy full security in its possession; and some of them even made contracts with their masters to work overtime and buy their freedom on the installment plan. In a word, the laws maintaining slavery in fact simply gave to the master a title to the control of his servants' labor and a claim upon his neighbors to aid in returning the servant to his service in case of an attempted flight. The actual adjustments between master and slave were very largely informal, extra-legal, and varied widely. The master's interest, however, and generally his inclination, lay in cultivating the good will and affection as well as in preserving the good health of his slave; for even a slave could be counted upon to do better work from loyalty and in the hope of rewards than from the fear of punishment. The great mass of plantation records, private correspondence, pamphlets, and newspapers preserved in the South, which the historians have failed to use, tend to show strongly that the average master realized that the range of possible relationships was very wide in the slavery system and that it was generally to the master's interest to be indulgent though firm, benevolent though autocratic. There were some severe, grasping, and harsh masters, however, and many of the slaves had so little of the docility and inertia of the typical Guinea negro for whose adjustment the system of slavery was framed, that they were a misfit in the system and were obviously and unjustly oppressed under it.

A few items written by men involved in the problem who had no thought that their letters, diaries or advertisements would ever be used for a historical purpose, will illustrate the regime more vividly than pages of description. The first is from a letter of Ralph Izard of South Carolina, then sojourning in New York City, to his neighbor, Peter Manigault, in Charleston, April 23, 1769:

Schermerhorn [a ship captain] will deliver my boy Andrew to you; he has run away, stolen, and given me an infinite deal of trouble. I must beg the favor of you to send him to Mr. Postell [Izard's overseer], as I find the discipline of a rice plantation is absolutely necessary for his welfare; if he was to stay long in this country he would certainly be hanged. (Ms.)

The next is a series of extracts from letters written in 1860, by William Capers, overseer of a rice plantation on Savannah River, to his employer, Charles Manigault, at Charleston. They show that a capable "driver" (i.e., foreman of a plantation gang) might fall into drunkenness and worthlessness when subjected to bad management, but might well be redeemed again under proper encouragement and control:

1. From a letter of August 5:

If he [John] is the man that I had as driver when at Mr. Pringle's, buy him by all means. There is but few negroes more competent than he is, and [he] was not a drunkard when under my management. . . . In speaking with John he does not answer like a smart negro, but [he] is quite so. You had better say to him who is to manage him on Savannah.

2. From a letter of August 11:

John arrived safe, and handed me yours of 9th inst. I congratulate you on the purchase of said negro. He says he is quite satisfied to be here and will do as he has always done during the time I have managed him. No drink will be offered him. All on my part will be done to bring John all right.

3. From a letter of October 15:

I have found John as good a driver as when I left him on Santee. Bad management was the cause of his being sold. [I] am glad you have been the fortunate man to get him. (MSS.)

The consideration often shown in the selling of slaves is illustrated in the following advertisement from the Augusta, Georgia, *Chronicle,* Sept. 2, 1809:

For sale, a likely Negro Fellow, sober and honest: he is a tolerable carpenter, a good cooper, and can make negro shoes, and in many respects is very useful on a plantation; he is used to the upper country, and does not like to live in the lower country, for which reason only he is to be sold.

The following letter of a citizen to the editor, printed in the Washington, Georgia, *News,* May 1, 1824, indicates the slackness of slave regulation. The burden of the letter is a complaint at the disorder prevailing in the village on the Sabbath:

I see crowds of negroes around the tippling houses. . . . They slip in and out, and some of them are seen drunk and rolling about the streets, oaths sounding in our own and our children's ears . . . . [Furthermore] I often and almost every Sabbath see load after load of wood, hay, fodder and other articles for market hauled through the streets in waggons, carts, etc., and stop in the square until the owner can go and find a purchaser. . . . Slaves have by these means every encouragement to become rogues.

The indulgence of favorite slaves in the matter of clothing may be gathered from the following advertisement by Mr. J. W. Gibbs of Charleston, offering rewards for two runaways, from the *South Carolina Gazette,* Dec. 10, 1784:

Fifty Dollars Reward. Ran away from the subscriber on Sunday morning, a short yellow wench named Sall, well known in this city; had on a blue woolen jacket and petticoat. Also ran away last night a Negro Fellow named Will, husband of the above wench, who took with him all the remainder of her cloathes, and several suits of his own; among the latter were a pair of black velveret breeches and waistcoat, pair of white dimity corded breeches, and two or three silk waistcoats, two or three pairs of linen overalls, a cinnamon-coloured broadcloth coat with a double row of white plated buttons on the breast, a Saxon green superfine broadcloth coat, almost as good as new, with white plated buttons, a drab coloured great coat with plated buttons, a small, round hat with a black band and plated buckle, with a number of other cloaths which cannot be remembered; also two new and four old blankets. These Negroes were absent once before for three years, a great part of which time they were in the employment of a Mr. Stirk, in Georgia, from whence they were brought back about a twelvemonth ago in rags. During their stay there they acquired a great number of acquaintances with Negroes run away from this State, many of whom are now in this City, and it is supposed are harbourers of them.

An ability to read and write increased the value of a slave, as is indicated by the following advertisement by A. Fleym in the Charleston *Morning Post* for March 6, 1787:

Negroes for Sale, viz. — A mulatto boy, sober, honest and industrious, can take care of horses, drive a coach, and is a good boatman, fisherman and house servant, 22 years old, and can read and write very well. . . .

The hardships suffered by those who refused to submit appear from this advertisement in the *Louisiana Gazette* (New Orleans), March 11, 1817:

A Negro man who has been two years in jail will be sold at the courthouse in the town of Baton Rouge, on the 4th day of April next, for jail fees. He is about sixty years of age, 5 feet 5 or 6 inches high, and says his name is Baptiste.

Or from this notice published in the *Virginia Gazette*, April 7, 1774, by Nathaniel Burwell, of King William County:

Run away in July last, Matt, a tall, slim Negro Man, by trade a carpenter, and about forty years old; he walks badly, having been Frost-bit in Prison some years ago, by which he lost one of his great Toes, and the Print of the Irons he then had on may be seen plainly on his legs. Whoever delivers him to me shall receive 3l. reward if taken within twenty miles of my House, and 5l. if at a greater Distance.

Likewise from the following by Henry Randolph, in the *Virginia Gazette*, Dec. 4, 1767:

Run away from the subscriber a Mulatto fellow named Aaron, about 5 feet 10 inches high, about 19 years old, and marked on each cheek I. R. . . .

The occasional severity of slave punishments is indicated by an extract from the diary of Henry Ravenal, of St. John Parish, South Carolina, April 9, 1818:

Set on a jury of inquest over the body of a negro woman named Sue, the property of Dr. Jordan. Verdict, came to her death by excessive punishment of his sister Rebecca Jordan.

Finally, the following letter from Mrs. S. R. Cobb, near Athens, Georgia, Jan. 9, 1843, to her daughter-in-law, Mrs. Howell Cobb, at Athens, illustrates the consideration often shown by the master class. The Matilda who is mentioned in it was a free negro, and Betty's relatives were of course slaves like herself:

Tell Howell I cannot agree for Betty to be hired to Matilda; her character [*i.e.*, Matilda's] is too bad. I know her of old, she is a drunkard, and is said to be bad in every respect. I should object to her being hired to any colored person no matter what their character was, and if she cannot get into a respectable family I had rather she came home and if she can't work out put her to spinning and weaving. Her relatives here beg she may not be hired to Matilda. She would not be worth a cent at the end of the year. (Ms.)

Problems of the Masters

The general tendency, as shown by the mass of plantation records and other material extant in the South, as well as by tradition and by many indications to be gathered even from the laws themselves, was for custom to be very much more kindly than the law. The legislators could deal with the theoretical situation as severely as they pleased, and suffer no personal discomfort; but the slaveholders in private life, day after day, year after year, in good times and in bad, in serenity or in stress had to make shift to get along with their slaves. An unfruitful servant could not be discharged. Reprimands were likely to be useless or worse than useless. Some slaves were beaten, some were cajoled, but with most of course some middle ground of treatment was followed. On the whole a great deal of slack-handed service was put up with. A West Indian planter wrote in his diary (Lewis, M. J., *Journal of a West India Proprietor,* under date of April 22, 1817):

Cubina is now twenty-five, and has all his life been employed about the stable; he goes out with my carriage twice every day; yet he has never been able to succeed in putting on the harness properly. Before we get to one of the plantation gates we are certain of being obliged to stop and put something or other to rights. . . . The girl, whose business it is to open the house each morning, has in vain been desired to unclose all the jalousies; she never fails to leave three or four closed, and when scolded for doing so, she takes care to open those three the next morning, and leaves three shut on the opposite side. Indeed the attempt to make them correct a fault is quite fruitless.

Mr. R. L. Dabney, of Virginia, wrote in familiar correspondence in 1840: "It seems to me there could be no greater curse inflicted on us than to be compelled to manage a parcel of negroes." Another Virginia planter said to F. L. Olmsted "that his negroes never worked so hard as to tire themselves — always were lively and ready to go off on a frolic at night. He did not think they ever did half a fair day's work. They could not be made to work hard; they never would lay out their strength freely, and it was impossible to make them do it." Some masters succeeded better than this in making their slaves work, usually because the masters themselves were high-grade captains of industry. . . .

Maladjustments under the Slavery Regime

The system of slavery was by no means perfect as a method of racial adjustment, nor was its working constantly smooth. There were always many slaves absconding from their masters, a few others being stolen by white thieves, and an indeterminate number more or less definitely plotting insurrection. At one extreme there were negroes too doggedly barbaric to submit to industrial discipline, and at the other there was a class, increasingly great as decades passed, of high-grade, intelligent, self-reliant negroes, mulattoes, and quadroons who were restless necessarily under the restraints of the system. With all its variety and its considerable elasticity the system of slavery was too rigid to be tolerable to all the extremely diverse people who were grouped in the so-called negro race.

Runaways and Desperadoes

A very conspicuous feature of any average newspaper of the slave-holding districts was the numerous advertisements offering rewards for the return of runaway slaves. Some of these runaways merely took to the woods for a vacation and returned to their work of their own accord at the end of the outing. The return of these was sometimes hastened by the noise of bloodhounds in the neighborhood. Others endeavored to establish themselves as free persons of color, or in the case of octoroons to pass as white persons, and perhaps to work their way in some fashion to the northward of Mason and Dixon's Line. Others became desperadoes and held localities in terror until raiding parties were sent against them. The following newspaper items are illustrative. The first which is taken from the *Louisiana Courier,* June 15, 1830, describes a case where provision in advance was made against the expenses of a long journey:

FIFTY DOLLARS REWARD will be paid for the apprehension of the negress slave named ANNY, aged about fifteen years, having a mark of a scald or burn on each shoulder. Said slave ran away from the residence of the subscriber, in the suburb Marigny on the night of the 11th inst., and took with her $300. in notes of the different Banks of this city. The above reward will be given for the apprehension of the said slave, and return the money; or $10. for taking up the Slave, should the money not be found. All persons are warned, under the penalties prescribed by law, for harbouring said slave.   ANTONIO ACOSTA.

Sometimes a whole group of negroes on a plantation would stampede for the woods or for the North together. A frequent cause in such cases was the maladroitness or the oppressiveness of the master or overseer. Sometimes a runaway would grow into a desperado and perhaps be declared an outlaw by the government with a price upon his head. One of these was mentioned, for example, in a news item from Raleigh, North Carolina, printed in the *Louisiana Gazette,* Feb. 24, 1819:

The notorious outlying negro Billy James, who has been so long depredating on the property of this vicinity, and for the apprehension of whom the Governor offers a reward of one hundred dollars, was on the plantation of Col. Wm. Hinton a few nights ago. The Col., being informed of it, hoped to surprise him, but hearing no doubt, from some of the negroes of the plantation, what was going on, he escaped.

Sometimes a fugitive when pursued stood at bay, and in a terrific fight sold his life most dearly. The following account is from the New Orleans *Daily Delta,* April 11, 1849:

It is our painful task, says the Houston (Miss.) Republican of the 31st. ult., to record one of the most shocking murders that has ever occurred within the bounds of our country, which happened in the prairie, near the quiet little village of Pikeville. It appears that Mr. J. Heggerson attempted to correct a negro man in his employ, who resisted, drew a knife and stabbed him (Mr. H.) in several places. Mr. J. C. Hobbs (a Tennesseean) ran to his assistance. Mr. Hobbs stooped to pick up a stick to strike the negro, and while in that position the negro rushed upon him, and with a dirk, inflicted a wound in his left breast, which caused his immediate death. The negro then fled to the woods, but was pursued with dogs, and soon overtaken. He had stopped in a swamp to fight the dogs, when the party who were pursuing came up and commanded him to give up, which he refused to do. He then made several efforts to stab them. Mr. Robertson, one of the party, gave him several blows on the head with a rifle gun; but this, instead of subduing, only increased his desperate revenge. Mr. R. then discharged his gun at the negro, and missing him, the ball struck Mr. Boon in the face, and felled him to the ground. The negro seeing Mr. Boon prostrated, attempted to rush up and stab him, but was prevented by the timely interference of some one of the party. He was then shot three times with a revolving pistol and once with a rifle, and after having his throat cut, he still kept the knife firmly grasped in his hand, and tried to cut their legs when they approached to put an end to his life. Mr. Boon is said to be seriously wounded. Mr. Heggerson's wounds are slight.

Sometimes groups of runaways would gather in some natural fastness and live for years in freedom. Thousands in the West Indies, particularly in Jamaica, flocked to the mountain defiles and with rude political and military organization held sway over wide areas. The colonial governments, despairing of any subjugation, would at times negotiate a *modus vivendi* with these maroons. On the continent, the Seminole Indians gave refuge to hundreds of runaway negroes, and swamp fastnesses in the Great Dismal or the Okefenokee or on the Savannah River or the Chattahoochee, the Mobile or the Mississippi gave havens where the fugitives could rally on their own initiative. An item from the Charleston *Observer*, July 21, 1827, relates an incident at such a rendezvous:

A nest of runaway negroes were lately discovered in the fork of the Alabama and Tombeckbee rivers, and broken up, after a smart skirmish by a party from Mobile county. Three of the negroes were killed, several taken and a few escaped. They had two cabins and were about to build a fort. Some of them had been runaway for years, and had committed many depredations on the neighboring plantations.

Outrages and Lynch Law

The doings of negro desperadoes are illustrated from the following account of a lynch law execution published in the Gallatin, Mississippi, *Signal,* Feb. 27, 1843, and reprinted in the *Louisiana Courier,* New Orleans, March 1:

NEGRO OUTRAGES. In the last number of our paper, we gave an imperfect account of the summary punishment of two negro men, belonging to a Mr. Burnly, of this county, who were hung according to a statute of Judge Lynch, in such cases made and provided. We have since learned the particulars of the circumstances which led to their execution; and the more we reflect upon them, the more we are inclined to justify almost any step calculated to punish them severely for such a revolting outrage as they themselves acknowledged was committed by them. It appears that they went to the house of Mr. N. during his absence, and ordered his wife to get them some liquor. On her refusing to do so, they cursed her in a most blasphemous manner and threatened her with death if she did not obey. After having got the liquor, they called for some hot coffee and cold victuals, which she told them they should have if they would not harm her and her children, which they promised to do. But after this, they forcibly took from her arms the infant babe and rudely throwing it upon the floor, they threw her down, and while one of them accomplished the fiendish design of a ravisher, the other pointing the muzzle of a loaded gun to her head, said he would blow out her brains if she resisted or made any noise.

They afterwards took quilts and blankets from the beds, broke open the trunks and drawers, and taking their contents, which consisted of forty dollars in specie and a quantity of clothing all of which they carefully put in the quilts and blankets, they even took the shoes from the feet of Mrs. N. and placing the whole of the plunder on the back of a horse which they had brought with them for the purpose, they made off.

We obtained these particulars from a gentleman of the highest respectability. He questioned the negroes on the subject, a few hours previous to their execution, and also interrogated Mrs. N. in a similar manner, and her answers agreed in every essential particular with the statement made by the negroes. What aggravates this affair is the fact that the unfortunate woman had but six weeks previous recovered from child-bed, and her body is bruised and much hurt from the rough treatment she received while in the hands of the negroes, the prints of whose fingers were visible on her neck. We have ever been, and now are, opposed to any kind of punishment being administered under the statutes of Judge Lynch; but when we reflect upon what must be the feelings of the husband and father, and the deep anguish which must pervade the bosom of the injured wife and outraged mother, a due regard for candor and the preservation of all that is held most sacred and all that is most dear to man, in the domestic circles of life, impels us to acknowledge the fact, that if the perpetrators of this excessively revolting crime had been burned alive, as was first decreed, their fate would have been too good for such diabolical and inhuman wretches.

Stolen Slaves

Some of the slaves were not lost or strayed but stolen. The *Athenian,* of Athens, Georgia, Aug. 19, 1828, related that

On July 23, a negro fellow belonging to Henry B. Thompson, of Taliaferro county, was met in the road while on his way to work by two waggoners with their waggon, who promised a treat to him if he would assist in moving a part of their loading; after he got in he was seized by the throat and confined, and one staid in the waggon for the purpose of keeping him quiet while the other drove.

But the negro preferred his old master to the new, and while his captors slept in camp that night he cut the thong that bound him and returned home.

When the slave to be stolen connived at the theft, as he frequently did in response to false promises by the thief, the stealing was easily accomplished. The slave could be carried off through the woods or by wagon or river boat or coasting vessel, and sold to some unsuspecting purchaser a hundred miles away, and the master might advertise over the whole countryside for his slave as a runaway and perhaps never gain trace of him; for the negro even if he declared he had been stolen would probably be disbelieved, particularly if he were being offered at a bargain to some not over-scrupulous employer in need of an extra workman. Numerous cases are reported where stolen slaves were packed in boxes or barrels for transportation by common carriers, whether steamboats or railroads. The following news item from Richmond, Virginia, was printed in the *Daily Delta* of New Orleans, May 7, 1849:

Early yesterday morning a negro drayman carried to the office of Adams & Co.'s Express, two large square boxes addressed to "Williamson, No.——, Buttonwood Street, Philadelphia." On being interrogated as to whence they came, the negro showed some confusion. Still the boxes were placed on the Express wagon and transported to the cars. As the driver of the wagon turned one of the boxes over rather roughly, he heard a sort of grunt, which proceeded from it. Suspicion was aroused, the boxes opened, and each one found to contain a stout negro, carefully folded up, with a small quantity of bread and a bladder of water, and one of them with a fan — a useful article in his warm situation. On examining the boxes, a large auger-hole was observed in each box, partially concealed by a stout rope knot, which could be withdrawn while in the cars, and allow the entrance of air. The negroes we hear, belonged, one to Mrs. C. Christian, of New Kent, the other to Mr. Govan's estate, and were employed as waiters, one at the Washington and the other at the Columbian Hotel. Their story is, that they had been prepared for transportation by Mr. S. A. Smith, who keeps a small shoe store on Broad street, in Mr. James Lyons' new buildings, and that they had paid him well (some 60 dollars each) for the job. This Smith formerly kept a shoe store at the sign of the "Red Boot," opposite the Old Market, and has also been a lottery-vendor. We hear that some years ago he was intimate with Blevins, the great negro-kidnapper (now in the penitentiary) and that on the trial of the latter, a letter to, or from, the same "P. Williamson," Philadelphia, was read in evidence.

Negro-stealers were of course no respectors of persons. A free negro could be kidnapped and sold into slavery as easily as a genuine slave — more easily in fact, because in a country controlled by white men's interests he had no master with an interest in him to safeguard. The following is from the New Orleans *Daily Tropic* of Jan. 13, 1846:

A CASE OF KIDNAPPING. — The Raleigh (N.C.) *Star*, notices the taking off of a little son of a poor blind free negro, in that vicinity, under such circumstances as to justify the suspicion that he was stolen to enslave him. A strange young man came to the house of the negro, and under pretence of desiring to find the way to a neighboring shop, took the boy behind him to shew him the road — since then neither of them have been heard of. The boy is a dark mulatto, eight years old, spare made, and is named Nelson Dudley Richardson. The young man who took him off was represented to be tall and slim, and between 21 and 25 years old.

Gangs of Kidnappers

In a few cases there were organized gangs of slave-stealers operating upon a large scale. A group led by John Washburn spent most of a decade, from 1827 until 1837 when their ringleader was hanged, in robbing river boats and mail coaches, picking pockets, rifling stores, murdering wayfarers, and stealing slaves. In 1820 they stole six negroes in one batch and peddled them out among the Louisiana planters for $4,600. A greater and more notorious gang was that under John A. Murrell, operating also in the Southwest, mainly between Memphis and New Orleans. Murrell had scores of accomplices, some of them apparently industrious farmers, others outright desperadoes, and he kept the whole region more or less terror stricken for some years before his final capture by Virgil A. Stewart, in 1835. The Murrell gang followed all the usual activities of desperadoes, but their favorite work was the seducing of slaves. Their most successful plan, and one which they carried out in a large number of cases, was for the thief to connive with a slave and promise if the negro would run with him and allow himself to be sold and then run away from the purchaser and meet his supposititious friend at a rendezvous agreed upon the thievish friend would then give him papers of freedom or help him to reach the free states. Sometimes the gang would sell a deluded negro three or four times in as many neighborhoods, and finally kill him to prevent his peaching on them. It was often a very inconvenient characteristic of slave property, accordingly, that such property could and did give aid in getting itself stolen.

Slave Conspiracies and Revolts

The liability of slaves to run away or to be stolen concerned their several masters only. Their liability to conspire and rise in insurrection, however, was a vital concern of the whole community in which they dwelt. On the continent of North America, it is true, the number of actual slave revolts was small, and each of those which occurred was quickly repressed. In the Spanish, French and British West Indies, on the other hand, there were numerous open attempts at revolt; there were constantly forces of rebel slaves living in the mountain fastnesses of Jamaica and San Domingo; and in the one case of Toussaint L'Ouverture's rising, the negro rebellion shattered the European control, expelled or massacred the whites, and established an independent negro state. News of all these occurrences was widely published and read in the slave-holding communities on the continent, and when added to the rumors of plots at home, was enough to foster from time to time a very serious anxiety.

The series of plots and rumors of plots for servile revolt on the continent extends through the whole period from the bringing of the blacks to America to the final destruction of slavery. There was a plot in Virginia, for example, in 1664, shared in by black and white bondmen, when the total negro population of the colony numbered hardly more than a thousand souls. In New York City there was a frenzy of fright in 1721 and again in 1741 at the report of negro conspiracies for rising and burning the city. Each of these alleged plots in New York was repressed with extreme severity, on the flimsiest of evidence. Severity of punishment was a fixed policy in servile conspiracy cases in all quarters; but the trials at law were usually far more adequate and even-tempered than in these New York instances.

In the colonies and states of denser black populations conspiracies were correspondingly early, and were more numerous and perhaps more disquieting than in Virginia and New York.

The preaching of the "rights of man" in the period of the American Revolution tended to stimulate longings for freedom; but the armies of the master class were mobilized in the period and the prospect poor for success in servile risings. The French revolutionists, fifteen years later, were more ecstatic in praise of liberty, and their preachings spread from the French colonies to the United States along with the slaves whom refugeeing masters carried from Hayti to new homes in and about New Orleans, Charleston, Norfolk, and Richmond. At or near each of these cities, as well as elsewhere, there were serious commotions within the eight years following the Haytien exodus of 1792. At Pointe Coupée, Louisiana, for example, in 1796 a plot was discovered of so alarming a nature that although a dozen negroes were hanged for it at the time, the whole community lived in dread and slept on its arms, so to speak, for years afterward.

The most important conspiracy of this period was that matured by the negro Gabriel, with its focus at Richmond in 1800. A thousand blacks and mulattoes were ready to rise at a signal, and the signal was given on scheduled time. The revolt occurred in terror-striking proportions, and the city would have been doomed had not a great freshet made the rivers impassable and delayed the insurgent march upon Richmond until the militia was organized and ready to oppose Gabriel's pikes with commonwealth bullets and bayonets. Gabriel's army scattered, the leaders were captured and executed, but the fright they had given was long fresh in the Virginian memories. A further source of disturbance was noted by John Randolph as early as 1811, when he said that the impetus given by the French revolution was being sustained and refreshed by emissaries from New England preaching disaffection among the Southern negroes, and that in consequence the whole South was living in a state of insecurity.

The next series of plots was in the period from 1816 to 1822, when the whites had relaxed from the tension of the foreign war. George Boxley, a white man, organized a more or less definite negro plot at Fredericksburg, Virginia, in 1816, which was betrayed before its maturity and repressed by hangings. A similar occurrence in the same year at Camden, South Carolina, was similarly punished, and others at Charleston in 1818 and at Augusta in 1819. Then came the great Denmark Vesey plot in Charleston in 1822, widely spread and well organized, but betrayed before its outbreak. After a large number of trials before a special tribunal Vesey and thirty-four of his fellows were hanged, and a number of others transported from the state. Police regulations were then stiffened in the locality and no further plots were rumored there for many years.

The next series of negro commotions began in 1831, and was attributed to incitement by the Northern abolitionists, whether through pamphlets and newspapers or through word of mouth. The only matured plot at this time was that organized by the negro preacher Nat Turner, which broke out in Southampton County, Virginia, and caused the death of about sixty white persons before it was suppressed. About the same time the discovery of plots, whether real or supposititious, was reported from localities in North Carolina, Georgia, Mississippi, Louisiana, and Kentucky. The wildest rumors flew, and at numerous places the greatest excitement prevailed. In 1832 Professor Dew published his epoch-making essay upon the existing regime as regards negro slavery, and scouted the possibility of any general uprising of the negroes. This promoted the return of confidence and sobriety. There were sporadic reports of plots — three for example in Louisiana in the early forties; in West Feliciana Parish in 1841, at Donaldsonville in 1843, and in Plaquemines Parish in 1845 — all of which were considered genuine and serious in the localities, but none of which matured or resulted in disaster to the whites. About 1855 and again more notably in 1860, rumors of plots were rife in the newspapers, and many citizens, it seems, were growing to apprehend a general rising. On the other hand, the complete failure of John Brown's dramatic attempt to incite the slave masses justified a sense of security in the minds of conservative men. A great number of Southerners at all times held the firm belief that the negro population was so docile, so little cohesive, and in the main so friendly toward the whites and so contented that a disastrous insurrection by them would be impossible. But on the whole there was much greater anxiety abroad in the land than the historians have told of, and its influence in shaping Southern policy was much greater than they have appreciated.

American Slave Insurrections before 1861

Harvey Wish

The romantic portrayal of *ante-bellum* society on the southern plantation, which depicts the rollicking black against a kindly patriarchal background, has tended to obscure the large element of slave unrest which occasionally shook the whole fabric of the planter's kingdom. Even the abolitionist, eager to capitalize upon such material, could make only vague inferences as to the extent of Negro insurrections in the South. The danger of inducing general panic by spreading news of an insurrection was a particularly potent factor in the maintenance of silence on the topic. Besides, sectional pride, in the face of anti-slavery taunts, prevented the loyal white Southerner from airing the subject of domestic revolt in the press. "Last evening," wrote a lady of Charleston during the Denmark Vesey scare of 1822, "twenty-five hundred of our citizens were under arms to guard our property and lives. But it is a subject not to be mentioned; and unless you hear of it elsewhere, say nothing about it."[1] Consequently, against such a conspiracy of silence the historian encounters unusual difficulties in reconstructing the true picture of slave revolts in the United States.

I. The Background of Slave Ship Mutinies

Before considering the nature of American slave insurrections, one may obtain a revelatory background by a survey of Negro uprisings upon the ships which carried the blacks from their African home. The horrors of the trade in human chattel have been frequently told and, for the most part, without serious exaggeration. Pious Captain John Hawkins, plying his profession on *The Jesus,* led the enterprising pioneers of the slave business. In time the miserable traffic was rationalized on religious and humanitarian grounds; but generally speaking, the stakes were

Harvey Wish, "American Slave Insurrections Before 1861, *"The Journal of Negro History,* XXII (July 1937), pp. 299–320. Reprinted by permission of the Association for the Study of Negro Life and History.

too high for any indulgence in sentimentality. George Scelle has written a detailed study of the enormous diplomatic factors involved, the constant rivalry for the much prized *assiento,* and the difficult social and administrative problems arising from the unceasing demand for cheap labor.[2]

It is unnecessary to account for slave ship mutinies by overstressing the revolting conditions which prevailed between decks. The desire for liberty was manifest from the very beginning and outbreaks would occur sometimes as the ship was being loaded, or as it sailed down the Gambia River, or along the West African Coast, as well as in the Middle Passage. Most instances of such insurrections seem to have taken place near the West African Coast, off such places as Sierra Leone, Goree, Cape Coast Castle, Cabinde, and Cape Malpas.

Some slave ship captains put their trust in the relative docility of certain African peoples. Captain Theodore Canot, for example, thought that the Negroes from Whydah were "distinguished for humble manners and docility"; yet he experienced a serious outbreak from these lambs. He believed that the Negroes from Benin and Angola were not as addicted to revolt as those north of the Gold Coast.[3] Frequent references appear in documentary accounts as to the refractory qualities of the "Coromantees."

The captives displayed a profound dejection and sought many devices to commit suicide. Sometimes they would jump overboard if the crew did not take every precaution to prevent this. Self-imposed starvation was common. One witness, testifying before a parliamentary committee, declared that compulsory feeding was used on every slave ship with which he was familiar.[4] Sick Negroes would refuse medicines, declaring that they wished only to die. Characteristic of many slavers was a "howling melancholy noise" with the women occasionally in hysterics. Sometimes the slaves were convinced that they were to be eaten.[5] The following type of evidence given in parliament appears in other accounts as well:

Mr. Towne says, that inquiring of the slaves into the cause of these insurrections he has been asked, what business he had to carry them from their own country. They had wives and children whom they wanted to be with.[6]

Despite the most elaborate precautions slave insurrections frequently broke out. Captain James Barbot, writing in 1700, tells of the meticulous daily search made into every corner of the ship for pieces of iron and wood, and for knives. Small arms for the crew were kept in readiness and sentinels stationed at all doorways. Such care he thought was unusual among other slavers, and, as he remarked, "If all those who carry slaves duly observed them (precautions) we should not hear of so many revolts as have happened."[7] The tense atmosphere which often preceded an outbreak has been graphically told by Captain Theodore Canot of the *Estrella:*

From the beginning there was manifest discontent among the slaves.   . . A few days after our departure a slave leaped overboard in a fit of passion and another choked himself during the night. These two suicides in twenty-four hours caused much uneasiness among the officers and induced me to make every preparation for a revolt.[8]

The insurrection itself was a desperate struggle waged with the courage of despair. Sometimes weapons would reach the slaves through the female captives who were frequently given comparative freedom on the deck. Naturally, in the greater number of cases, the revolt was doomed to failure, and the retribution was swift and terrible. Every refinement of torture was utilized by the captain, and the ring leaders, at least, were killed. Captain Harding, for example, borrowed the methods of savagery by compelling the rebels to eat the heart and liver of a sailor who had been killed, and hanged a woman leader by her thumbs, whipping and slashing her with knives.[9] Occasionally the slaves were successful in overpowering the crew and escaped by compelling the pilot to direct them homeward.

There is evidence of a special form of insurance to cover losses arising specifically from insurrections. An insurance statement of 1776 from Rhode Island, for example, has this item: "Wresk of Mortality and Insurrection of 220 slaves, Value £9000 Ste'g at 5 per cent is Pr Month = £37,10s."[10] A captain's statement of August 11, 1774, contains a request for insurrection insurance.[11] In a Negro mutiny case of May 3, 1785, the court awarded payment in conformance with a policy provision for insurrection insurance.[12] Sometimes the captain of a slaver would throw sick Negroes overboard to profit by the insurance payments given in such contingencies.

From the following summary of slave ship revolts based largely on documentary sources, it is evident that such insurrections occurred very frequently, sometimes recurring on the same ship.[13]

Date	Ship or Captain
1. August 22, 1699	The Albion [14]
2. August, 1700	Captain James Barbot[15]
3. —— 1703	Captain Ralph Ash, The Tyger [16]
4. —— 1704	The Eagle [17]
5. June, 1717	The Ann [18]
6. —— 1721	Captain Harding, The Robert [19]
7. —— 1721	Captain Snelgrave, The Henry [20]
8. —— 1722	Captain Messervy, Ferrers [21]
9. June, 1730	Little George [22]
10. Nov. 14, 1730	Captain William Martin, The Guinea [23]
11 Dec. 7, 1731	(Glasgow vessel)[24]
12. —— 1731	Captain George Scott[25]
13. —— 1731	Captain Jump[26]
14. August, 1732	Captain John Major[27]
15. Feb. 5, 1733	Captain Williams[28]
16. —— 1735	The Dolphin [29]
17. March 16, 1737	Captain Japhet Bird, Prince of Orange [30]

18. May, 1747   Captain Beers[31]
19. April 14, 1750   *The Ann* [32]
20. May 8, 1750   *King David* [33]
21. May 28, 1750   (Liverpool vessel)[34]
22. —— 1754   Captain Smith, *The Jubilee* [35]
23. Jan. 12, 1759   *The Perfect* [36]
24. —— 1761   Captain Nichols[37]
25. Sept., 1761   Captain Day, *The Thomas* [38]
26. March, 1764   *The Hope* [39]
27. June, 1764   Captain Joseph Muller[40]
28. Winter, 1764   Captain Toman, *Three Friends* [41]
29. Aug. 16, 1764   Captain Faggot, *Extraordinary* [42]
30. Nov. 25, 1765   Captain Rogers[43]
31. —— 1765   Captain Hopkins[44]
32. —— 1773   Captain Gogart, *The Industry* [45]
33. July, 1776   Captain Peleg Clark, *The Phoenix* [46]
34. Nov. 8, 1776   *The Thames* [47]
35. Dec. 8, 1776   Captain Bell[48]
36. Feb., 1785   (Rhode Island vessel)[49]
37. May 3, 1785   (Bristol vessel)[50]
38. Dec., 1787   *The Ruby* [51]
39. April 23, 1789   Captain Fairfield[52]
40. —— 1793   Captain J. B. Cooke, *The Nancy* [53]
41. —— 1793   Captain Joseph Hawkins, *The Charleston* [54]
42. —— 1795   (Boston vessel)[55]
43. June 10, 1796   *The Mary* [56]
44. —— 1797   Captain Thomas Clarke, *The Thames* [57]
45. May, 1797   *The Cadiz Dispatch* [58]
46. Sept., 1797   *The Thomas* [59]
47. April, 1799   *The Thomas* [60]
48. Aug. 2, 1799   *The Trelawney* [61]
49. Feb., 1804   *The Anne* [62]
50. Aug. 1, 1807   Captain Joseph Viale, *The Nancy* [63]
51. March 19, 1808   *The Leander* [64]
52. May 11, 1808   *The Coralline* [65]
53. —— 1829   Captain Theodore Canot, *L'Estrella* [66]
54. June, 1839   Captain Ramon Ferrer, *Amistad* [67]
55. March, 1845   *The Creole* [68]

II. Slave Insurrections in the United States

The desire for freedom on the part of the African, evidenced by his struggle on the slave ships, did not die in the New World. On the plantations of Latin-

America, in the British and French Indies, and finally in the American cotton, rice, and sugar fields, the aspirations of the Negro, blocked by the white master, gave birth to plots and uprisings. The lesson of San Domingo particularly was suggestive to both whites and blacks. Repressive black codes and emergency patrols frequently converted the plantation into an armed camp. Governor Robert Y. Hayne of South Carolina declared to the Assembly in 1833, two years after the Nat Turner Insurrection:[69]

A state of military preparation must always be with us a state of perfect domestic security. A period of profound peace and consequent apathy may expose us to the danger of domestic insurrection.

Professor Thomas R. Dew, militant apologist of slavery, sought, in an address that year before the Virginia Legislature, to minimize the fears of insurrection:

This is the evil, after all, let us say what we will, which really operates most powerfully upon the schemers and emancipating philanthropists of those sections where slaves constitute the principal property. . . . We cannot fail to derive the greatest consolation from the fact that although slavery has existed in our country for the last two hundred years, there have been but three attempts at insurrection — one in Virginia, one in South Carolina, and we believe, one in Louisiana — and the loss of lives from this cause has not amounted to one hundred persons in all.[70]

Despite the serious understatement of the number of insurrections, Dew's remarks are actually revelatory of the fears aroused among the planters. A graphic illustration of the cyclic fears of Negro uprisings during the 1830's is afforded by the remarks of several whites of Mississippi in 1859 to Frederick L. Olmsted:

Where I used to live (Alabama) I remember when I was a boy — must ha' been about twenty years ago — folks was dreadful frightened about the niggers. I remember they built pens in the woods where they could hide and Christmas time they went and got into the pens, fraid the niggers was risin'.[71]

The speaker's wife added her recollection to this comment:

I remember the same time where we was in South Carolina, we had all our things put up in bags so we could tote 'em if we heard they was comin' our way.[72]

Slave outbreaks and plots appeared both North and South during the Colonial period. Sometimes the white indentured servants made common cause with the Negroes against their masters. This was the case in 1663 when a plot of white servants and Negroes was betrayed in Gloucester County, Virginia.[73] The eastern counties of Virginia, where the Negroes were rapidly outnumbering the whites, suffered from repeated scares in 1687, 1709, 1710, 1722, 1723, and 1730.[74] A patrol system was set up in 1726 in parts of the state and later extended. Attempts were made here as elsewhere to check the importation of slaves by high duties.

Two important slave plots, one a serious insurrection, disturbed the peace of New York City in 1712 and 1741. In revenge for ill-treatment by their masters, twenty-three Negroes rose on April 6, 1712, to slaughter the whites and killed nine before they were overwhelmed by a superior force. The retaliation showed an unusual barbarous strain on the part of the whites. Twenty-one Negroes were executed, some were burnt, others hanged, and one broken on the wheel.[75] In 1741 another plot was reported in New York involving both whites and blacks. A white, Hewson (or Hughson), was accused of providing the Negroes with weapons. He and his family were executed; likewise, a Catholic priest was hanged as an accomplice. Thirteen Negro leaders were burnt alive, eighteen hanged, and eighty transported.[76] Popular fears of further insurrections led the New York Assembly to impose a prohibitive tax on the importation of Negroes. This tax, however, was later rescinded by order of the British Commissioner for Trade and Plantations.[77]

The situation in colonial South Carolina was worse than in her sister states. Long before rice and indigo had given way to King Cotton, the early development of the plantation system had yielded bumper crops of slave uprisings and plots. An insurrection, resulting in the deaths of three whites, is reported for May 6, 1720.[78] Ten years later an elaborate plot was discovered in St. John's Parish by a Negro servant of Major Cordes'. This plan was aimed at Charleston, an attack that was to inaugurate a widespread war upon the planters. Under the pretense of conducting a "dancing bout" in the city and in St. Paul's Parish the Negroes gathered together ready to seize the available arms for the attack. At this point the militia descended upon the blacks and killed the greater number, leaving few to escape.[79]

Owing partly to Spanish intrigues the same decade in South Carolina witnessed many more uprisings. An outbreak is reported for November, 1738.[80] The following year, on September 9, the Stono uprising created panic throughout the southeast. About twenty Angola Negroes assembled at Stono under their captain, Tommy, and marched toward Spanish territory, beating drums and endeavoring to attract other slaves. Several whites were killed and a number of houses burnt or plundered. As the "army" paused in a field to dance and sing they were overtaken by the militia and cut down in a pitched battle.[81] The following year an insurrection broke out in Berkeley County.[82] Charleston was threatened repeatedly by slave plots.[83] These reports are confirmed officially in the petition of the South Carolina Assembly to the King on July 26, 1740. Among the grievances of 1739 the Assembly complained of:

. . . an insurrection of our slaves in which many of the Inhabitants were murdered in a barbarous and cruel manner; and that no sooner quelled than another projected in Charles Town, and a third lately in the very heart of the Settlements, but happily discovered in time enough to be prevented.[84]

Repercussions of slave uprisings in South Carolina sometimes affected Georgia as well. This was particularly true in 1738.[85] In 1739 a plot was discovered in Prince George County.[86] To many slaves St. Augustine on Spanish soil seemed a welcome refuge from their masters.

Indications of many other insurrections in the American Colonies may be inferred from the nature of early patrol laws: The South Carolina law of 1704 for example contains a reference in its preamble to recent uprisings in that Colony.[87] In the British and French possessions to the south, particularly in the West Indies, affairs were much worse and put the planter of the North in constant fear of importing rebellious slaves and the contagion of revolt.

In considering the insurrections of the national period, it is at once evident that abolitionist propaganda played a relatively minor role despite the charges of southern politicians after 1831. The genealogy of revolt extends much further back than the organized efforts of anti-slavery advocates. It is true, however, that white men played an important role in many Negro uprisings, frequently furnishing arms, and even leadership, as well as inspiration.[88] The motives for such assistance varied from philanthropy to unadulterated self-interest. As might be expected, insurrections tended to occur where King Cotton and his allies were most firmly entrenched and the great plantation system established.

Slave unrest seems to have been far greater in Virginia rather than in the states of the Lower South. Conspiracies like those of Gabriel in 1800 and Nat Turner in 1831 attained national notoriety. The Gabriel plot was developed in the greatest secrecy upon the plantation of a harsh slavemaster, Thomas Prosser, several miles from Richmond. Under the leadership of a young slave, Gabriel, and inspired by the examples of San Domingo and the emancipation of the ancient Israelites from Egypt, some eleven hundred slaves had taken an oath to fight for their liberty. Plans were drawn for the seizure of an arsenal and several other strategic buildings of Richmond which would precede a general slaughter of all hostile whites. After the initial successes, it was expected that fifty thousand Negroes would join the standard of revolt. Beyond this point, the arrangements were hazy.[89] A faithful slave however exposed the plot and Governor James Monroe took rapid measures to secure the cooperation of the local authorities and the federal cavalry. Bloodshed was averted by an unprecedented cloudburst on the day set for the conspiracy and the utter demoralization of the undisciplined "army." Writing to his friend, President Jefferson, the Governor declared:

It (the Gabriel plot) is unquestionably the most serious and formidable conspiracy we have ever known of the kind. While it was possible to keep it secret, which it was till we saw the extent of it, we did so. . . .[90]

With the opening of the slave trials, hysteria swept the South and many inno-cent blacks were compelled to pay for this with their lives. Rumors of new plots sprang up everywhere much to the distraction of Monroe. The results of the Gabriel incident were significant. An impetus was given to the organization of the American Colonization Society which took definite form in 1816. The slave patrol laws became very stringent, and the example was copied elsewhere in the South. The incipient feeling of sectional diversity received a new impetus.

Between Gabriel's abortive plot and the Nat Turner uprising, several more incidents occurred which disturbed the sleep of Virginians. In January, 1802, Gover-nor Monroe received word of a plot in Nottaway County. Several Negroes suspected of participation were executed.[91] That same year came disclosures of a projected slave uprising in Goochland County aided by eight or ten white men.[92] Several plots were reported in 1808 and 1809 necessitating almost continuous patrol service.[93] The War of 1812 intensified the apprehensions of servile revolt. Petitions for troops and arms came during the summer of 1814 from Caroline County and Lynchburg.[94] Regiments were called out during the war in anticipation of insurrections along the tidewater area. During the spring of 1816 confessions were wrung from slaves concerning an attack upon Fredericksburg and Richmond. The inspiration for this enterprise was attributed to a white military officer, George Boxley. The latter claimed to be the recipient of divine revelations and the instrument of "omnipo-tence" although he denied any intention of leading an insurrection. His relatives declared that he was insane, but his neighbors in a complaint to the governor showed serious misgivings on this point:

On many occasions he has declared that the distinction between the rich and the poor was too great; that offices were given to wealth than to merit; and seemed to be an advocate for a more leveling system of Government. For many years he has avowed his disapprobation of the slavery of the Negroes and wished they were free.[95]

Boxley was arrested but escaped. About thirty Negroes were sentenced to death or deportation in consequence.

The years preceding the Nat Turner insurrection brought further news of plots discovered. During the middle of July, 1829, the governor received requests for aid from the counties of Mathews, Gloucester, the Isle of Wight and adjacent counties.[96] The ease with which "confessions" were obtained under duress casts doubt upon the reality of such outbreaks, but the reports are indicative of the ever-present fear of attack.

Nat Turner's insurrection of August 21, 1831, at Southhampton, seventy miles from Richmond, raised fears of a general servile war to their highest point. The contemporary accounts of the young slave, Nat, tend to overemphasize his leanings towards mysticism and under-state the background of unrest.[97] As a "leader" or lay preacher, Nat Turner exercised a strong influence over his race. On the fatal

August night, he led his followers to the plantations of the whites killing fifty-five before the community could act. The influence of the Southhampton insurrection upon the South was profound. Gradually the statesmen of that section began to reexamine their "peculiar" institution in the rival aspects of humanitarianism, the race problem, and the economic requirements for a cheap labor supply. How the friends of emancipation failed is familiar history. The immediate results were also far-reaching. Laws against the free Negro were made more restrictive, the police codes of the slave states were strengthened, and Negro education became more than ever an object of suspicion.[98] Virginia's lucrative business of supplying slaves to the lower South was gradually undermined by the recurrent insurrections. Frederic Bancroft, the historian of the domestic slave trade, has written:

Believing that as a result of actual or feared insurrections Virginia and other States were taking pains to sell to the traders the most dangerous slaves and criminal free Negroes, Alabama, Mississippi, Louisiana, and other States passed laws forbidding all importations for sale.[99]

Rumors of slave plots continued to disturb Virginia up to the era of emancipation. During 1856, the state, in common with other slaveholding states, shared in the general feeling that a widespread conspiracy, set for December 25, was maturing. Requests for aid came to the Governor from the counties of Fauquier, King and Queen, Culpeper, and Rappahannock; and particularly from the towns of Lynchburg, Petersburg, and Gordonsville.[100] As for John Brown's visionary deed at Harper's Ferry in the autumn of 1859, the aftermath can be easily imagined. The spectre of a general insurrection again haunted the minds of the white citizenry and large patrols were kept in constant service to prevent Negro meetings of all types.[101]

Maryland and North Carolina, although more fortunate than their slave-ridden neighbor, did not escape unscathed. The news of Nat Turner and John Brown brought panic to the other states. In Maryland, baseless rumors of conspiracies, rather than actual outbreaks, seemed to be the rule. In 1845 a plot was "disclosed" in Charles County, Maryland, and a number of Negroes were subsequently sold out of the state.[102] Ten years later there was general excitement over alleged uprisings in Dorchester, Talbot and Prince George's Counties. Resolutions were adopted at the time by various citizens asking that slaveholders keep their servants at home.[103] The reaction to John Brown's raid of 1859 was more intense than had ever before been experienced over insurrections in Maryland. The newspapers for days were full of nothing else but the Harper's Ferry incident. Large patrols were called out everywhere and talk was general of a concerted uprising of all the slaves in Maryland and Virginia. A martial atmosphere prevailed.[104]

In 1802 an insurrection was reported in Bertie County, North Carolina, necessitating an elaborate patrol system.[105] A decade later, another outbreak in Rockingham County was narrowly averted;[106] and in 1816 further plots were discovered at Tarboro, New Bern, Camden and Hillsboro.[107] Several minor disturbances occurred in 1821 among the slaves of Bladen, Carteret, Jones, and Onslow Counties.[108] On October 6, 1831, a Georgia newspaper reported an extensive slave conspiracy in North Carolina with ramifications in the eastern counties of Duplin, Sampson, Wayne, New Hanover, Lenoir, Cumberland, and Bladen.[109]

Slave plots in South Carolina during the national period seem to have been abortive for the most part, but several of the projects could easily have been uprisings of the first magnitude. During November, 1797, slave trials in Charleston disclosed a plot to burn the city. Two Negroes were hanged and three deported.[110] The Camden plot of June, 1816, was a very serious affair and envisaged a concerted attempt to burn the town and massacre its inhabitants. A favorite slave reported the plot to his master, Colonel Chesnut, who thereupon informed Governor Williams. Six of the slave leaders were executed and patrol measures were strengthened.[111]

The outstanding threat of insurrection in the State was the Denmark Vesey plot of 1822. The leader, Denmark, was a free Negro of Charleston, a native of St. Thomas in the West Indies, who had purchased his freedom in 1800 from the proceeds of a lottery prize and had since worked in the city as a carpenter. He desired to emulate the Negro leaders of San Domingo and win the freedom of his people. Preaching that conditions had become intolerable for the slave, he urged a war against the slave-holder. A white man was to purchase guns and powder for his proposed army; Charleston was to be captured and burnt, the shipping of the town seized, and all would sail away for the West Indies to freedom. Again a "faithful slave" — or spy — exposed the plot and severe reprisals were instituted. Thirty-five Negroes were executed and thirty-seven sold out of the state.[112]

Because of the number of free Negroes involved, the Legislature passed an act preventing such persons from entering the state. To avoid, as far as possible, the contagion of abolitionist and kindred ideas, the purchase of slaves was forbidden from the West Indies, Mexico, South America, Europe, and the states north of Maryland. Slaves, who had resided in these forbidden areas, were likewise denied entrance into South Carolina.[113] A Charleston editor, Benjamin Elliott, penned a sharp reply to the Northern accusations of cruelty, by pointing out that New York in the insurrection of 1741 had executed thirty-five and deported eighty-five. He demanded that the Federal Government act under its power to suppress insurrection.[114] In July, 1829, another plot was reported in Georgetown County[115] and in 1831, the year of Nat Turner's attack, one in Laurens County.[116]

Georgia, like South Carolina, was able to avert the worst consequences of repeated slave plots. One was reported in Greene County in 1810;[117] a plan to destroy Atlanta came to light in May, 1819;[118] during 1831, disquieting rumors came from Milledgeville and Laurens County;[119] four years later, a plot for a general uprising on the Coast was disclosed;[120] in 1851 another plot in Atlanta was reported;[121] and in 1860, similar reports came from Crawford and Brooks Counties.[122]

Florida experienced an uprising in March, 1820, along Talbot Island which was put down by a detachment of federal troops.[123] Another was reported in December, 1856; in Jacksonville.[124] Alabama discovered a plot in January, 1837, believed to have been instigated by a free Negro, M'Donald.[125] Mississippi seems to have been the central area of a widespread slave plot in July, 1835, threatening the entire Cotton Kingdom. Far-reaching plans of revolt had been drawn up by a white, John A. Murrell, who enjoyed a reputation as a Negro kidnapper and land pirate. Ten or fifteen Negroes and a number of whites were hanged for participation in the plot.[126]

Next to Virginia, Louisiana had the greatest difficulty among the southern states in coping with repeated attempts at insurrection. Governor Claiborne of the Mississippi Territory received frequent letters concerning plots in various parts of Louisiana. In 1804, New Orleans seems to have been threatened.[127] Several months later another alarm came from the plantations at Pointe Coupee.[128] In 1805, the attempt of a Frenchman to teach the doctrine of equality to slaves, led to general fears of an uprising.[129]

An actual outbreak occurred in January, 1811. Beginning from a plantation in the parish of St. John the Baptist, about thirty-six miles above New Orleans, a concerted slave uprising spread along the Mississippi. The Negroes formed disciplined companies to march upon New Orleans to the beating of drums. Their force, estimated to include from 180 to 500 persons, was defeated in a pitched battle with the troops.[130] According to one historian many of those executed were decapitated and their heads placed on poles along the river as an example to others.[131]

Another uprising took place in the same area in March, 1829, causing great alarm before it was suppressed. Two leaders were hanged.[132] Other plots were reported in 1835, 1837, 1840, 1841 and 1842.[133] An uprising occurred in August, 1856, at New Iberia.[134]

The situation in Tennessee, Kentucky, and Texas may be briefly summarized. In Tennessee, plots were disclosed during 1831, 1856, and 1857.[135] Kentucky, in December, 1856, hanged several ringleaders of an attempted insurrection at Hopkinsville, in which a white man was involved.[136] That same year, two Negroes were punished by being whipped to death in Texas for an alleged conspiracy at Columbus, Colorado County.[137]

Owing to the nature of such a study any claim to an exhaustive treatment would be mere pretense. An analysis of slave patrol history alone would suggest the existence of far more conspiracies and outbreaks than those already mentioned. It is clear however that *ante-bellum* society of the South suffered from a larger degree of domestic insecurity than the conventional view would indicate. No doubt many Negroes made the required adjustments to slavery but the romantic picture of careless abandon and contentment fails to be convincing. The struggle of the Negro for his liberty, beginning with those dark days on the slave ship, was far from sporadic in nature, but an ever-recurrent battle waged everywhere with desperate courage against the bonds of his master.

Notes

[1] T. W. Higginson, "Gabriel's Defeat," *The Atlantic Monthly*, X (1862), 337–345.

[2] George Scelle, *Histoire politique de la traite négriere aux Indes de Castille*, (Paris, 1902), 2 vols. Profits to the slave trader of 600% and 1000% were not unusual. *The Ninth Annual Report of the British and Foreign Anti-Slavery Society*, (London, 1848), 20.

[3] Brantz Mayer, *Adventures of an African Slaver*, (New York, 1928), 265.

[4] *An Abstract of the Evidence Delivered Before a Select Committee of the House of Commons, 1790–91*, (London, 1791), 39.

[5] Elizabeth Donnan (ed.), *Documents Illustrative of the Slave Trade to America*, (Washington, 1930–5), I, 462–3; hereafter referred to as *D.S.T.*

[6] *An Abstract of the Evidence ———, 44.*

[7] *D.S.T.*, I, 462. It should be added that the cautious Barbot later experienced an insurrection when off Cabinde and overpowered the rebels only after terrific slaughter. *Ibid,* 457.

[8] Mayer, *Adventures of an African Slaver*, 264.

[9] *D.S.T.*, II, 266.

[10] *Ibid.*, III, 325.

[11] *Ibid.*, 293.

[12] Helen H. Catterall (ed.), *Judicial Cases Concerning American Slavery and the Negro*, (Washington, 1926), I, 19; hereafter referred to as *J.C.N.* For other illustrations of insurrection insurance see *ibid.*, III, 568 and *D.S.T.*, III, 217.

[13] This list of insurrections is undoubtedly far from exhaustive. In a few cases there may even be duplications.

[14] George Francis Dow, *Slave Ships and Slaving*, (Salem, 1927), 83.

[15] *D.S.T.*, I, 463.

[16] *Ibid.*, 5 ff.

[17] William Snelgrave, *A New Account of Some Parts of Guinea and the Slave Trade*, (London, 1734), 164.

[18] *D.S.T.*, II, 232.

[19] *Ibid.*, 266.

[20] Snelgrave, *A New Account of — Guinea and the Slave Trade*, 164.

[21] *Ibid.*, 185.

[22] *D.S.T.*, III, 119.

[23] *Ibid.*, II, 397.

[24] *Ibid.*, 431 ff.

[25] Joshua Coffin, *An Account of Some of the Principal Slave Insurrections*, (New York, 1860), 14.

[26] *D.S.T.*, III, 37.

[27] *Ibid.*, 42 ff.; also Coffin, — *Principal Slave Insurrections*, 14.

[28] *D.S.T.*, II, 410.

[29] Coffin, — *Principal Slave Insurrections*, 14.

[30] *D.S.T.*, II, 460.

[31] *Ibid.*, III, 51; also Coffin, — *Principal Slave Insurrections*, 15.

[32] *D.S.T.*, II, 485–6.

[33] *Ibid.*, 486–7.

[34] *Ibid.*, 485.

[35] Sylvanus Urban (ed.), *Gentleman's Magazine,* XXIV, (London, 1754), 141.

[36] Edmund B. D'Auvergne, *Human Livestock,* (London, 1933), 73.

[37] Coffin, *Principal Slave Insurrections,* 15; also *D.S.T.,* III, 452.

[38] *Ibid.,* 67–70.

[39] *Ibid.,* 71.

[40] *Ibid.,* 71, 207.

[41] *Ibid.,* 209 ff.

[42] *Ibid.,* 2.

[43] *Ibid.,* 201.

[44] *Ibid.,* 213.

[45] *Gentleman's Magazine,* XLIV, 1774, 469.

[46] *D.S.T.,*III, 318.

[47] *Ibid.,* 331.

[48] *Ibid.,* 323.

[49] *Ibid.,* 341.

[50] *J.C.N.,* I, 19.

[51] Dow, *Slave Ships and Slaving,* 175.

[52] *D.S.T.,* III, 82–3.

[53] *Ibid.,* 358–9.

[54] Joseph Hawkins, *A History of a Voyage to the Coast of Africa,* (Philadelphia, 1797), 145–9.

[55] *D.S.T.,* III, 101.

[56] *Ibid.,* 375.

[57] *Ibid.,* II, 665.

[58] *J.C.N.,* I, 22.

[59] D'Auvergne, *Human Livestock,* 73.

[60] *J.C.N.,* I, 22.

[61] *D.S.T.,* II, 644.

[62] *J.C.N.,* I, 25.

[63] *D.S.T.,* III, 394–6; also Dow, *Slave Ships and Slaving,* 272.

[64] *J.C.N.,* II, 292.

[65] Dow, *Slave Ships and Slaving,* 207.

[66] Mayer, *Adventures of an African Slaver,* 264–5.

[67] Coffin, *Principal Slave Insurrections,* 33.

[68] *J.C.N.,* III, 565.

[69] *Message of Governor Robert Y. Hayne to the Senate and House of Representatives of South Carolina,* (Columbia, November 26, 1833).

[70] *The Political Register,* (Washington, 1833), III, (1833), 823.

[71] Frederick Law Olmsted, *A Journey in the Back Country,* (New York, 1860), 203.

[72] *Ibid.*

[73] Ulrich B. Phillips, *American Negro Slavery,* (New York, 1918), 472.

[74] William P. Palmer (ed.), *Calendar of Virginia State Papers,* (Richmond, 1875), I, (1652–1781), 129–130; also James Curtis Ballagh, *A History of Slavery in Virginia,* (Baltimore, 1902), 79–80; also Coffin, *Principal Slave Insurrections,* 11.

[75] Letter of Governor Robert Hunter to the Lords of Trade, in E. B. O'Callaghan (ed.), *Documents Relative to the Colonial History of the State of New York,* (Albany, 1855), V, (1707–1733), 341–2.

[76] *Gentleman's Magazine,* XI, (1741), 441.

34   The Classic Debate: Accommodation vs. Resistance

77 *D.S.T.*, III, 409. Joshua Coffin also reports plots and actual outbreaks in other slave-holding areas in the Northern Colonies. East Boston is said to have experienced a minor uprising in 1638. In 1723, a series of incendiary fires in Boston led the selectmen to suspect a slave plot and the militia was ordered to police the slaves. Another plot was reported in Burlington, Pennsylvania during 1734. Coffin, *Principal Slave Insurrections,* 10, 11, 12.

78 Coffin, *Principal Slave Insurrections,* 11.

79 Edward Clifford Holland, *A Refutation of the Calumnies Circulated Against the Southern and Western States Respecting the Institution and Existence of Slavery,* (Charleston, 1822), 68–9, 81.

80 Ralph Betts Flander, *Plantation Slavery in Georgia,* (Chapel Hill, 1933), 24.

81 *Gentleman's Magazine,* X, (1740), 127–8.

82 See the Constable's bill in the *Magazine of American History,* XXV, (1891), 85–6

83 Edward McGrady, *The History of South Carolina Under the Royal Government,* (1719–1776), (New York, 1899), 5.

84 Appendix to Holland, *A Refutation of the Calumnies,* —, 71. Another plot of December 17, 1765, is mentioned in *D.S.T.,* IV, 415.

85 Flanders, *Plantation Slavery in Georgia,* 24; similarly, South Carolina's slave plots sometimes required the assistance of North Carolina as in the scare of 1766. William L. Saunders, (ed.), *Colonial Records of North Carolina,* (Raleigh, 1890), VIII, (1769–1771), 559.

86 Jeffrey R. Brackett, *The Negro in Maryland,* (Baltimore, 1889), 93.

87 H. M. Henry, *The Police Control of the Slave in South Carolina,* (Vanderbilt University, 1914), 30.

88 One aspect of this subject is discussed in James Hugo Johnston's article, "The Participation of White Men in Virginia Negro Insurrections," *Journal of Negro History,* XVI, (1931), 158–167.

89 Details of the Gabriel Plot are in the *Calendar of Virginia State Papers,* X, (1808–1835), 140–173, *et passim;* T. W. Higginson, "Gabriel's Defeat," *The Atlantic Monthy,* X, (1862), 337–345; Robert R. Howison, *A History of Virginia,* (Richmond, 1848), II, 390–3).

90 Monroe to Jefferson, September 15, 1800; S. M. Hamilton, (ed.), *Writings of James Monroe,* (New York, 1893–1903), III, 201. Much of the Gabriel affair can be followed from the letters of Monroe.

91 Hamilton, (ed.) *Writings of James Monroe,* III, 328–9.

92 James H. Johnston, "The Participation of White Men in Virginia Negro Insurrections," 161.

93 *Calendar of Virginia State Papers,* X, (1808–1835), 31, 62.

94 *Ibid.,* 367, 388.

95 *Calendar of Virginia State Papers,* X, 433–6.

96 *Ibid.,* 567–9.

97 Thomas Gray, (ed.), *Nat Turner's Confession,* (Richmond, 1832); Samuel Warner, (ed.), *The Authentic and Impartial Narrative of The Tragical Scene of the Twenty Second of August, 1831,* New York, 1831, (a Collection of accounts by eye witnesses); and William Sidney Drewry, *Slave Insurrections in Virginia, 1830–1865,* (Washington, 1900), *passim.*

98 The immediate results of the Nat Turner affair are summarized in John W. Cromwell's "The Aftermath of Nat Turner's Insurrection," *The Journal of Negro History,* V, (1920), 208–234.

99 Frederick Bancroft, *Slave-Trading in the Old South,* (Baltimore, 1931), 18.

100 *Calendar of Virginia State Papers,* XI, (1836–1869), 50. Other rumors of unrest during 1856 came from the towns of Williamsburg and Alexandria, and from Montgomery County. See Laura A. White, "The South in the 1850's as seen by British Consuls," *The Journal of Southern History,* I, (1935), 44.

101 Brackett, *The Negro in Maryland,* 97–99.

[102] Brackett, *The Negro in Maryland*, 96.

[103] *Ibid.*, 97.

[104] *Ibid.*, 97–99.

[105] John Spencer Bassett, *Slavery in the State of North Carolina*, Johns Hopkins University Studies in Historical and Political Science, XVIII, (Baltimore, 1899), 332. The nature of North Carolina laws during 1777–1788 regarding insurrections indicates the keen fears entertained of slave uprisings. One preamble of 1777 begins ". . . Whereas the evil and pernicious practice of freeing slaves in this State, ought at this alarming and critical time to be guarded against by every friend and well-wisher to his country . . . ." This idea is repeated in the insurrection laws of 1778 and 1788. Walter Clark (ed.), *The State Records of North Carolina*, (Goldsboro, N. C., 1905), XXIV, (1777–1788), 14, 221, 964. The laws regulating manumission were made increasingly stringent for fear of creating a dangerous class of free Negroes.

[106] *Calendar of Virginia State Papers*, X, (1808–1835), 120–2.

[107] A. H. Gordon, "The Struggle of the Negro Slaves for Physical Freedom," *Journal of Negro History*, XIII, (1928), 22–35.

[108] Hugh T. Lefler (ed.), *North Carolina History Told by Contemporaries*, (Chapel Hill, 1934), 265.

[109] Milledgeville (Georgia) *Federal Union*, October 6, 1831, quoted in *ibid.;* The repercussion of the Nat Turner insurrection at Murfreesboro, Hertford County, has been graphically described by an eye witness, "It was court week and most of our men were twelve miles away at Winton. Fear was seen in every face, women pale and terror stricken, children crying for protection, men fearful and full of foreboding, but determined to be ready for the worst." Quoted from the Baltimore *Gazette*, November 16, 1831, by Stephen B. Weeks, "The Slave Insurrection in Virginia," *American Magazine of History*, XXV, (1891), 456.

[110] H. M. Henry, *The Police Patrol of the Slave in South Carolina*, 150.

[111] Holland, *A Refutation of the Calumnies*, —, 75.

[112] J. Hamilton (ed.), *An Account of the Late Intended Insurrection* (Boston, 1822); also Holland, *A Refutation of the Calumnies*, —, 77–82; *Niles Register*, XXIII, (1822–3), 9–12.

[113] *An Act of the Legislature of South Carolina Passed at the Session in December to Prevent Free Negroes and Persons of Color from Entering This State*, (Charleston, 1824).

[114] Appendix to Holland, *A Refutation of the Calumnies*, 81.

[115] *J.C.N.*, 340.

[116] Henry, *The Police Control of the Slave in South Carolina*, 153.

[117] Flanders, *Plantation Slavery in Georgia*, 274.

[118] *Niles Register*, XVI (1819), 213.

[119] Flanders, *Plantation Slavery in Georgia*, 274.

[120] *Niles Register*, XLIX, (1935–6), 172.

[121] Flanders, *Plantation Slavery in Georgia*, 275. Georgia suffered in common with the other southern states during the scare of 1856; White, "The South in the 1850's as Seen by British Consuls," 43.

[122] Flanders, *Plantations Slavery in Georgia*, 275–6, 186. The abolitionists were accused of organizing the slave plots of the thirties and thereafter. One New England abolitionist, Kitchel, who opened a school for Negroes in Tarversville, Twigg County, Georgia, in 1835, was driven out of the community because he was said to have incited the slaves to revolt. *Ibid.*, 275.

[123] *J.C.N.*, III, 327.

[124] James Stirling, *Letters from the Slave States*, (London, 1857), 299.

[125] *J.C.N.*, III, 141. Alabama had two rumors of slave plots reported in 1860, White, "The South in the 1850's as Seen by British Consuls," 47.

[126] *Niles Register*, XLIX, (1835–6), 119; also Elizur Wright (ed.), *Quarterly Anti-Slavery Magazine*, (New York, 1837), II, 104–11.

[127] Dunbar, Rowland (ed.), *Official Letter Book of W.C.C. Claiborne,* (Jackson, 1917), II, (1801–1816), 337–8.

[128] *Ibid.,* III, (1804–1806), 6.

[129] *Ibid.,* 187.

[130] *Ibid.,* V, (1809–1811), 93–142.

[131] Francois Xavier Martin, *The History of Louisiana,* (New Orleans, 1829), II, 300–301. During the fall of the following year another plot was reported. *J.C.N.,* III, 449.

[132] *Niles Register,* XXVI, (1829), 53.

[133] *Ibid.,* LIII, (1837–8), 129; LX, (1841), 368; LXIII, (1842–3), 212.

[134] V. Alton Moody, *Slavery on the Louisiana Sugar Plantations,* (Univ. of Michigan Press, 1924), 41; also Phillips, *American Negro Slavery,* 486; *J.C.N.,* III, 648.

[135] Caleb P. Patterson, *The Negro in Tennessee,* Univ. of Texas Bulletin No. 225, (Austin, February 1, 1922), 49; *J.C.N.,* II, 565–6; Stirling, *Letters from the Slave States,* 294.

[136] *J.C.N.,* 299.

[137] Frederick Law Olmsted, *A Journey Through Texas,* (New York, 1857), 513–4; Stirling, *Letters From the Slave States,* 300.

Day to Day Resistance to Slavery[1]

Raymond A. Bauer
Alice H. Bauer

The tradition that has grown up about Negro slavery is that the slaves were docile, well adapted to slavery, and reasonably content with their lot. A standard work on the Negro problem in the United States says:

The Negroes brought into the New World situation and presently reduced to a perpetual servitude became very rapidly accommodated to the environment and status. The explanation of the comparative ease with which this was brought about doubtless lies in the peculiar racial traits of the Negro peoples themselves. They are strong and robust in physique and so everywhere sought after as laborers. In disposition they are cheerful, kindly and sociable: in character they are characteristically extrovert, so readily obedient and easily contented. More than most other social groups they are patiently tolerant under abuse and oppression and little inclined to struggle against difficulties. These facts of racial temperament and disposition make the Negroes more amenable to the condition of slavery than perhaps any other racial group.[2]

This concept is gradually being changed as the study of slave revolts, and of the social tension caused by the constant threat of revolt progresses.[3] In answer to the question, " 'Are the masters afraid of insurrection?' (a slave) says, 'They live in constant fear upon this subject. The least unusual noise at night alarms them greatly. They cry out, 'What is that?' 'Are the boys all in'?"[4]

The purpose of this paper is to study a less spectacular aspect of slavery — the day to day resistance to slavery, since it is felt that such a study will throw some further light on the nature of the Negro's reaction to slavery. Our investigation has made it apparent that the Negroes not only were very discontented, but that they developed effective protest techniques in the form of indirect retaliation for their enslavement. Since this conclusion differs sharply from commonly accepted belief, it would perhaps be of value if a brief preliminary statement were made of how belief

Raymond A. Bauer and Alice H. Bauer, "Day to Day Resistance to Slavery," *Journal of Negro History,* XXVII (October 1942), pp. 388–419. Reprinted by permission of the Association for the Study of Negro Life and History.

so at variance with the available documentary materials could gain such acceptance.

The picture of the docile, contented Negro slave grew out of two lines of argument used in ante-bellum times. The pro-slavery faction contended that the slaves came of an inferior race, and that they were happy and contented in their subordinate position, and that the dancing and singing Negro exemplified their assumption. Abolitionists, on the other hand, tended to depict the Negro slave as a passive instrument, a good and faithful worker exploited and beaten by a cruel master. As one reads the controversial literature on the slavery question, it soon becomes apparent that both sides presented the Negro as a docile creature; one side because it wished to prove that he was contented, the other because it wished to prove that he was grossly mistreated. Both conceptions have persisted to the present time. Writers who romanticize the "Old South" idealize the condition of the slaves, and make of them happy, willing servitors, while those who are concerned with furthering the interests of the Negroes are careful to avoid mention of any aggressive tendencies which might be used as a pretext for further suppressing the Negroes.

Many travelers in the South have accepted the overt behavior of the slaves at its face value. The "yas suh, Cap'n," the smiling, bowing, and scraping of the Negroes have been taken as tokens of contentment. Redpath's conversations with slaves indicated how deep seated this behavior was.[5] This point of view, however, neglects the fact that the whites have always insisted on certain forms of behavior as a token of acceptance of inferior status by the Negro. The following quotation from Dollard is pertinent:

An informant already cited has referred to the Negro as a 'Dr. Jekyll and Mr. Hyde.' He was making an observation that is well understood among Negroes — that he has a kind of dual personality, two rôles, one that he is forced to play with white people and one the 'real Negro' as he appears in his dealings with his own people. What the white Southern people see who 'know their Negroes' is the rôle that they have forced the Negro to accept, his caste role.[6]

The conceptual framework within which this paper is written is that the Negro slaves were forced into certain outward forms of compliance to slavery; that, except for the few who were able to escape to the North, the Negroes had to accept the institution of slavery and make their adjustments to that institution. The patterns of adjustment which we have found operative are: slowing up of work, destruction of property, malingering and self-mutilation.

The sources of our material are: (1) general works on slavery, labor, and the Negro; (2) the journals and the travel accounts of southerners and of visitors to the slave territory; and (3) the biographies and autobiographies of slaves. Most of the secondary sources take some cognizance of the fact that slaves slowed up their work, feigned illness, and the like, but this behavior is regarded as a curiosity. There has been no attempt by those writers who set down such facts to understand their social and economic significance. The journals and travel-books vary greatly in the amount of information they contain. This, of course, is due to the authors' variations in interest and acuteness. Olmsted's *Seaboard Slave States,* for instance, abounds in anecdotes, and in expressions of opinion as to the extent of loafing and malingering. Susan Smedes' *Memorials of a Southern Planter,* on the other hand, contains just one foot-noted reference to any such behavior. Life stories of ex-slaves emphasize running away, forms of punishment, and other aspects of slavery that would make interesting reading. Yet while references to slowing up work, or feigning illness, are thus few in number, where they are made they are stated in such a way that they leave no doubt that there was a persistent pattern of such behavior.

Slaveholders ever underrate the intelligence with which they have to grapple. I really understood the old man's mutterings, attitudes and gestures, about as well as he did himself. But slaveholders never encourage that kind of communication, with the slaves, by which they might learn to measure the depths of his knowledge. Ignorance is a high virtue in a human chattel; and as the master studies to keep the slave ignorant, the slave is cunning enough to make the master think he succeeds. The slave fully appreciates the saying, 'where ignorance is bliss 'tis folly to be wise.'[7]

We have felt it wise to quote extensively. Much of the meaning of incidents and interpretations lies in the phrasing of the author — in sensing his own emphasis on what he says. Methodologically, in attempting to analyze an existing stereotype, as we are trying to do here, it would seem wisest to present the picture as it appeared to contemporaries, and thus as given in their own words.

II

The Negroes were well aware that the work they did benefited only the master. "The slaves work and the planter gets the benefit of it."[8] "The conversation among the slaves was that they worked hard and got no benefit, that the masters got it all."[9] It is thus not surprising that one finds many recurring comments that a slave did not do half a good day's work in a day. A northerner whom Lyell met in the South said:

Half the population of the south is employed in seeing the other half do their work, and they who do work, accomplish half what they might do under a better system.[10]

An English visitor, with a very strong pro-slavery bias corroborates this:

The amount of work expected of the field hand will not be more than one half of what would be demanded of a white man; and even that will not be properly done unless he is constantly overlooked.[11]

Statements of other writers are to the same effect:

It is a common remark of those persons acquainted with slave-labour, that their proportion is as one to two. This is not too great an estimate in favour of the free-labourer; and the circumstances of their situation produce a still greater disparity.[12]

A capitalist was having a building erected in Petersburg, and his slaves were employed in carrying up the brick and mortar for the masons on their heads: a Northerner, standing near, remarked to him that they moved so indolently that it seemed as if they were trying to see how long they could be in mounting the ladder without actually stopping. The builder started to reprove them, but after moving a step turned back and said: 'It would only make them move more slowly still when I am not looking at them, if I should hurry now. *And what motive have they to do better?* It's no concern of theirs how long the masons wait. I am sure if I was in their place, I shouldn't move as fast as they do.'[13]

A well-informed capitalist and slave-holder remarked,

In working niggers, we always calculate that they will not labor at all except to avoid punishment, and they will never do more than just enough to save themselves from being punished, and no amount of punishment will prevent their working carelessly or indifferently. It always seems on the plantations as if they took pains to break all the tools and spoil all the cattle that they possibly can, even when they know they'll be directly punished for it.[14]

Just how much of this was due to indifference and how much due to deliberate slowing up is hard to determine. Both factors most probably entered. A worker who had to devote himself to a dull task from which he can hope to gain nothing by exercising initiative soon slips into such a frame of mind that he does nothing more than go through the motions. His chief concern is to escape from the realities of his task and put it in the back of his mind as much as possible.

There is, indeed, a strong possibility that this behavior was a form of indirect aggression. While such an hypothesis cannot be demonstrated on the basis of the available contemporary data, it is supported by Dollard's interpretation of similar behavior which he found in Southern towns.

If the reader has ever seen Stepin Fetchit in the movies, he can picture this type of character. Fetchit always plays the part of a well-accommodated lower-class Negro, whining, vacillating, shambling, stupid, and moved by very simple cravings. There is probably an element of resistance to white society in the shambling, sullenly slow pace of the Negro; it is the gesture of a man who is forced to work for ends not his own and who expresses his reluctance to perform under these circumstances.[15]

Certainly description after description emphasizes the mechanical plodding of the slave workers:

John Lamar wrote, 'My man Ned the carpenter is idle or nearly so at the plantation. He is fixing gates and, like the idle groom in Pickwick, trying to fool himself into the belief that he is doing something — He is an eye servant.'[16]

Those I saw at work appeared to me to move very slowly and awkwardly, as did those engaged in the stables. These also were very stupid and dilatory in executing any orders given them, so that Mr. C. would frequently take the duty off their hands into his own, rather than wait for them, or make them correct their blunders; they were much, in these respects, what our farmers call *dumb Paddees* — that is, Irishmen who do not readily understand the English language, and who are still weak and stiff from the effects of the emigrating voyage. At the entrance gate was a porter's lodge, and, as I approached I saw a black face peeping at me from it, but both when I entered and left, I was obliged to dismount and open the gate myself.

Altogether, it struck me — slaves coming here as they naturally did in comparison with free laborers, as commonly employed on my own and my neighbors' farms, in exactly similar duties — that they must have been difficult to direct efficiently, and that it must be irksome and trying to one's patience, to have to superintend their labor.[17]

To what extent this reluctant labor was the rule may be appreciated when it is pointed out that a southern doctor classified it under the name *Dysaesthesia Aethiopica* as a mental disease peculiar to Negroes. Olmsted quotes this Dr. Cartwright as follows:

From the careless movements of the individual affected with this complaint, they are apt to do much mischief, which appears as if intentional, but it is mostly owing to the stupidness of mind and insensibility of the nerves induced by the disease. Thus, they break, waste, and destroy everything they handle — abuse horses and cattle — tear, burn, or rend their own clothing, and, paying no attention to the rights of property, steal others to replace what they have destroyed. They wander about at night, and keep in a half nodding state by day. They slight their work — cut up corn, cotton and tobacco, when hoeing it, as if for pure mischief. They raise disturbances with their overseers, and among their fellow servants, without cause or motive, and seem to be insensible to pain when subjected to punishment.

. . . The term "rascality" given to this disease by overseers, is founded on an erroneous hypothesis, and leads to an incorrect empirical treatment, which seldom or never cures it.[18]

There are only two possible interpretations of the doctor's statement. Either the slaves were so extraordinarily lazy that they gave the appearance of being mentally diseased, or the doctor was describing cases of hebephrenic schizophrenia. Either situation is startling. The phenomenon was obviously widespread, and if it was actually a mental disease it certainly would indicate that Negroes did not become "easily adjusted to slavery."

Whatever the case, it is certain that the slaves consciously saved their energy. Olmsted, who always had his eye open for such incidents, reported:

The overseer rode among them, on a horse, carrying in his hand a raw-hide whip, constantly directing and encouraging them; but, as my companion and I, both, several times noticed, as often as he visited one line of the operations, the hands at the other end would discontinue their labor, until he turned to ride toward them again.[19]

The few statements on this point we have by ex-slaves seem to indicate that the slaves as a group made a general policy of not letting the master get the upper hand.

I had become large and strong; and had begun to take pride in the fact that I could do as much hard work as some of the older men. There is much rivalry among slaves, at times, as to which can do the most work, and masters generally seek to promote such rivalry. But some of us were too wise to race with each other very long. Such racing, we had the sagacity to see, was not likely to pay. We had times out for measuring each other's strength, but we knew too much to keep up the competition so long as to produce an extraordinary day's work. We knew that if, by extraordinary exertion, a large quantity of work was done in one day, the fact, becoming known to the master, might lead him to require the same amount every day. This thought was enough to bring us to a dead halt whenever so much excited for the race.[20]

Writer after writer, describing incidents in which slaves were compelled to assist in punishing other slaves states that they did so with the greatest of reluctance.

The hands stood still; — they knew Randall — and they knew him also [able to] take a powerful man, and were afraid to grapple with him. As soon as Cook had ordered the men to seize him, Randall turned to them, and said — 'Boys, you all know me; you know that I can handle any three of you, and the man that lays hands on me shall die. This white man can't whip me himself, and therefore he has called you to help him.' The overseer was unable to prevail upon them to seize and secure Randall, and finally ordered them all to go to their work together.[21]

In some cases it was noted that the slave resisting punishment took pains not to treat his fellows with any more than the absolute minimum of violence.

With such demonstrations of solidarity among the slaves it is not surprising to find a slave telling of how he and his fellows "captured" the institution of the driver. The slave Solomon Northup was such a driver. His task was to whip the other slaves in order to make them work.

'Practice makes perfect,' truly; and during eight years' experience as a driver I learned to handle the whip with marvelous dexterity and precision, throwing the lash within a hair's breadth of the back, the ear, the nose without, however, touching either of them. If Epps was observed at a distance, or we had reason to apprehend he was sneaking somewhere in the vicinity, I would commence plying the lash vigorously, when, according to arrangement, they would squirm and screech as if in agony, although not one of them had in fact been grazed. Patsey would take occasion, if he made his appearance presently, to mumble in his hearing some complaints that Platt was whipping them the whole time, and Uncle Abram, with an appearance of honesty peculiar to himself would declare roundly I had just whipped them worse than General Jackson whipped the enemy at New Orleans.[22]

Williams, another slave whose task was to drive his fellows, said:

He was at these periods terribly severe to his hands, and would order me to use up the cracker of my whip every day upon the poor creatures who were toiling in the field; and in order to satisfy him, I used to tear it off when returning home at night. He would then praise me for a good fellow and invite me to drink with him.[23]

The amount of slowing up of labor by the slaves must, in the aggregate, have caused a tremendous financial loss to plantation owners. The only way we have of estimating it quantitatively is through comparison of the work done in different plantations and under different systems of labor. The statement is frequently made that production on a plantation varied more than 100% from time to time. Comparison in the output of slaves in different parts of the South also showed variations of over 100%. Most significant is the improvement in output obtained under the task, whereby the slaves were given a specific task to fulfill for their day's work, any time left over being their own. Olmsted gives us our best information on this point:

These tasks certainly would not be considered excessively hard by a northern laborer; and, in point of fact, the more industrious and active hands finished them often by two o'clock. I saw one or two leaving the field soon after one o'clock, several about two; and between three and four, I met a dozen women and several men coming home to their cabins, having finished their day's work.

Under this 'Organization of Labor' most of the slaves work rapidly and well. In nearly all ordinary work, custom has settled the extent of the task, and it is difficult to increase it. The driver who marks it out, has to remain on the ground until it is finished, and has no interest in overmeasuring it; and if it should be systematically increased very much, there is danger of a general stampede to the swamp, a danger the slave can always hold before his master's cupidity.[24]

It is the custom of tobacco manufacturers to hire slaves and free negroes at a certain rate of wages each year. A task of 45 pounds per day is given them to work up, and all they choose to do more than this, they are paid for — payment being made once a fortnight; and invariably this over-wages is used by the slave for himself, and is usually spent in drinking, licentiousness, and gambling. The man was grumbling that he had saved but $20 to spend at the holidays. One of the manufacturers offered to show me by his books, that nearly all gained by over-work $5 a month, many $20 and some as much as $28.[25]

He (the speaker) was executor of an estate in which, among other negroes, there was one very smart man, who, he knew perfectly well, ought to be earning for the estate $150 a year, and who could if he chose, yet whose wages for a year being let out by the day or job, had amounted to but $18, while he had paid for medical attendance upon him $45.[26]

The executor of the estate finally arranged for this man to work out his freedom, which he readily accomplished.

A quantitative estimate can be made from another situation which Olmsted observed. Rain during a previous day had made certain parts of the work more difficult than others. The slaves were therefore put on day work, since it would not be possible to lay out equitable tasks.

Ordinarily it is done by tasks — a certain number of the small divisions of the field being given to each hand to burn in a day; but owing to a more than usual amount of rain having fallen lately, and some other causes, making the work harder in some places than in others, the women were now working by the day, under the direction of a 'driver,' a negro man, who walked about among them, taking care they had left nothing unburned. Mr. X inspected the ground they had gone over, to see whether the driver had done his duty. It had been sufficiently well burned, but not more than a quarter as much ground had been gone over, he said, as was usually burned in tasked work, — and he thought they had been very lazy, and reprimanded them for it.[27]

Most revealing of all is this statement:

'Well, now, old man,' said I, 'you go and cut me two cords today!' 'Oh, massa! two cords! Nobody could do dat. Oh! massa, dat is too hard! Neber heard o' nobody's cuttin' more 'n a cord o' wood in a day, round heah. No nigger couldn't do it.' 'Well, old man, you have two cords of wood cut to-night or to-morrow morning you shall get two hundred lashes — that's all there is about it. So look sharp.' And he did it and ever since no negro ever cut less than two cords a day for me, though my neighbors never get but one cord. It was just so with a great many other things — mauling rails — I always have two hundred rails mauled in a day; just twice what it is the custom of the country to expect of a negro, and just twice as many as my negroes had been made to do before I managed them myself.

These estimates, let it be recollected in conclusion, are all deliberately and carefully made by gentlemen of liberal education, who have had unusual facilities of observing both at the North and the South.[28]

The slaves were well aware of their economic value, and used it to good advantage. The skilled laborers among the slaves knew their worth, and frequently rebelled against unsatisfactory work situations. Slaves who were hired out would run away from the masters who had hired them, and then either return home, or remain in hiding until they felt like returning to work.

The slave, if he is indisposed to work, and especially if he is not treated well, or does not like the master who has hired him, will sham sickness — even make himself sick or lame — that he need not work. But a more serious loss frequently arises, when the slave, thinking he is worked too hard, or being angered by punishment or unkind treatment,'getting the sulks,' takes to 'the swamp.' and comes back when he has a mind to. Often this will not be till the year is up for which he is engaged, when he will return to his owner, who, glad to find his property safe, and that it has not died in the swamp, or gone to Canada, forgets to punish him, and immediately sends him for another year to a new master.

'But, meanwhile, how does the negro support life in the swamp?' I asked.

'Oh, he gets sheep and pigs and calves, and fowls and turkey; sometimes they will kill a small cow. We have often seen the fires, where they were cooking them, through the woods in the swamp yonder. If it is cold, he will crawl under a fodder stack, or go into the cabin with some of the other negroes, and in the same way, you see, he can get all the corn, or almost anything else he wants.'

'He steals them from his master?'

'From anyone: frequently from me. I have had many a sheep taken by them.'[29]

'It is a common thing, then?'

'Certainly it is, very common, and the loss is sometimes exceedingly provoking. One of my neighbors here was going to build, and hired two mechanics for a year. Just as he was ready to put his house up, the two men, taking offense at something, both ran away, and did not come back at all, till their year was out, and then their owner immediately hired them out again to another man.'[30]

One plantation overseer wrote to the plantation owner concerning a carpenter he had hired out to one G. Moore:

Not long before Jim run away G More (sic.) wanted him to make some gates and I sent him theireselves (sic.) and he run away from him and cum home and then he left me withow (sic.) a cause.[31]

Even the threat of a whipping did not deter such slaves from running off for a time when they were displeased. The quotation from Olmsted below is typical of a constantly recurring pattern of statements:

The manager told me that the people often ran away after they have been whipped or something else had happened to make them angry. They hide in the swamp and come into the cabins at night to get food. They seldom remain away more than a fortnight and when they come in they are whipped.[32]

Some of the resistance took on the aspects of organized strikes:

Occasionally, however, a squad would strike in a body as a protest against severities. An episode of this sort was recounted in a letter of a Georgia overseer to his absent employer: 'Sir: I write you a few lines in order to let you know that six of your hands has left the plantation — every man but Jack. They displeased me with their work and I give some of them a few lashes, Tom with the rest. On Wednesday morning they were missing. I think they are lying out until they can see you or your Uncle Jack.' The slaves could not negotiate directly at such a time, but while they lay in the woods they might make overtures to the overseer through slaves on a neighboring plantation as to terms upon which they would return to work, or they might await their master's posthaste arrival and appeal to him for a redress of grievances. Humble as their demeanor might be, their power of renewing the pressure by repeating their act could not be ignored.[33]

John Holmes, an escaped slave, told how he ran off and hid in the swamp after an overseer attempted to whip him.

At last they told all the neighbors if I would come home, they wouldn't whip me. I was a great hand to work and made a great deal of money for our folks.[34]

The same overseer had further trouble with the slaves.

She (a slave) was better with her fists, and beat him, but he was better at wrestling and threw her down. He then called the men to help him, but all hid from him in a brush where we were working. . . . Then (later) the calculation was to whip us every one, because we did not help the overseer. . . . That night everyone of us went away into the woods. . . . We went back, but after a while (the overseer) came back too, and stayed the year out. He whipped the women but he did not whip the men, of fear they would run away.[35]

III

The indifference of the slaves to the welfare of the masters extended itself to complete contempt for property values. The slaves were so careless with tools that they were equipped with special tools, and more clumsy than ordinary ones:

The 'nigger hoe' was first introduced into Virginia as a substitute for the plow, in breaking up the soil. The law fixes its weight at four pounds, — as heavy as the woodman's axe. It is still used, not only in Virginia, but in Georgia and the Carolinas. The planters tell us, as the reason for its use, that the negroes would break a Yankee hoe in pieces on the first root, or stone that might be in their way. An instructive commentary on the difference between free and slave labor![36]

The absence of motive, and the consequent want of mental energy to give vigor to the arm of the slave is the source of another great drawback upon the usefulness of his labour. His implements or tools are at least one-third (in some instances more than twofold) heavier and stronger than the northern man's to counteract his want of skill and interest in his work. A Negro hoe or scythe would be a curiosity to a New England farmer.[37]

Not only tools but livestock suffered from the mistreatment by the slaves. Olmsted found not only the "nigger hoe" but even discovered that mules were substituted for horses because horses could not stand up under the treatment of the slaves.

. . . . I am shown tools that no man in his senses, with us, would allow a laborer, to whom he was paying wages, to be encumbered with; and the excessive weight and clumsiness of which, I would judge, would make work at least ten per cent greater than those ordinarily used with us. And I am assured that, in the careless and clumsy way they must be used by the slaves, anything lighter or less crude could not be furnished them with good economy, and that such tools as we constantly give our laborers and find profit in giving them, would not last out a day in a Virginia corn-field — much lighter and more free from stones though it be than ours.

So, too, when I ask why mules are so universally substituted for horses on the farm, the first reason given, and confessedly the most conclusive one, is, that horses cannot bear the treatment they always must get from negroes; horses are always soon foundered or crippled by them but mules will bear cudgeling, and lose a meal or two now and then, and not be materially injured, and they do not take cold or get sick if neglected or overworked. But I do not need to go further than to the window of the room in which I am writing, to see, at almost any time, treatment of cattle that would insure the immediate discharge of the driver, by almost any farmer owning them in the North.[38]

Redpath verifies Olmsted's statement — by telling how he saw slaves treat stock. It is important to note that Redpath was a strong abolitionist and most sympathetic toward the slaves.

He rode the near horse, and held a heavy cowhide in his hand, with which from time to time he lashed the leaders, as barbarous drivers lash oxen when at work. Whenever we came to a hill, especially if it was very steep, he dismounted, lashed the horses with all his strength, varying his performances by picking up stones, none of them smaller than half a brick, and throwing them with all his force, at the horses' legs. He seldom missed.

The wagon was laden with two tons of plaster in sacks.

This is a fair specimen of the style in which Negroes treat stock.[39]

The indifference to livestock is well illustrated by an incident which Olmsted recounts:

I came, one afternoon, upon a herd of uncommonly fine cattle as they were being turned out of a field by a negro woman. She had given herself the trouble to let down but two of the seven bars of the fence, and they were obliged to leap over a barrier at least four feet high. Last of all came, very unwillingly, a handsome heifer, heavy with calf; the woman urged her with a cudgel and she jumped, but lodging on her belly, as I came up she lay bent, and, as it seemed, helplessly hung upon the top bar. . . . The woman struck her severely and with a painful effort she boggled over.[40]

In the Sea Islands off the coast of Georgia, Kemble reported that the slaves started immense fires, destroying large sections of woods through carelessness or maliciousness.

The 'field hands' make fires to cook their midday food wherever they happen to be working, and sometimes through their careless neglect, but sometimes, too, undoubtedly on purpose, the woods are set fire to by these means. One benefit they consider . . . is the destruction of the dreaded rattlesnakes.[41]

The slaves on Lewis' West Indies plantation let cattle get into one of his best cane-pieces because they neglected to guard them, being more interested in a dance which was going on. They were fully aware that the cattle were ruining the sugar cane, but kept right on singing and dancing. Lewis was able to get only a handful of house servants to drive the cattle out of the cane, and that not until the cane-piece was ruined.[42]

One tobacco planter complained that his slaves would cut the young plants indiscriminately unless they were watched. When it became late in the season and there was need of haste to avoid frost they would work only the thickest leaving the sparser ones untouched.[43] Another planter said that he could cultivate only the poorer grades of tobacco because the slaves would not give necessary attention to the finer sort of plants.[44] An English visitor said:

The kitchens and out-offices are always at the distance of several yards from the principal dwelling. This is done as well to guard against the house-Negroes through carelessness setting the houses on fire, for they generally sit over it half the night, as to keep out their noise. (sic.)[45]

The full import of these practices strikes home fully only when they are read in the words of the original observers. Olmsted's comments, and the ease with which he found incidents to illustrate them, are most valuable. So important is his testimony that we must once more quote him at some length.

Incidents, trifling in themselves, constantly betray to a stranger the bad economy of using enslaved servants. The catastrophe of one such occurred since I began to write this letter. I ordered a fire to be made in my room, as I was going out this morning. On my return, I found a grand fire — the room door having been closed and locked upon it 'out of order.' Just now, while I was writing, down tumbled upon the floor, and rolled away close to the valance of the bed, half a hod-full of ignited coal, which had been so piled upon the diminutive grate, and left without a fender or any guard, that this result was almost inevitable. If I had not returned at the time I did, the house would have been fired.[46]

On the rice plantation which I have particularly described, the slaves were, I judge, treated with at least as much discretion and judicious consideration of economy, consistently with humane regard to their health, comfort, and morals, as on any other in all the Slave States; yet I could not avoid observing — and I certainly took no pains to do so, nor were any special facilities offered me for it — repeated instances of that waste and misapplication of labor which it can never be possible to guard against, when the agents of industry are slaves. Many such evidences of waste it would not be easy to specify; and others, which remain in my memory after some weeks, do not adequately account for the general impression that all I saw gave me; but there were, for instance, under my observation gates left open and bars left down, against standing orders; rails removed from fences by the negroes (as was conjectured, to kindle their fires with, mules lamed, and implements broken, by careless usage; a flat boat, carelessly secured, going adrift on the river; men ordered to cart rails for a new fence depositing them so that a double expense of labor would be required to lay them, more than would have needed if they had been placed, as they might have almost as easily been, by a slight exercise of forethought . . . making statements which their owner was obliged to receive as sufficient excuse, though, he told me, he felt assured they were false — all going to show habitual carelessness, indolence, and mere eye-service.[47]

But not only did the Negro slaves refuse to work, and not only did they destroy property, but they even made it impossible for planters to introduce new work techniques by feigning clumsiness. They prevented the introduction of the plow in this way on many plantations.[48] Olmsted here cites many instances. Lewis, quoted in *Plantation Documents*, found the same thing to be true in Jamaica.

It appears to me that nothing could afford so much relief to the negroes, under the existing system of Jamaica, as the substituting of labor of animals for that of slaves in agriculture wherever such a measure is practicable. On leaving the island, I impressed this wish of mine upon the mind of my agents with all my power; but the only result has been the creating a very considerable expense in the purchase of ploughs, oxen and farming implements; the awkwardness and still more the obstinacy of the few negroes, whose services were indispensable, was not to be overcome: they broke plough after plough, and ruined beast after beast, till the attempt was abandoned in despair.[49]

IV

Malingering was a well-known phenomenon throughout the slave states.[50] The purpose of feigning illness was generally to avoid work, although occasionally a slave who was being sold would feign a disability either to avoid being sold to an undesirable master, or to lower his purchase price so as to obtain revenge on a former master. The women occasionally pretended to be pregnant, because pregnant women were given lighter work assignments and were allowed extra rations of food.

In a situation such as this in which physical disability was an advantage, one would expect much malingering. One might also expect to find functional mental disorders, hysterical disorders which would get one out of work. There is some evidence that many had such functional disorders.

There are many complaints described in Dr. Cartwright's treatise, to which the Negroes, in slavery, seem to be peculiarly subject.

'Negro-consumption,' a disease almost unknown to medical men of the Northern States and of Europe, is also sometimes fearfully prevalent among the slaves. 'It is of importance,' says the Doctor, 'to know the pathognomic signs in its early stages, not only in regard to its treatment but to detect impositions, as negroes, afflicted with this complaint are often for sale; the acceleration of the pulse, on exercise, incapacitates them for labor, as they quickly give out, and have to leave their work. This induces their owneres to sell them, although they may not know the cause of their inability to labor. Many of the negroes brought South, for sale, are in the incipient stages of this disease; they are found to be inefficient laborers, and sold in consequence thereof. The effect of superstition — a firm belief that he is poisoned or conjured — upon the patient's mind, already in a morbid state (dysaesthesia), and his health affected from hard usage, overtasking or exposure, want of wholesome food, good clothing, warm, comfortable lodging, with the distressing idea (sometimes) that he is an object of hatred or dislike, both to his master or fellow-servants, and has no one to befriend him, tends directly to generate that erythism of mind which is the essential cause of negro consumption.' '. . . Remedies should be assisted by removing the *original cause*[51] of the dissatisfaction or trouble of mind, and by using every means to make the patient comfortable, satisfied and happy.'[52]

Of course it is impossible to determine the extent of these disorders. Assuming that Dr. Cartwright's assumption was correct, very few observers would be qualified to make an adequate diagnosis, and a very small proportion of these would be inclined to accept his interpretation. After all, functional disorders are in many cases almost impossible to tell from real disorders or from feigning, since the behavior which Cartwright describes could very easily be interpreted on another, and easier, level by a less acute observer.

Of the extent to which illness was feigned there can, however, be little doubt. Some of the feigning was quite obvious, and one might wonder why such flagrant abuses were tolerated. The important thing to remember is that a slave was an important economic investment. Most slave owners sooner or later found out that it was more profitable to give the slave the benefit of the doubt. A sick slave driven to work might very well die.

But the same gentleman admitted that he had sometimes been mistaken and had made men go to work when they afterwards proved to be really ill; therefore, when one of his people told him he was not able to work, he usually thought, 'very likely he'll be all the better for a day's rest, whether he's really ill or not,' and would let him off without being very particular in his examination. Lately he had been getting a new overseer, and when he was engaging him he told him that this was his way. The observer replied, 'It's my way too, now; it didn't used to be, but I had a lesson. There was a nigger one day at Mr. ———'s who was sulky and complaining; he said he couldn't work. I looked at his tongue, and it was right clean, and I thought it was nothing but damned sulkiness so I paddled him, and made him go to work; but, two days after, he was under ground. He was a good eight hundred dollar nigger, and it was a lesson to me about taming possums, that I ain't going to forget in a hurry.'[53]

So one might find situations like this:

At one, which was evidently the 'sick house' or hospital, there were several negroes, of both sexes, wrapped in blankets, and reclining on the door steps or on the ground, basking in sunshine. Some of them looked ill, but all were chatting and laughing as I rode up to make inquiry.[54]

The situation turned in on itself. The masters were always suspicious of the sick slaves, so that slaves who were moderately sick accentuated their symptoms in order to make out a convincing case.

It is said to be nearly as difficult to form a satisfactory diagnosis of negroes' disorders, as it is of infants', because their imagination of symptoms is so vivid, and because not the smallest reliance is to be placed on their accounts of what they have felt or done. If a man is really ill, he fears lest he should be thought to be simulating, and therefore exaggerates all his pains, and locates them in whatever he supposes to be the most vital parts of his system.

Frequently the invalid slaves will neglect or refuse to use the remedies prescribed for their recovery. They will conceal pills, for instance, under their tongue, and declare they have swallowed them, when, from their producing no effect, it will be afterwards evident that they have not. This general custom I heard ascribed to habit acquired when they were not very disagreeably ill and were loth to be made quite well enough to have to go to work again.[55]

Fortunately in this field we have some quantitative estimates which enable us to appreciate fully the extent of these practices. Sydnor has digested the records of sickness on various plantations. From the Wheeles plantation records he found that of 1,429 working days 179 were lost on account of sickness, a ratio of almost one to seven. On the Bowles' plantation, in one year 159½ days were missed on account of sickness but only five days were on Sundays. This is a recurrent pattern, everybody sick on Saturday, and scarcely anybody sick on Sunday. On the Leigh plantation, where thirty persons were working there were 398 days of sickness. In examining this record Sydnor discovered that the rate of sickness was greatest at the times of the year when there was the most work to be done.[56] Olmsted says that he never visited a plantation on which twenty Negroes were employed where he did not find one or more not at work on some trivial pretext.[57]

Lewis' anecdote is typical:

On Saturday morning there were no fewer than forty-five persons (not including children) in the hospital; which makes nearly a fifth of my whole gang. Of these the medical people assured me that not above seven had anything whatever the matter with them. . . . And sure enough on Sunday morning they all walked away from the hospital to amuse themselves, except about seven or eight.[58]

Sometimes the feigning did not work, as is shown by two incidents that Olmsted relates:

A Mr. X asked if there were any sick people.
'Nobody, oney dat boy Sam, sar.'
'What Sam is that?'
'Dat little Sam, sar; Tom's Sue's Sam, sar.'
'What's the matter with him?'
'Don' spec der's nothing much de matter wid him now, sar. He came in Sa'dy, complaining he had de stomach-ache, an' I give him some ile, sar, 'spec he mus' be well dis time, but he din go out dis mornin'.
'Well, I see to him.'
Mr. X went to Tom's Sue's cabin, looked at the boy and concluded that he was well, though he lay abed, and pretended to cry with pain, ordered him to go out to work.[59]

A planter asked the nurse if anyone else was sick.

'Oney dat woman Caroline.'
'What do you think is the matter with her?'
'Well, I don't think there is anything de matter wid her, masser; I mus answer you for true, I don't tink anything de matter wid her, oney she's a little sore from dat whipping she got.'
The manager found the woman groaning on a dirty bed and after examining her, scolded her and sent her to work.[60]

The prevalence of malingering may be better appreciated when one realizes that despite the fact that Olmsted refers to it throughout four volumes of his works, in one place he has five whole pages of anecdotes concerning it.[61]

Pretending to be pregnant was a type of escape in a class by itself, since the fraud must inevitably have been discovered. This in itself may give us some insight into the Negroes' attitude toward the relative advantages of escaping work and of escaping punishment. Just as the slave who ran off into the woods for a temporary relief from work, the pseudo-pregnant woman must have realized in advance that she would inevitably be punished.

I will tell you of a most comical account Mr. ——— has given me of the prolonged and still protracted pseudo-pregnancy of a woman called Markie, who for many more months than are generally required for the process of continuing the human species, pretended to be what the Germans pathetically and poetically call 'in good hope' and continued to reap increased rations as the reward of her expectation, till she finally had to disappoint the estate and receive a flogging.[62]

One woman sought to escape from the consequences of her fraud. The results were quite tragic:

A young slave woman, Becky by name, had given pregnancy as the reason for a continued slackness in her work. Her master became skeptical and gave notice that she was to be examined and might expect the whip in case her excuse were not substantiated. Two days afterwards a Negro midwife announced that Becky's baby had been born; but at the same time a neighboring planter began search for a child nine months old which was missing from his quarter. This child was found in Becky's cabin, with its two teeth pulled and the tip of its navel cut off. It died; and Becky was convicted only of manslaughter.[63]

An outstanding example of malingering is given by Smedes, a writer who insisted so emphatically on the devotion of the slaves to their masters.
The cook's husband, who for years had looked on himself as nearly blind, and therefore unable to do more than work about her, and put her wood on the fire, sometimes cutting a stick or two, made no less than eighteen good crops for himself when the war was over. He was one of the best farmers in the country.[64]

The most effective means of retaliation against an unpopular master which the slave had at his command was by feigning disability on the auction block. How often this was done we do not know, but Phillips accepts it as a recognized pattern.

Those on the block often times praised their own strength and talents, for it was a matter of pride to fetch high prices. On the other hand if a slave should bear a grudge against his seller, or should hope to be bought only by someone who would expect but light service he might pretend a disability though he had it not.[65]

Coleman offers the same opinion:

Similar actions were not unknown in slave sales. Frequently on such occasions there is a strong indispositon in such creatures to be sold, and that by stratagem to avoid sale, they may frequently feign sickness, or magnify any particular complaint with which they are affected.[66]

As was customary at a public auction of slaves, the auctioneer announced that Mr. Anderson, the master, would give a bill of sale for his slave with the usual guarantee — 'sound of mind and body and a slave for life.' While there began a lively bidding among the Negro traders, George suddenly assumed a strange appearance — his head was thrown back, his eyes rolled wildly, his body and limbs began to twitch and jerk in an unheard of manner.

'What's the matter with your boy, Mr. Anderson?' one of the traders asked the owner, who, astonished and puzzled, drew nearer the block. But Mr. Anderson did not answer the question. George was now foaming at the mouth, and the violent twitching and jerking increased precipitously.

'What's the matter with you, boy?' gruffly demanded the trader. 'O, I 'es fits I has!' exclaimed George, whereupon his body doubled up and rolled off the block.

Of course the auction was hastily terminated. George was hustled off to jail, and a doctor sent for, but, after a careful examination; the medical man was somewhat mystified as to the slave's actual condition. He advised the master to leave George in the jailer's custody for a while, promising to look in on him the next morning. Under his master's instruction, the wily slave was put to bed in the debtor's room, where he soon sank, apparently, into a sound sleep.

Next morning when the jailer brought in breakfast, he found the bed empty. George was gone, and nothing was heard of him again until word came, several weeks later, that he was safe in Canada.[67]

Or, again, we read:

A young girl, of twenty years or thereabouts, was the next commodity put up. Her right hand was entirely useless — 'dead,' as she aptly called it. One finger had been cut off by a doctor, and the auctioneer stated that she herself chopped off the other finger — her forefinger — because it hurt her, and she thought that to cut it off would cure it.

'Didn't you cut your finger off?' asked a man, 'kase you was mad?'

She looked at him quietly, but with a glance of contempt, and said:

'No, you see it was a sort o' sore, and I thought it would be better to cut it off than be plagued with it.'

Several persons around me expressed the opinion that she had done it willfully, to spite her master or mistress, or to keep her from being sold down South.[68]

Another instance is described as follows:

As I came up, a second-rate plantation hand of the name of Noah, but whom the crier persisted in calling 'Noey,' was being offered, it being an administrator's sale. Noey, on mounting the steps, had assumed a most drooping aspect, hanging his head and affecting the feebleness of old age. He had probably hoped to have avoided sale by a dodge, which is very common in such cases. But the first bid — $1,000 — startled him, and he looked eagerly to the quarter whence it proceeded. 'Never mind who he is, he has got the money. Now, gentlemen, just go on; who will say fifty.' and so the crier proceeds with his monotonous calling. 'I ain't worth all that, mass'r; I ain't much count no how,' cried Noey energetically to the first bidder. 'Yes you are, Noey — ah, $1,000, thank you, sir,' replies the crier.[69]

The strength of Negro resistance to slavery becomes apparent in the extent to which the slaves mutilated themselves in their efforts to escape work. A girl on Lewis' plantation who had been injured tied pack thread around her wounds when they started to heal and then rubbed dirt in them. In her anxiety to avoid work she gave herself a very serious infection.[70] But this action was mild compared to that of others.

General Leslie Coombs, of Lexington, owned a man named Ennis, a house carpenter. He had bargained with a slave-trader to take him and carry him down the river. Ennis was determined not to go. He took a broadaxe and cut one hand off; then contrived to lift the axe, with his arm pressing it to his body, and let it fall upon the other, cutting off the ends of the fingers.[71]

'*But some on 'em would rather be shot then be took, sir,*' he added simply.

A farmer living near a swamp confirmed this account, and said he knew of three or four being shot on one day.[72]

Planters had much trouble with slaves fresh from Africa, the new slaves committing suicide in great numbers. Ebo Landing in the Sea Islands was the site of the mass suicide of Ebo slaves who simply walked in a body into the ocean and drowned themselves. A planter writing on the handling of slaves mentions the difficulty of adjusting the Africans to slavery. He advocates mixing them in with seasoned slaves.

It too often happens that poor masters, who have no other slaves or are too greedy, require hard labor of these fresh negroes, exhaust them quickly, lose them by sickness and more often by grief. Often they hasten their own death; some wound themselves, others stifle themselves by drawing in the tongue so as to close the breathing passage, others take poison, or flee and perish of misery and hunger.[73]

The one problem of Negro resistance to slavery which is most enticing is that of the attitude of slave mothers toward their children. There are frequent references in the literature to Negro women who boasted about the number of "niggers they hade for the massah," but breeding was probably quite secondary to sex activity. It would be interesting to discover the motives behind this apparent pleasure in presenting babies to the master. Some of the women may have been sincere in their pride. What makes this problem peculiarly important is the presence of much indirect evidence that, the Negro mothers either had no affection for their children, or did not want them to be raised as slaves.

We know quite well that African Negroes are (at least reasonably) able to take care of their children, and that the slave women efficiently tended the children of the plantation mistress. Yet one runs across comment after comment that the Negro mothers were ignorant, and careless, and did not know how to care for their own offspring. Typical of such statements is this:

> The Negro mothers are often so ignorant and indolent, that they cannot be trusted to keep awake and administer medicine to their own children; so that the mistress has often to sit up all night with a sick Negro child.[74]

Guion Johnson states that plantation owners in the Sea Islands offered the mothers rewards to take good care of their children. They were paid for those who survived the first year! This at least would indicate that there was something to be desired in their attitude toward their children.

Occasionally one runs across a reference to a slave mother killing her child, but the statements are almost invariably incomplete. For instance, Catterall[75] has a record of a trial, the details of which are: "The prisoner was indicted for murder of her own child," no more. Or a plantation overseer writes, "Elizabeth's child died last night. She smothered it somehow."[76] There is no indication as to whether or not the smothering was deliberate.

Several cases, where it was certain that parents killed their children to keep them from slavery, have been described. They are important enough to be given in detail.

Of all the cases of slave rendition, the saddest and probably the most circulated at the time was that of Margaret Garner. Winter was the best time for flight across the Ohio River, for when it was frozen over the difficulties of crossing were fewer. Simeon Garner, with his wife Margaret and two children, fled from slavery in Kentucky during the cold winter of 1856 and, after crossing the frozen stream at night, made their ways to the house of a free Negro in Cincinnati.

Quickly tracing the fugitive Negroes to their hideout in Cincinnati, the armed pursuers, after some resistance, broke down the door and entered the house. There they found Margaret, the mother, who, preferring death to slavery for her children, had striven to take their lives, and one child lay dead on the floor. The case was immediately brought into court, where despite the efforts made by sympathetic whites, rendition was ordered. On their return to slavery, Margaret in despair attempted to drown herself and child by jumping into the river but even the deliverance of death was denied her, for she was recovered and soon thereafter sold to a trader who took her to the cotton fields of the Far South.[77]

Not only were slaves known to take the lives of their masters or overseers, but they were now and then charged with the murder of their own children, sometimes to prevent them from growing up in bondage. In Covington a father and mother, shut up in a slave baracoon and doomed to the southern market, 'when there was no eye to pity them and no arm to save,' did by mutual agreement 'send the souls of their children to Heaven rather than have them descend to the hell of slavery,' and then both parents committed suicide.[78]

'Take off your shoes, Sylva,' said Mrs. A., 'and let this gentleman see your feet.'

'I don't want to,' said Sylva.

'But I want you to,' said her mistress.

'I don't care if you do,' replied Sylva sullenly.

'You must,' said the mistress firmly.

The fear of punishment impelled her to remove the shoes. Four toes on one foot, and two on the other were wanting! 'There!' said the mistress, 'my husband, who learned the blacksmith's trade for the purpose of teaching it to the slaves, to increase their market value, has, with his own hands, pounded off and wrung off all those toes, when insane with passion. And it was only last week that he thought Sylva was saucy to me, and he gave her thirty lashes with the horse whip. She was so old that I could not bear to see it, and I left the house.

'Sylva says,' Mrs. A. continued, 'that she had been the mother of thirteen children, every one of whom she has destroyed with her own hands, in their infancy, rather than have them suffer slavery'!'[79]

V

The patterns of resistance to slavery studied in this paper are: (1) deliberate slowing up of work; (2) destruction of property, and indifferent work (3) feigning illness and pregnancy; (4) injuring one's self; (5) suicide; (6) a possibility that a significant number of slave mothers killed their children.

The motivation behind these acts was undoubtedly complex. The most obvious of the motives was a desire to avoid work. It has been demonstrated that the slaves were acutely conscious of the fact that they had nothing to gain by hard work except in those instances where they were working under the task system. The destruction of property and the poor quality of the slaves' work was mainly due to their indifference to their tasks. There is enough evidence that they could, and did, work hard and well when sufficiently motivated to refute any contention that the Negro slaves were congenitally poor workers.

Many of the slaves reacted to the institution of slavery in a far more drastic fashion than could be manifested by a mere desire to avoid work. Some of these slaves committed suicide; others killed members of their families, usually their children, in order that they might not grow up as slaves.

Possibly the most significant aspect of these patterns of resistance is the aggression against the white masters they imply. Unfortunately, however, though this aspect may be the most significant, it is the least subject to proof. On the plane of logic, there is every reason to believe that a people held in bondage would devise techniques such as have been described above as an indirect means of retaliation. The statement of Dollard, previously quoted,[80] indicates that such techniques (slowness, inefficiency, etc.) are used at the present time as a means of indirect aggression.

The material presented here suggests the need for a reconsideration of the concept of the Negro's easy adjustment to slavery. He was not a cheerful, efficient worker, as has been assumed. Rather, he was frequently rebellious, and almost always sullen, as any person faced with a disagreeable situation from which he cannot escape will normally be. Nor, can the belief that racial inferiority is responsible for inefficient workmanship on his part be supported. For such deficiencies of his workmanship as he manifested, or, indeed, may still be manifested, are seen to be explainable in terms that are in no sense to be couched in the conventional mold of inherent racial differences.

Notes

[1] We wish to express our appreciation to Professor M. J. Herskovits, under whose direction this research has been carried on.

[2] Reuter, E. B., *The American Race Problem,* New York, 1927, p. 7.

[3] Cf. Aptheker, Herbert, "American Negro Slave Revolts," *Science and Society,* 1:512–538, 1937; Wish, Harvey, "American Slave Insurrections before 1861," *Journal of Negro History,* 23:435–450, 1928; Wish, Harvey, "The Slave Insurrection Panic of 1856," *Journal of Southern History,* 5:206–222, 1939; see also Herskovits, M. J., *The Myth of the Negro Past,* pp. 99–106.

[4] Clarke, Lewis, *Narratives of the Sufferings of Lewis and Milton Clarke,* Boston, 1846, p. 123.

[5] Redpath, James, *The Roving Editor: or, Talks with Slaves in the Southern States,* New York, 1859.

[6] Dollard, John, *Caste and Class in a Southern Town,* New Haven, 1937, pp. 255, 256.

[7] Douglass, Frederick, *Life and Times of Frederick Douglass,* p. 8.

[8] Wm. Brown, an escaped slave; in: Benjamin Drew, *The Refugee,* Boston, 1856, p. 281.

[9] Thomas Hedgebeth, a free Negro, in: Benjamin Drew, *The Refugee,* Boston, 1856, p. 276.

[10] Lyell, Sir Charles, *A Second Visit to the United States of America,* New York, 1849, II, 72.

[11] Ozanne, T. D., *The South as It Is,* London, 1863, pp. 165, 166.

[12] Anon., *An Inquiry Into the Condition and Prospects of the African Race,* Philadelphia, 1839, p. 83.

[13] Olmsted, F. L., *A Journey in the Seaboard Slave States,* New York, 1863, p. 210.

[14] *Ibid.,* p. 104.

[15] Dollard, *op. cit.,* p. 257.

[16] Phillips, U. B., *American Negro Slavery,* New York, 1918, p. 192.

[17] Olmsted, *op. cit.,* p. 11.

[18] Olmsted, *op. cit.,* pp. 192, 193.

[19] *Ibid.,* p. 388.

[20] Douglass, *op. cit.,* p. 261.

[21] Brown, W. W., *Life of Williams Welles Brown, A Fugitive Slave,* Boston, 1848, p. 18. See also Williams, James, *Narratives of James Williams,* Boston, 1838, pp. 56, 62, 65.

[22] Northup, Solomon, *Twelve Years a Slave,* 1853, pp. 226, 227.

[23] Williams, James, *Narratives of James Williams,* Boston, 1838, p. 43.

[24] Olmsted, *op. cit.,* pp. 435, 436.

[25] *Ibid.,* p. 103.

[26] *Ibid.,* p. 103.

[27] *Ibid.,* p. 430.

[28] *Ibid.,* p. 207.

[29] The speaker had freed his slaves.

[30] Olmsted, *op. cit.,* pp. 100, 101.

[31] Bassett, J. S., *The Southern Plantation Overseer as Revealed in His Letters,* Northampton, Mass., 1925, p. 66.

[32] Olmsted, F. L., *A Journey in the Back Country,* New York, 1863, p. 79.

[33] Phillips, U. B., *American Negro Slavery,* pp. 303, 304.

[34] Drew, B., *The Refugee,* p. 164.

[35] *Ibid.,* p. 167.

[36] Parson, C. G., *Inside View of Slavery,* Boston, 1853, p. 94.

[37] Anon., *An Inquiry Into the Condition and Prospects of the African Race,* Philadelphia, 1839, p. 83.

[38] Olmsted, F. L., *A Journey in the Seaboard Slave States,* pp. 46, 47.

[39] Redpath, *op. cit.,* p. 241.

[40] Olmsted, F. L., *A Journey in the Back Country,* p. 227.

[41] Kemble, F. A. *Journal of a Residence on a Georgian Plantation in 1838–1839,* New York, 1863, p. 242.

[42] Lewis, M. G., *Journal of a West Indian Proprietor, 1815–1817,* London, 1929, p. 267.

[43] Phillips, U. B., *Plantation and Frontier Documents, 1649–1863,* Cleveland, 1909, p. 34.

[44] Olmsted, F. L., *A Journey in the Seaboard Slave States,* p. 91.

[45] Hanson, C. W., *The Stranger in America,* London, 1807, p. 357.

[46] Olmsted, F. L., *A Journey in the Seaboard Slave States,* p. 145.

[47] *Ibid.,* p. 480.

[48] *Ibid.,* pp. 481–484.

[49] Phillips, U. B., *Plantation and Frontier Documents,* 1694–1863, p. 137.

[50] Since this paper was written a significant contribution has appeared which throws a new light on the subject of slave illness. (Felice Swados, "Negro Health on the Ante Bellum Plantations," *Bulletin of the History of Medicine,* vol. x, no. 3, October, 1941.) Though Swados demonstrated that the rate of actual sickness among the Negroes was very high, she leaves

some doubt as to what proportion of sickness was feigned. For instance, in a footnote (p. 472) she refers to Sydnor's compilations of the records of sickness on several plantations as indications of the extent of actual sickness, even going so far as to note that on one plantation most of the sickness occurred during the picking season. Sydnor, himself, indicates that he believes that these records demonstrate that a great deal of the sickness was feigned.

[51] Cartwright's italics.

[52] Olmsted, F. L., *A Journey in the Seaboard Slave States*, p. 193.

[53] *Ibid.*, p. 189.

[54] *Ibid.*, pp. 416, 417.

[55] *Ibid.*, p. 187.

[56] Sydnor, C. S., *Slavery in Mississippi*, New York, 1933, pp. 45 ff.

[57] Olmsted, F. L., *A Journey in the Seaboard Slave States*, p. 187.

[58] Lewis, M. G., *Journal of a West Indian Proprietor, 1815–1817*, London, 1929, p. 168.

[59] Olmsted. F. L., *A Journey in the Seaboard Slave States*, pp. 423, 424.

[60] Olmsted, F. L., *A Journey in the Back Country*, p. 77.

[61] Olmsted, F. L., *A Journey in the Seaboard Slave States*, pp. 187–191.

[62] Kemble, F. A., *op. cit.*, p. 235.

[63] Phillips, U. B., *American Negro Slavery*, p. 436.

[64] Smedes, S., *Memorials of a Southern Planter*, Baltimore, 1887, p. 80.

[65] Phillips, U. B., *American Negro Slavery*, p. 199.

[66] Coleman, J. W., *Slavery Times in Kentucky*, Chapel Hill, N.C., 1940, p. 130.

[67] *Ibid.*, pp. 129–130.

[68] Redpath, *op. cit.*, pp. 253–254.

[69] Pollard, E. A., *The Southern Spy*, Washington, 1859, pp. 13–14.

[70] Lewis, *op. cit.*, p. 168.

[71] Clarke, *op. cit.*, p. 125.

[72] Olmsted, F. L., *A Journey in the Seaboard Slave States*, p. 160.

[73] Phillips, U. B., *Plantation and Frontier Documents*, II, p. 31.

[74] Lyell, *op. cit.*, p. 264.

[75] Catterall, H. H. (ed.), *Judicial Cases Concerning American Slavery and the Negro*, Washington, D.C., 1926–1937, Vol. II, p. 59.

[76] Bassett, *op. cit.*, p. 59.

[77] Coleman, J. W., *op. cit.*, p. 208.

[78] *Ibid.*, p. 269.

[79] Parson, C. G. *op. cit.*, p. 212.

[80] See above, p. 41.

A Troublesome Property

Kenneth M. Stampp

Slaves apparently thought of the South's peculiar institution chiefly as a system of labor extortion. Of course they felt its impact in other ways — in their social status, their legal status, and their private lives — but they felt it most acutely in their lack of control over their own time and labor. If discontented with bondage, they could be expected to direct their protests principally against the master's claim to their work. Whether the majority were satisfied with their lot, whether they willingly obeyed the master's commands, has long been a controversial question.

It may be a little presumptuous of one who has never been a slave to pretend to know how slaves felt; yet defenders of slavery did not hesitate to assert that most of them were quite content with servitude. Bondsmen generally were cheerful and acquiescent — so the argument went — because they were treated with kindness and relieved of all responsibilities; having known no other condition, they unthinkingly accepted bondage as their natural status. "They find themselves first existing in this state," observed a Northerner who had resided in Mississippi, "and pass through life without questioning the justice of their allotment, which, if they think at all, they suppose a natural one."[1] Presumably they acquiesced, too, because of innate racial traits, because of the "genius of African temperament," the Negro being "instinctively . . . contented" and "quick to respond to the stimulus of joy, quick to forget his grief." Except in rare instances when he was cruelly treated, his "peaceful frame of mind was not greatly disturbed by the mere condition of slavery."[2]

Though sometimes asserted with such assurance, it was never proved that the great majority of bondsmen had no concept of freedom and were therefore contented. It was always based upon inference. Most masters believed they understood their slaves, and most slaves apparently made no attempt to discourage this belief. Instead, they said the things they thought their masters wanted to hear, and they conformed with the rituals that signified their subservience. Rare, no doubt, was the master who never heard any of his humble, smiling bondsmen affirm their loyalty and contentment. When visitors in the South asked a slave whether he wished to be free, he usually replied: "No, massa, me no want to be free, have good massa, take care of me when I sick, never 'buse nigger; no, me no want to be free."[3]

This was dubious evidence, as some slaveholders knew and others learned. (They would have acknowledged the validity of an affirmation later to be made by a post-bellum South Carolinian: "the white man does not know the Negro so well as he thinks he does."⁴) A Virginia master believed that slaves had their faculties "sharpened by constant exercise" and that their perceptions were "extremely fine and acute." An overseer decided that a man who "put his confidence in a Negro . . . was simply a Damned Fool." A Georgia planter concluded: "So deceitful is the Negro that as far as my own experience extends I could never in a single instance decipher his character. . . . We planters could never get at the truth."⁵ When advertising for runaways, masters repeatedly confirmed these opinions by describing them as being "very artful," as acting and conversing in a way "calculated to deceive almost any one," and (most frequently) as possessing a "pretty glib and plausible tongue." Yet proslavery writers swallowed whole the assurances of contentment which these glib-tongued "scoundrels" gave them.

Since there are few reliable records of what went on in the minds of slaves, one can only infer their thoughts and feelings from their behavior, that of their masters, and the logic of their situation. That they had no understanding of freedom, and therefore accepted bondage as their natural condition, is hard to believe. They had only to observe their masters and the other free men about them to obtain a very distinct idea of the meaning and advantages of freedom. All knew that some Negroes had been emancipated: they knew that freedom was a *possible* condition for any of them. They "continually have before their eyes, persons of the same color, many of whom they have known in slavery . . . freed from the control of masters, working where they please, going whither they please, and expending their money how they please." So declared a group of Charleston whites who petitioned the legislature to expel all free persons of color from South Carolina.⁶

Untutored slaves seldom speculated about freedom as an abstraction. They naturally focused their interest upon such immediate and practical benefits as escaping severe discipline and getting increased compensation for less labor. An ex-slave explained simply what freedom meant to her: "I am now my own mistress, and need not work when I am sick. I can do my own thinkings, without having any to think for me, — to tell me when to come, what to do, and to sell me when they get ready.'"⁷ Though she may never have heard of the doctrine of natural rights, her concept of freedom surely embraced more than its incidental aspects.

If slaves had some understanding of the pragmatic benefits of freedom, no doubt most of them desired to enjoy these benefits. Some, perhaps the majority, had no more than a vague, unarticulated yearning for escape from burdens and restraints. They submitted, but submission did not necessarily mean enjoyment or even contentment. And some slaves felt more than a vague longing, felt a sharp pang and saw a clear objective. They struggled toward it against imposing obstacles, expressing their discontent through positive action.

Were these, the actively discontented, to be found only among slaves exposed to great physical cruelty? Apparently not. Slaves of gentle masters might seek freedom as eagerly as those of cruel ones. Frederick Douglass, the most famous refugee from slavery, testified:

Beat and cuff your slave, keep him hungry and spiritless, and he will follow the chain of his master like a dog, but feed and clothe him well, — work him moderately — surround him with physical comfort, — and dreams of freedom intrude. Give him a *bad* master, and he aspires to a *good* master; give him a good master, and he wishes to become his *own* master.[8]

Here was a problem confronting conscientious slaveholders. One confessed that slaveownership subjected

the man of care and feeling to more dilemmas than perhaps any other vocation he could follow. . . . To moralize and induce the slave to assimilate with the master and his interest, has been and is the great desideratum aimed at; but I am sorry to say I have long since desponded in the completion of this task.[9]

Another slaveholder who vaguely affirmed that his bondsmen were "as contented as their nature will permit" was in reality agreeing with what a white man once bluntly stated before the Louisiana Supreme Court: The desire for freedom "exists in the bosom of *every* slave — whether the recent captive, or him to whom bondage has become a habit."[10]

Slaves showed great eagerness to get some — if they could not get all — of the advantages of freedom. They liked to hire their own time, or to work in tobacco factories, or for the Tredegar Iron Company, because they were then under less restraint than in the fields, and they had greater opportunities to earn money for themselves. They seized the chance to make their condition approximate that of freemen.

But they were not satisfied with a mere loosening of the bonds. Former slaves affirmed that one had to "know the *heart* of the poor slave — learn his secret thoughts — thoughts he dare not utter in the hearing of the white man," to understand this. "A man who has been in slavery knows, and no one else can know, the yearnings to be free, and the fear of making the attempt." While he was still in bondage Douglass wondered how white people knew that God had made black people to be slaves. "Did they go up in the sky and learn it? or, did He come down and tell them so?"[11] A slave on a Louisiana sugar plantation assured Olmsted that slaves did desire freedom, that they talked about it among themselves, and that they speculated about what they would do if they were emancipated. When a traveler in Georgia told a slave he understood his people did not wish to be free, "His only answer was a short, contemptuous laugh."[12]

If slaves yielded to authority most of the time, they did so because they usually saw no other practical choice. Yet few went through life without expressing discontent somehow, some time. Even the most passive slaves, usually before they reached middle age, flared up in protest now and then. The majority, as they grew older, lost hope and spirit. Some, however, never quite gave in, never stopped fighting back in one way or another. The "bad character" of this "insolent," "surly," and "unruly" sort made them a liability to those who owned them, for a slave's value was measured by his disposition as much as by his strength and skills. Such rebels seldom won legal freedom, yet they never quite admitted they were slaves.

Slave resistance, whether bold and persistent or mild and sporadic, created for all slaveholders a serious problem of discipline. As authors or as readers they saw the problem discussed in numberless essays with such titles as "The Management of Negroes," essays which filled the pages of southern agricultural periodicals. Many masters had reason to agree with the owner of a hundred slaves who complained that he possessed "just 100 troubles," or with the North Carolina planter who said that slaves were "a troublesome property."[13]

The record of slave resistance forms a chapter in the story of the endless struggle to give dignity to human life. Though the history of southern bondage reveals that men *can* be enslaved under certain conditions, it also demonstrates that their love of freedom is hard to crush. The subtle expressions of this spirit, no less than the daring thrusts for liberty, comprise one of the richest gifts the slaves have left to posterity. In making themselves "troublesome property," they provide reassuring evidence that slaves seldom wear their shackles lightly.

The record of the minority who waged ceaseless and open warfare against their bondage makes an inspiring chapter, also, in the history of Americans of African descent. True, these rebels were exceptional men, but the historian of any group properly devotes much attention to those members who did extraordinary things, men in whose lives the problems of their age found focus, men who voiced the feelings and aspirations of the more timid and less articulate masses. As the American Revolution produced folk heroes, so also did southern slavery — heroes who, in both cases, gave much for the cause of human freedom. . . .

According to Dr. Cartwright, there was a second disease peculiar to Negroes which he called *Drapetomania:* "the disease causing negroes to run away." Cartwright believed that it was a "disease of the mind" and that with "proper medical advice" it could be cured. The first symptom was a "sulky and dissatisfied" attitude. To forestall the full onset of the disease, the cause of discontent must be determined and removed. If there were no ascertainable cause, then "whipping the devil out of them" was the proper "preventive measure against absconding."[14]

Though Cartwright's dissertations on Negro diseases are mere curiosities of medical history, the problem he dealt with was a real and urgent one to nearly every slaveholder. Olmsted met few planters, large or small, who were not more or less troubled by runaways. A Mississippian realized that his record was most unusual when he wrote in his diary: "Harry ran away; *the first* negro that ever ran from me." Another slaveholder betrayed his concern when he avowed that he would "rather a negro would do anything Else than runaway."[15]

The number of runaways was not large enough to threaten the survival of the peculiar institution, because slaveholders took precautions to prevent the problem from growing to such proportions. But their measures were never entirely successful, as the advertisements for fugitives in southern newspapers made abundantly clear. Actually, the problem was much greater than these newspapers suggested, because many owners did not advertise for absconding property. (When an owner did advertise, he usually waited until his slave had been missing for several weeks.) In any case, fugitive slaves were numbered in the thousands every year. It was an important form of protest against bondage.

Who were the runaways? They were generally young slaves, most of them under thirty, but occasionally masters searched for fugitives who were more than sixty years old. The majority of them were males, though female runaways were by no means uncommon. It is not true that most of them were mulattoes or of predominantly white ancestry. While this group was well represented among the fugitives, they were outnumbered by slaves who were described as "black" or of seemingly "pure" African ancestry. Domestics and skilled artisans — the ones who supposedly had the most intimate ties with the master class — ran away as well as common field-hands.

Some bondsmen tried running away only once, or on very rare occasions. Others tried it repeatedly and somehow managed to escape in spite of their owners' best efforts to stop them. Such slaves were frequently identified as "habitual" or "notorious" runaways. While a few of them were, according to their masters, "unruly scoundrels" or "incorrigible scamps," most of them seemed to be "humble," inoffensive," or "cheerful" slaves. Thus an advertisement for a Maryland fugitive stated: he "always appears to be in a good humor, laughs a good deal, and runs on with a good deal of foolishness." A Louisiana master gave the following description of three slaves who escaped from him: the first was "very industrious" and always answered "with a smile" when spoken to; the second, a "well-disposed and industrious boy," was "very timid" and spoke to white men "very humbly, with his hand to his hat"; and the third addressed whites "humbly and respectfully with a smile."[16] Slaves such as these apparently concealed their feelings and behaved as they were expected to — until one day they suddenly made off.

Runaways usually went singly or in small groups of two or three. But some escaped in groups of a dozen or more, and in a few instances in groups of more than fifty. They ran off during the warm summer months more often than during the winter when sleeping out of doors was less feasible and when frost-bitten feet might put an end to flight.

Many fugitives bore the marks of cruelty on their bodies, but humane treatment did not necessarily prevent attempts to escape. More than a few masters shared the bewilderment of a Marylander who advertised for his slave Jacob: "He has no particular marks, and his appearance proves the fact of the kind treatment he has always received." Slaveholders told Olmsted that slaves who were treated well, fed properly, and worked moderately ran away even when they knew that it would cause them hardship and, eventually, severe punishment. "This is often mentioned to illustrate the ingratitude and especial depravity of the African race."[17]

In advertising for a runaway, owners frequently insisted that he had absconded for no cause, or for none that they could understand. A Virginia slave ran off without the excuse "either of whipping, or threat, or angry word"; the slaves Moses and Peter left an Alabama plantation "without provocation." A small Virginia planter recorded in his diary that he had punished a slave woman for running away, because there was "no cause" for it but "badness."[18] "Poor ignorant devils, for what do they run away?" asked a puzzled master. "They are well clothed, work easy and have all kinds of plantation produce."[19] Some masters, it appears, were betrayed by their own pessimistic assumptions about human nature, especially about the nature of Negroes!

When slaves protested against bondage (or some specific aspect of it) by flight, however, they normally had a clear personal grievance or an obvious objective. One of their most common grievances was being arbitrarily separated from families and friends. Hired slaves often became fugitives as they attempted to get back to their homes. Many of the runaways had recently been carried from an eastern state to the Southwest; torn by loneliness they tried frantically to find their ways back to Virginia or to one of the Carolinas. Sometimes a timid slave had never before attempted escape until he was uprooted by sale to a trader or to another master.

The advertisements for runaways were filled with personal tragedies such as the following: "I think it quite probable that this fellow has succeeded in getting to his wife, who was carried away last Spring out of my neighborhood." Lawrence, aged fourteen, was trying to make his way from Florida to Atlanta where "his mother is supposed to be." Mary "is no doubt lurking about in the vicinity of Goose Creek, where she has children." Will, aged fifty, "has recently been owned in Savannah, where he has a wife and children."[20] Items such as these appeared regularly in the southern press.

Occasionally running away enabled a slave to defeat an attempt to move him against his will. A North Carolina slave fled to the woods when his master tried to take him to Tennessee, and a Georgia slave escaped to his old home after being taken to Alabama. In both cases the owners decided to sell them to owners in the neighborhoods where they wished to remain, rather than be troubled with potential "habitual runaways."[21]

Flight was also a means by which slaves resisted attempts to work them too severely. The heavier labor burdens as well as the more favorable climatic conditions accounted for the higher incidence of runaways in summer. Cotton growers found the number increasing at picking time, sugar growers during the grinding season. Planters who used the task system faced the danger of "a general stampede to the 'swamp' " when they attempted to increase the standardized tasks. The overseer on a Florida plantation, dissatisfied with the rate at which the hands were picking cotton, tried "pushing them up a Little," whereupon some of them retaliated by absconding. Sometimes these escapes resembled strikes, and master or overseer had to negotiate terms upon which the slaves would agree to return. A small slaveholder in Louisiana once wrote in his diary: "I arose this morning as usual to proceed to the day's work, but there were none to do it, with the exception of Sib and Jess." The rest had run off in protest against his work regimen.[22]

Slaves ran away to avoid punishment for misdeeds or to get revenge for punishments already received. Most masters knew that it was folly to threaten slaves with "correction," for this usually caused them to disappear. An overseer reported the escape of a slave to his employer: "I went to give him a Floging for not coming to work in due time and he told me that he would not take it and run off."[23] Olmsted learned that slaves "often ran away after they had been whipped, or something else has happened to make them angry." Those who advertised for fugitives confirmed this fact; they frequently stated that a bondsman "was well paddled before he left," or that "on examination he will be found to have been severely whipped." Slaveholders discovered that some of their human chattels would not tolerate being "dealt harshly with — otherwise they will run off — and if once the habit of absconding is fixed, it is difficult to conquer it."[24]

In other cases escape was simply the result of a longing for at least temporary relief from the restraints and discipline of slavery. "John's running off," explained an overseer, "was for no other cause, than that he did not feel disposed to be governed, by the same rules and regulations that the other negroes . . . are governed by."[25] This seemed to be the most common motive, and in spite of severe punishment some ran away time after time. The most talented fugitives reduced the technique to a science. For example, Remus and his wife Patty escaped from James Battle's Alabama plantation; were caught and jailed in Montgomery; escaped again; were caught and jailed in Columbus, Georgia; escaped again; and were then still at large. Battle urged the next jailer to "secure Remus well."[26]

Slaves like Remus set "evil" examples for others. A small slaveholder in South Carolina was distressed by his "runaway fellow" Team: "this is the 2^d or 3^d time he has ranaway, and lost together nearly a years work, I cannot afford to keep him at this rate, he will spoil the rest of my people by his bad example." Moreover, the skilled, "habitual" runaway often persuaded friends or relatives to decamp with him. A Mississippian advertised for his slave Jim, "a dangerous old scoundrel to be running at large, as he has the tact of exercising great influence with other negroes to induce them to run away."[27] No punishment could break the spirit of such a slave, and he remained an "incorrigible scamp" as long as he lived.

In most cases the runaways were at large for only a short time — a few days or, at most, a few weeks — before they were caught or decided to return voluntarily. But some of them, though remaining in the South, eluded their pursuers with amazing success. It took a South Carolinian a year to catch a slave woman who was over fifty years old. A Florida master advertised for a slave who had been a fugitive for three years. In 1832, a Virginia master was still searching for two slaves who had escaped fifteen years earlier. And a jailer in Jones county, North Carolina, gave notice that he had captured a bondsman who had been a runaway for twenty-five years.[28]

The success of runaway expeditions depended upon the willingness of other slaves to give the fugitives aid. Some of them were helped by literate bondsmen who provided them with passes. One slave carpenter made a business of writing passes for his friends; when he was finally detected he ran away himself.[29] Slaveholders knew that their bondsmen fed and concealed runaways, but they were unable to stop them. In Louisiana a fugitive was found to have been "lurking" about his master's premises for nearly a year while sympathetic bondsmen "harbored" him.[30]

A few slaves betrayed runaways, but usually it was futile for a master to expect their help in catching his property. Even domestics often refused to be informers. One house servant was whipped for not reporting that she had heard a runaway "talking in the yard." James H. Hammond demoted two domestics to field labor for aiding runaways and cut off the meat allowance of all his slaves until they would help him bring them in. A Mississippi planter wrote angrily that his slave woman Nancy, who had been treated "with the greatest indulgence," was "taken in the very act" of carrying food to some runaways. "there is no gratitude among them," he concluded, "and there is nothing more true, than that they will not bear indulgence."[31]

Bands of fugitives sometimes fled into the fastness of a forest or swamp where they established camps and lived in rude huts. Occasionally they tried to grow their own food, but more often they obtained it by raiding nearby farms. One such camp in South Carolina was in a "clearing in a very dense thicket" from which the runaways "killed the hogs and sheep and robbed the fields of the neighbors." A party hunting fugitives in the same state found another camp which was "well provided with meal, cooking utensils, blankets, etc.," and near which "corn, squashes, and peas were growing." Slaves rarely betrayed the locations of these camps. A Louisiana planter, searching for runaways, "very foolish[ly]" tried to force a captured slave woman to lead him to their camp and thus "fooled the day off to no purpose."[32]

Some bold fugitives, because of the lightness of their complexions or because they possessed forged "free papers," made no attempt to conceal themselves. An Alabama master sounded a warning that appeared frequently in fugitive-slave advertisements: Daniel would "no doubt change his name and have a free pass, or pass to hire his time as he has done before."[33] This Negro was, in effect, trying to work and live as a free man while remaining in the south. A fugitive blacksmith repeatedly wrote passes for himself authorizing him to travel about and work at his trade; another managed to find employment in the turpentine industry for nearly two years.[34] Still others, pretending to be "free persons of color," were eventually caught working in the fisheries, on the wharves, or on river boats. They could scarcely have given stronger evidence of their longing for freedom and of their ability to take care of themselves.

But slaves who ran away with the hope of gaining permanent freedom usually attempted to get out of the South. This fearful enterprise involved a dangerous journey along the back ways in the dead of night. Most of the time it ended in the tragedy of failure, which meant certain punishment and possibly no second opportunity. When it ended in success, the fugitive at best faced an uncertain future among strangers. But a passionate desire for a new and better life in freedom caused many bondsmen to take all these risks. How often they succeeded there is no way of knowing accurately. The claim of a southern judge in 1855 that the South had by then lost "upwards of 60,000 slaves" to the North was a reasonable estimate.[35] In any case, the number was large enough to keep southern masters on guard and to remind Northerners that defenders of slavery did not speak for the slaves.

Most of the fugitives who tried to reach the free states naturally came from the Upper South where the distance was relatively short and the chance of success accordingly greater. In 1847, a Louisville newspaper reported that nearly fifty Kentucky slaves had recently escaped across the Ohio River; slave property, the paper commented, was becoming "entirely insecure" in the river counties.[36] Maryland lacked even a river barrier, and probably more bondsmen fled to the North through this state than through any other. In Cecil County, slaves were reported in 1848 to be "running away in droves." In Charles County, a "strange and singular spirit" once came over the bondsmen, with the result that more than eighty fled in a single group. (Their recapture made it evident again that it was foolhardy to attempt escape in groups of this size.) On various occasions Maryland slaveholders assembled to consider measures "to put a stop to the elopement" of Negroes.[37] They never succeeded.

Fear of being sold to the Deep South, as well as fear of having their families broken, often caused bondsmen in the Upper South to flee to the North. Many ran away when the estates of deceased masters were being settled. Sometimes the mere threat of a sale was sufficient provocation. A Virginia Negro who escaped to Canada recalled: "Master used to say, that if we didn't suit him, he would put us in his pocket quick — meaning he would sell us."[38]

A few runaways from the Deep South also attempted to reach the free states in spite of their slender chances of success. An Alabama master advertised for his slave Gilbert, "a carpenter by trade and an excellent workman," who would probably "endeavor to get to Ohio, as he ran away . . . once before, and his aim was to get to that state." Archy and his wife Maria escaped from their master in Wilkes County, Georgia: "They will make for a free State, as the boy Archy has heretofore made several attempts to do." Prince, a South Carolina fugitive, was doubtless aiming for a free state, "having runaway . . . [before] and got as far as Salisbury, N.C., before he was apprehended."[39] These slaves often tried to reach a seaport and get aboard a vessel bound for the North. Generally they were caught before the vessel left port.

Abraham, who lived in Mobile and was for many years his master's "confidential servant," was one of the few slaves from the Deep South who actually got all the way to a free state. "By dint of his ingenuity and adroitness at forgery, and a good share of cunning," Abraham made his way unhindered until he reached Baltimore. Here he was arrested and taken before a magistrate, "but his fictitious papers were so well executed . . . [that] he was at once suffered to go free." He then went on to New York where he found employment as a hotel porter. Eventually, however, his master found him and under the provisions of the fugitive-slave law carried him back to bondage.[40] Not many runaways from the Deep South experienced Abraham's bitter disappointment, because not many came so close to having freedom within their grasp. . . .

Notes

[1] [Ingraham], *South-West,* II, p. 201.

[2] Francis P. Gaines, *The Southern Plantation: A Study in the Development and the Accuracy of a Tradition* (New York, 1924), p. 244.

[3] Ethan A. Andrews, *Slavery and the Domestic Slave Trade in the United States* (Boston, 1836), pp. 97–99.

[4] Mason Crum, *Gullah: Negro Life in the Carolina Sea Islands* (Durham, 1940), p. 80.

[5] Abdy, *Journal,* II, pp. 216–17; Manigault Ms. Plantation Records, summary of plantation events, May, 1863–May, 1864; entry for March 22, 1867.

[6] Phillips (ed.), *Plantation and Frontier,* II, pp. 108–11.

[7] Drew, *The Refugee,* p. 177.

[8] Douglass, *My Bondage,* pp. 263–64.

[9] *Southern Agriculturist,* III (1830), p. 238.

[10] Ebenezer Pettigrew to Mrs. Mary Shepard, September 22, 1847, Pettigrew Family Papers; Catterall (ed.), *Judicial Cases,* III, p. 568.

[11] Northup, *Twelve Years a Slave,* pp. 206–207; Drew, *The Refugee,* pp. 43, 115; Douglass, *My Bondage,* pp. 89–91.

[12] Olmsted, *Seaboard,* pp. 679–80; James Stirling, *Letters from the Slave States* (London, 1857), p. 201.

[13] Gustavus A. Henry to his wife, November 25, 1849, Henry Papers; William S. Pettigrew to James C. Johnston, January 6, 1847 (copy), Pettigrew Family Papers.

[14] *De Bow's Review,* XI (1851), pp. 331–33.

[15] Olmsted, *Back Country,* p. 476; Newstead Plantation Diary, entry for June 7, 1860; Davis (ed.), *Diary of Bennet H. Barrow.* p. 165.

[16] Baltimore *Sun,* September 25, 1856; New Orleans *Picayune,* March 17, 1846.

[17] Baltimore *Sun,* August 1, 1840; Olmsted, *Seaboard,* pp. 190–91.

[18] Richmond *Enquirer,* August 1, 1837; John Walker diary, entry for December 16, 1848.

[19] Sellers, *Slavery in Alabama,* pp. 13–14.

[20] Huntsville *Southern Advocate,* December 11, 1829; Tallahassee *Floridian and Journal,* May 20, 1854; Charleston *Courier,* April 10, 1847; March 10, 1856.

[21] Balie Peyton to Samuel Smith Downey, January 6, March 7, 1831, Samuel Smith Downey Papers; John C. Pickens to Samuel Pickens, June 28, 1827, Pickens Papers.

[22] Olmsted, *Seaboard,* pp. 100–101, 434–36; Phillips and Glunt (eds.), *Florida Plantations Records,* p. 95; Phillips, *American Negro Slavery,* p. 303; John Spencer Bassett, *The Southern Plantation Overseer As Revealed in His Letters* (Northampton, Mass., 1925), p. 18; Marston Diary, entry for May 19, 1828.

[23] Phillips and Glunt (eds.), *Florida Plantation Records,* p. 57.

[24] Olmsted, *Back Country*, p. 79; Memphis *Daily Appeal*, July 23, 1859; New Orleans *Picayune*, October 5, 1847; Stephen Duncan to Thomas Butler, September 20, 1851, Butler Family Papers.

[25] Elisha Cain to Alexander Telfair, October 10, 1829, Telfair Plantation Records.

[26] Milledgeville *Southern Recorder*, February 16, 1836.

[27] Gavin Diary, entry for July 4, 1857; Vicksburg *Weekly Sentinel*, August 9, 1849.

[28] Wilmington (N.C.) *Journal*, September 5, 1851; July 5, 1855; Tallahassee *Floridian*, March 13, 1847; Richmond *Enquirer*, September 4, 1832.

[29] Rachel O'Connor to Mary C. Weeks, April 9, 1833, David Weeks and Family Collection.

[30] Davis (ed.), *Diary of Bennet H. Barrow*, pp. 226–27; Northup, *Twelve Years a Slave*, pp. 236–49.

[31] Mrs. Andrew McCollam Ms. Diary, entry for April 20, 1847; Hammond Diary, entries for July 1, 18, 19, 1832; Stephen Duncan to Thomas Butler, July 1, 1823, Butler Family Papers.

[32] Catterall (ed.), *Judicial Cases*, II, p. 434; Howell M. Henry, *The Police Control of the Slaves in South Carolina* (Emory, Va., 1914), p. 121; Davis (ed.), *Diary of Bennet H. Barrow*, pp. 341–43.

[33] Pensacola *Gazette*, November 3, 1838.

[34] Milledgeville *Southern Recorder*, July 18, 1843; Raleigh *North Carolina Standard*, November 7, 1855.

[35] Catterall (ed.), *Judicial Cases*, III, pp. 45–46; Franklin, *From Slavery to Freedom*, p. 255–56.

[36] Louisville *Democrat*, September 6, 1847; Coleman, *Slavery Times in Kentucky*, p. 219.

[37] Baltimore *Sun*, July 10, 14, 22, 1845; April 22, 1848.

[38] Drew, *The Refugee, Passim*.

[39] Mobile *Commercial Register*, March 17, 1834; Nashville *Republican Banner*, July 3, 1843; Columbia *South Carolina*, July 20, 1847.

[40] Baltimore *Sun*, August 15, 1842.

Elkins and His Critics

2

Slave Personality and the Concentration Camp Analogy

Stanley Elkins

The system of the concentration camps was expressly devised in the 1930's by high officials of the German government to function as an instrument of terror. The first groups detained in the camps consisted of prominent enemies of the Nazi regime; later, when these had mostly been eliminated, it was still felt necessary that the system be institutionalized and made into a standing weapon of intimidation — which required a continuing flow of incoming prisoners. The categories of eligible persons were greatly widened to include all real, fancied, or "potential" opposition to the state. They were often selected on capricious and random grounds, and together they formed a cross-section of society which was virtually complete: criminals, workers, businessmen, professional people, middle-class Jews, even members of the aristocracy. The teeming camps thus held all kinds — not only the scum of the underworld but also countless men and women of culture and refinement. During the war a specialized objective was added, that of exterminating the Jewish populations of subject countries, which required special mass-production methods of which the gas chambers and crematories of Auschwitz-Birkenau were outstanding examples. Yet the basic technique was everywhere and at all times the same: the deliberate infliction of various forms of torture upon the incoming prisoners in such a way as to break their resistance and make way for their degradation as individuals. These brutalities were not merely "permitted" or "encouraged"; they were prescribed. Duty in the camps was a mandatory phase in the training of SS guards, and it was here that particular efforts were made to overcome their scruples and to develop in them a capacity for relishing spectacles of pain and anguish.

The concentration camps and everything that took place in them were veiled in the utmost isolation and secrecy. Of course complete secrecy was impossible, and a continuing stream of rumors circulated among the population. At the same time so repellent was the nature of these stories that in their enormity they transcended

From Stanley Elkins, *Slavery: A Problem in American Institutional and Intellectual Life* (Chicago: University of Chicago Press, 1959), pp. 104–15, 128–32. Copyright © 1959 by the University of Chicago Press. Reprinted by permission of the University of Chicago Press and Stanley Elkins.

the experience of nearly everyone who heard them; in self-protection it was somehow necessary to persuade oneself that they could not really be true. The results,
therefore, contained elements of the diabolical. The undenied existence of the camps
cast a shadow of nameless dread over the entire population; on the other hand the
individual who actually became a prisoner in one of them was in most cases devas-
tated with fright and utterly demoralized to discover that what was happening to
him was not less, but rather far more terrible than anything he had imagined. The
shock sequence of "procurement," therefore, together with the initial phases of the
prisoner's introduction to camp life, is not without significance in assessing some
of the psychic effects upon those who survived as long-term inmates.

The arrest was typically made at night, preferably late; this was standing
Gestapo policy, designed to heighten the element of shock, terror, and unreality
surrounding the arrest. After a day or so in the police jail came the next major
shock, that of being transported to the camp itself. "This transportation into the
camp, and the 'initiation' into it," writes Bruno Bettelheim (an ex-inmate of Dachau
and Buchenwald), "is often the first torture which the prisoner has ever experienced
and is, as a rule, physically and psychologically the worst torture to which he will
ever be exposed."[1] It involved a planned series of brutalities inflicted by guards
making repeated rounds through the train over a twelve- to thirty-six-hour period
during which the prisoner was prevented from resting. If transported in cattle cars
instead of passenger cars, the prisoners were sealed in, under conditions not dissimi-
lar to those of the Middle Passage.[2] Upon their arrival — if the camp was one in
which mass exterminations were carried out — there might be sham ceremonies
designed to reassure temporarily the exhausted prisoners, which meant that the
fresh terrors in the offing would then strike them with redoubled impact. An SS
officer might deliver an address, or a band might be playing popular tunes, and it
would be in such a setting that the initial "selection" was made. The newcomers
would file past an SS doctor who indicated, with a motion of the forefinger, whether
they were to go to the left or to the right. To one side went those considered capable
of heavy labor; to the other would go wide categories of "undesirables"; those in
the latter group were being condemned to the gas chambers.[3] Those who remained
would undergo the formalities of "registration," full of indignities, which cul-
minated in the marking of each prisoner with a number.[4]

There were certain physical and psychological strains of camp life, especially
debilitating in the early stages, which should be classed with the introductory shock
sequence. There was a state of chronic hunger whose pressures were unusually
effective in detaching prior scruples of all kinds; even the sexual instincts no longer
functioned in the face of the drive for food.[5] The man who at his pleasure could
bestow or withhold food thus wielded, for that reason alone, abnormal power.
Another strain at first was the demand for absolute obedience, the slightest deviation
from which brought savage punishments.[6] The prisoner had to ask permission — by
no means granted as a matter of course — even to defecate.[7] The power of the SS
guard, as the prisoner was hourly reminded, was that of life and death over his body.

A more exquisite form of pressure lay in the fact that the prisoner had never a moment of solitude: he no longer had a private existence; it was no longer possible, in any imaginable sense, for him to be an "individual."[8]

Another factor having deep disintegrative effects upon the prisoner was the prospect of a limitless future in the camp. In the immediate sense this meant that he could no longer make plans for the future. But there would eventually be a subtler meaning: it made the break with the outside world a *real* break; in time the "real" life would become the life of the camp, the outside world an abstraction. Had it been a limited detention, whose end could be calculated, one's outside relationships — one's roles, one's very "personality" — might temporarily have been laid aside, to be reclaimed more or less intact at the end of the term. Here, however, the prisoner was faced with the apparent impossibility of his old rules or even his old personality ever having any future at all; it became more and more difficult to imagine himself resuming them.[9] It was this that underlay the "egalitarianism" of the camps; old statuses had lost their meaning.[10] A final strain, which must have been particularly acute for the newcomer, was the omnipresent threat of death and the very unpredictable suddenness with which death might strike. Quite aside from the periodic gas-chamber selections, the guards in their sports and caprices were at liberty to kill any prisoner any time.[11]

In the face of all this, one might suppose that the very notion of an "adjustment" would be grotesque. The majority of those who entered the camps never came out again, but our concern here has to be with those who survived — an estimated 700,000 out of nearly eight million.[12] For them, the regime must be considered not as a system of death but as a way of life. These survivors did make an adjustment of some sort to the system; it is they themselves who report it. After the initial shocks, what was the nature of the "normality" that emerged?

A dramatic species of psychic displacement seems to have occurred at the very outset. This experience, described as a kind of "splitting of personality," has been noted by most of the inmates who later wrote of their imprisonment. The very extremity of the initial tortures produced in the prisoner what actually amounted to a sense of detachment; these brutalities went so beyond his own experience that they became somehow incredible — they seemed to be happening no longer to him but almost to someone else. "[The author] has no doubt," writes Bruno Bettelheim, "that he was able to endure the transportation, and all that followed, because right from the beginning he became convinced that these horrible and degrading experiences somehow did not happen to 'him' as a subject, but only to 'him' as an object."[13] This subject-object "split" appears to have served a double function: not only was it an immediate psychic defense mechanism against shock,[14] but it also acted as the first thrust toward a new adjustment. This splitting-off of a special "self" — a self which endured the tortures but which was not the "real" self — also provided the first glimpse of a new personality which, being not "real," would not need to feel bound by the values which guided the individual in his former life. "The prisoners' feelings," according to Mr. Bettelheim, "could be summed up by the following sentence: 'What I am doing here, or what is happening to me, does not count at all; here everything is permissible as long and insofar as it contributes to helping me survive in the camp.' "[15]

One part of the prisoner's being was thus, under sharp stress, brought to the crude realization that he must thenceforth be governed by an entire new set of standards in order to live. Mrs. Lingens-Reiner puts it bluntly: "Will you survive, or shall I? As soon as one sensed that this was at stake everyone turned egotist."[16] ". . . I think it of primary importance," writes Dr. Cohen, "to take into account that the superego acquired new values in a concentration camp, so much at variance with those which the prisoner bore with him into camp that the latter faded."[17] But then this acquisition of "new values" did not all take place immediately; it was not until some time after the most acute period of stress was over that the new, "unreal" self would become at last the "real" one.

"If you survive the first three months you will survive the next three years." Such was the formula transmitted from the old prisoners to the new ones,[18] and its meaning lay in the fact that the first three months would generally determine a prisoner's capacity for survival and adaptation. "Be inconspicuous": this was the golden rule.[19] The prisoner who called attention to himself, even in such trivial matters as the wearing of glasses, risked doom. Any show of bravado, any heroics, any kind of resistance condemned a man instantly. There were no rewards for martyrdom: not only did the martyr himself suffer, but mass punishments were wreaked upon his fellow inmates. To "be inconspicuous" required a special kind of alertness — almost an animal instinct[20] — against the apathy which tended to follow the initial shocks.[21] To give up the struggle for survival was to commit "passive suicide"; a careless mistake meant death. There were those, however, who did come through this phase and who managed an adjustment to the life of the camp. It was the striking contrasts between this group of two- and three-year veterans and the perpetual stream of newcomers which made it possible for men like Bettelheim and Cohen to speak of the "old prisoner" as a specific type.

The most immediate aspect of the old inmates' behavior which struck these observers was its *childlike* quality. "The prisoners developed types of behavior which are characteristic of infancy or early youth. Some of these behaviors developed slowly, others were immediately imposed on the prisoners and developed only in intensity as time went on."[22] Such infantile behavior took innumerable forms. The inmates' sexual impotence brought about a disappearance of sexuality in their talk;[23] instead, excretory functions occupied them endlessly. They lost many of the customary inhibitions as to soiling their beds and their persons.[24] Their humor was shot with silliness and they giggled like children when one of them would expel wind. Their relationships were highly unstable. "Prisoners would, like early adolescents, fight one another tooth and nail . . . only to become close friends within a few minutes."[25] Dishonesty became chronic. "Now they suddenly appeared to be pathological liars, to be unable to restrain themselves, to be unable to make objective evaluation, etc."[26] "In hundreds of ways," writes Colaço Belmonte, "the soldier, and to an even greater extent the prisoner of war, is given to understand that he is a child. . . . Then dishonesty, mendacity, egotistic actions in order to obtain more food or to get out of scrapes reach full development, and theft becomes a veritable affliction of camp life."[27] This was all true, according to Elie Cohen, in the concentration camp as well.[28] Benedikt Kautsky observed such things in his own behavior: "I myself can declare that often I saw myself as I used to be in my school days, when by sly dodges and clever pretexts we avoided being found out, or could 'organize' something."[29] Bruno Bettelheim remarks on the extravagance of the stories told by the prisoners to one another. "They were boastful, telling tales about what they had accomplished in their former lives, or how they succeeded in cheating foremen or guards, and how they sabotaged the work. Like children they felt not at all set back or ashamed when it became known that they had lied about their prowess."[30]

This development of childlike behavior in the old inmates was the counterpart of something even more striking that was happening to them: *"Only very few of the prisoners escaped a more or less intensive identification with the SS."*[31] As Mr. Bettelheim puts it: "A prisoner had reached the final stage of adjustment to the camp situation when he had changed his personality so as to accept as his own the values of the Gestapo."[32] The Bettelheim study furnishes a catalogue of examples. The old prisoners came to share the attitude of the SS toward the "unfit" prisoners; newcomers who behaved badly in the labor groups or who could not withstand the strain became a liability for the others, who were often instrumental in getting rid of them. Many old prisoners actually imitated the SS; they would sew and mend their uniforms in such a way as to make them look more like those of the SS — even though they risked punishment for it. "When asked why they did it, they admitted that they loved to look like . . . the guards." Some took great enjoyment in the fact that during roll call "they really had stood well at attention." There were cases of nonsensical rules, made by the guards, which the older prisoners would continue to observe and try to force on the others long after the SS had forgotten them.[33] Even the most abstract ideals of the SS, such as their intense German nationalism and anti-Semitism, were often absorbed by the old inmates — a phenomenon observed among the politically well-educated and even among the Jews themselves.[34] The final quintessence of all this was seen in the "Kapo" — the prisoner who had been placed in a supervisory position over his fellow inmates. These creatures, many of them professional criminals, not only behaved with slavish servility to the SS, but the way in which they often outdid the SS in sheer brutality became one of the most durable features of the concentration-camp legend.

To all these men, reduced to complete and childish dependence upon their masters, the SS had actually become a father-symbol. "The SS man was all-powerful in the camp, he was the lord and master of the prisoner's life. As a cruel father he could, without fear of punishment, even kill the prisoner and as a gentle father he could scatter largesse and afford the prisoner his protection."[35] The result, admits Dr. Cohen, was that "for all of us the SS was a father image. . . ."[36] The closed system, in short, had become a kind of grotesque patriarchy.

The literature provides us with three remarkable tests of the profundity of the experience which these prisoners had undergone and the thoroughness of the changes which had been brought about in them. One is the fact that few cases of real resistance were ever recorded, even among prisoners going to their death.

With a few altogether insignificant exceptions, the prisoners, no matter in what form they were led to execution, whether singly, in groups, or in masses, never fought back! . . . there were thousands who had by no means relapsed into fatal apathy. Nevertheless, in mass liquidations they went to their death with open eyes, without assaulting the enemy in a final paroxysm, without a sign of fight. Is this not in conflict with human nature, as we know it?[37]

Even upon liberation, when revenge against their tormentors at last became possible, mass uprisings very rarely occurred. "Even when the whole system was overthrown by the Allies," says David Rousset writing of Buchenwald, "nothing happened. . . . The American officer appointed to command of the camp was never called upon to cope with any inclination toward a popular movement. No such disposition existed."[38]

A second test of the system's effectiveness was the relative scarcity of suicides in the camps.[39] Though there were suicides, they tended to occur during the first days of internment, and only one mass suicide is known; it took place among a group of Jews at Mauthausen who leaped into a rock pit three days after their arrival.[40] For the majority of prisoners the simplicity of the urge to survive made suicide, a complex matter of personal initiative and decision, out of the question. Yet they could, **when** commanded by their masters, go to their death without resistance.

The third test lies in the very absence, among the prisoners, of hatred toward the SS. This is probably the hardest of all to understand. Yet the burning spirit of rebellion which many of their liberators expected to find would have had to be supported by fierce and smoldering emotions; such emotions were not there. "It is remarkable," one observer notes, "how little hatred of their wardens is revealed in their stories."[41]

It is hoped that the very hideousness of a special example of slavery has not disqualified it as a test for certain features of a far milder and more benevolent form of slavery. But it should still be possible to say, with regard to the individuals who lived as slaves within the respective systems, that just as on one level there is every difference between a wretched childhood and a carefree one, there are, for other purposes, limited features which the one may be said to have shared with the other.

Both were closed systems from which all standards based on prior connections had been effectively detached. A working adjustment to either system required a childlike conformity, a limited choice of "significant others." Cruelty per se cannot be considered the primary key to this; of far greater importance was the simple "closedness" of the system, in which all lines of authority descended from the master and in which alternative social bases that might have supported alternative standards were systematically suppressed.[42] The individual, consequently, for his very psychic security, had to picture his master in some way as the "good father,"[43] even when, as in the concentration camp, it made no sense at all.[44] But why should it not have made sense for many a simple plantation Negro whose master did exhibit, in all the ways that could be expected, the features of the good father who was really "good"? If the concentration camp could produce in two or three years the results that it did, one wonders how much more pervasive must have been those attitudes, expectations, and values which had, certainly, their benevolent side and which were accepted and transmitted over generations.

For the Negro child, in particular, the plantation offered no really satisfactory father-image other than the master. The "real" father was virtually without authority over his child, since discipline, parental responsibility, and control of rewards and punishments all rested in other hands; the slave father could not even protect the mother of his children except by appealing directly to the master. Indeed, the mother's own role loomed far larger for the slave child than did that of the father. She controlled those few activities — household care, preparation of food, and rearing of children — that were left to the slave family. For that matter, the very etiquette of plantation life removed even the honorific attributes of fatherhood from the Negro male, who was addressed as "boy" — until, when the vigorous years of his prime were past, he was allowed to assume the title of "uncle."

From the master's viewpoint, slaves had been defined in law as property, and the master's power over his property must be absolute. But then this property was still human property. These slaves might never be quite as human as *he* was, but still there were certain standards that could be laid down for their behavior: obedience, fidelity, humility, docility, cheerfulness, and so on. Industry and diligence would of course be demanded, but a final element in the master's situation would undoubtedly qualify that expectation. Absolute power for him meant absolute dependency for the slave — the dependency not of the developing child but of the perpetual child. For the master, the role most aptly fitting such a relationship would naturally be that of the father. As a father he could be either harsh or kind, as he chose, but as a *wise* father he would have, we may suspect, a sense of the limits of his situation. He must be ready to cope with *all* the qualities of the child, exasperating as well as ingratiating. He might conceivably have to expect in this child — besides his loyalty, docility, humility, cheerfulness, and (under supervision) his diligence — such additional qualities as irresponsibility, playfulness, silliness, laziness, and (quite possibly) tendencies to lying and stealing. Should the entire prediction prove accurate, the result would be something resembling "Sambo."

The social and psychological sanctions of role-playing may in the last analysis prove to be the most satisfactory of the several approaches to Sambo, for, without doubt, of all the roles in American life that of Sambo was by far the most pervasive. The outlines of the role might be sketched in by crude necessity, but what of the finer shades? The sanctions against overstepping it were bleak enough,[45] but the rewards — the sweet applause, as it were, for performing it with sincerity and feeling — were something to be appreciated on quite another level. The law, untuned to the deeper harmonies, could command the player to be present for the occasion, and the whip might even warn against his missing the grosser cues, but could those things really insure the performance that melted all hearts? Yet there was many and many a performance, and the audiences (whose standards were high) appear to háve been for the most part well pleased. They were actually viewing their own masterpiece. Much labor had been lavished upon this chef d'oeuvre, the most genial resources of Southern society had been available for the work; touch after touch had been applied throughout the years, and the result — embodied not in the unfeeling law but in the richest layers of Southern lore — had been the product of an exquisitely rounded collective creativity. And indeed, in a sense that somehow transcended the merely ironic, it was a labor of love. "I love the simple and unadulterated slave, with his geniality, his mirth, his swagger, and his nonsense," wrote Edward Pollard. "I love to look upon his countenance shining with content and grease; I love to study his affectionate heart; I love to mark that peculiarity in him, which beneath all his buffoonery exhibits him as a creature of the tenderest sensibilities, mingling his joys and his sorrows with those of his master's home.[46] Love, even on those terms, was surely no inconsequential reward.

But what were the terms? The Negro was to be a child forever. "The Negro . . . in his true nature, is always a boy, let him be ever so old. . . ."[47] "He is . . . a dependent upon the white race; dependent for guidance and direction even to the procurement of his most indispensable necessaries. Apart from this protection he has the helplessness of a child — without foresight, without faculty of contrivance, without thrift of any kind."[48] Not only was he a child; he was a happy child. Few Southern writers failed to describe with obvious fondness the bubbling gaiety of a plantation holiday or the perpetual good humor that seemed to mark the Negro character, the good humor of an everlasting childhood.

The role, of course, must have been rather harder for the earliest generations of slaves to learn. "Accommodation," according to John Dollard, "involves the renunciation of protest or aggression against undesirable conditions of life and the organization of the character so that protest does not appear, but acceptance does. It may come to pass in the end that the unwelcome force is idealized, that one identifies with it and takes it into the personality; it sometimes even happens that what is at first resented and feared is finally loved."[49]

Notes

¹ Bruno Bettelheim, "Individual and Mass Behavior in Extreme Situations," *Journal of Abnormal Psychology,* XXXVIII (October, 1943), 424.

² A description of such a trip may be found in Olga Lengyel, *Five Chimneys: The Story of Auschwitz* (Chicago, 1947), pp. 7–10. See also Eugen Kogon, *The Theory and Practice of Hell* (New York: Farrar, Straus, 1946), p. 67.

³ Elie Cohen, *Human Behavior in the Concentration Camp* (New York: Norton, 1953), pp. 118–22; Kogon, *Theory and Practice,* pp. 66–76; Lengyel, *Five Chimneys,* pp. 12–22.

⁴ One aspect of this registration ceremony involved a sham "inspection" of the body, whose effect on the women prisoners in particular was apparently very profound. See Lengyel, *Five Chimneys,* p. 19; Ella Lingens-Reiner, *Prisoners of Fear* (London: Victor Gollancz, 1948), p. 26. This may be compared with Degrandpré's description of a similar "inspection" on the African slave coast in the 1780's; see his *Voyage,* II, 55–56. "Apart from the fact that for every newcomer his transformation into a 'prisoner' meant a degradation," writes an ex-prisoner of Auschwitz and Mauthausen, "there was also the *loss of his name.* That this was no trifling circumstance should be apparent from the great importance which, according to Freud, a man attaches to his name. This is, in Freud's view, sufficiently proven by 'the fact that savages regard a name as an essential part of a man's personality. . . .' Anyhow, whether one agrees with Freud or not, the loss of one's name is not without significance, for the name is a personal attribute. Because he no longer had a name, but had become a number, the prisoner belonged to the huge army of the nameless who peopled the concentration camp." Cohen, *Human Behavior,* pp. 145–46.

⁵ *Ibid.,* pp. 134–35, 140–43.

⁶ These punishments are discussed most vividly in Kogon, *Theory and Practice,* pp. 102–8, 207–11.

⁷ Bettelheim, "Individual and Mass Behavior," p. 445.

⁸ The effects of never being alone are noted in Cohen, *Human Behavior,* pp. 130–31, and David Rousset, *The Other Kingdom* (New York: Reynal & Hitchcock, 1947), p. 133.

⁹ "When the author [Bettelheim] expressed to some of the old prisoners his astonishment that they seemed not interested in discussing their future life outside the camp, they frequently admitted that they could no longer visualize themselves living outside the camp, making free decisions, taking care of themselves and their families." Bettelheim, "Individual and Mass Behavior," p. 439.

¹⁰ M. Rousset tells of how, on one of the death marches, a prisoner came to him bringing a French compatriot and begging his protection for the wretched man. "He told me that he was a lawyer from Toulouse, and it was only the greatest difficulty that I kept from laughing aloud. For this social designation, *lawyer,* no longer fitted the poor wretch in the slightest. The incongruity of the thought was irresistibly comic. And it was the same with all of us." Rousset, *Other Kingdom,* p. 77.

¹¹ Kogon, *Theory and Practice,* p. 274; Cohen, *Human Behavior,* p. 155; Hilde O. Bluhm, "How Did They Survive?" *American Journal of Psychotherapy,* II (January, 1948), 5.

¹² Kogon, *Theory and Practice,* p. 277.

¹³ Bettelheim, "Individual and Mass Behavior," p. 431. See also Cohen, *Human Behavior,* pp. 116–17, 172.

¹⁴ "Many kept their bearings only by a kind of split personality. They surrendered their bodies resistlessly to the terror, while their inner being withdrew and held aloof." Kogon, *Theory and Practice,* p. 71. "I arrived at that state of numbness where I was no longer sensitive to either club or whip. I lived through the rest of that scene almost as a spectator." Lengyel, *Five Chimneys,* p. 20.

¹⁵ Bettelheim, "Individual and Mass Behavior," p. 432. "We camp prisoners," writes

Mrs. Lingens-Reiner, "had only one yardstick: whatever helped our survival was good, and whatever threatened our survival was bad, and to be avoided." *Prisoners of Fear,* p. 142.

[16] Lingens-Reiner, *Prisoners of Fear,* p. 23.

[17] *Human Behavior,* p. 136. The "superego," Freud's term for the "conscience," is discussed below, pp. 116–18.

[18] Bettelheim, "Individual and Mass Behavior," p. 438.

[19] Cohen, *Human Behavior,* p. 169.

[20] This should in no sense be considered as a calculating, "rational" alertness, but rather as something quite primitive. "Of myself," writes Dr. Cohen, "I know that I was not continuously occupied by the reflection: I am going to win through. The actions which contributed to my survival were performed instinctively rather than consciously. . . . Like animals warned by their instinct that danger is imminent, we would act instinctively at critical moments. These instinctive acts must, I think, be considered as manifestations of the life instinct. If the life instinct is not strong enough, the instinct will desert the individual, and instead of rising to the emergency, the individual will succumb, whereas a stronger life instinct would have seen him through." *Human Behavior,* p. 163.

[21] Those who had in fact succumbed to this apathy — who had given up the struggle, and for whom death would be a mere matter of time — were known as "Moslems." See above, n. 17.

[22] Bettelheim, "Individual and Mass Behavior," p. 141.

[23] Says Dr. Cohen, "I am not asserting that sex was never discussed; it was, though not often. Frankl also states 'that in contrast to mass existence in other military communities . . . here (in the concentration camp) there is *no smut talk.*'" *Human Behavior,* p. 141.

[24] "With reference to this phenomenon Miss Bluhm has pointed out that it is not at all unusual that people in extraordinary circumstances, for example soldiers in wartime, 'are able to give up their habitual standards of cleanliness without deeper disturbance; yet only up to certain limits.' The rules of anal cleanliness, she adds, are not disregarded. 'Their neglect means return to instinctual behavior of childhood.'" *Ibid.,* p. 175.

[25] Bettelheim, "Individual and Mass Behavior," p. 445.

[26] *Ibid.,* p. 421.

[27] Quoted in Cohen, *Human Behavior,* p. 176.

[28] *Ibid.*

[29] *Ibid.,* p. 174.

[30] Bettelheim, "Individual and Mass Behavior," pp. 445–46. This same phenomenon is noted by Curt Bondy: "They tell great stories about what they have been before and what they have performed." "Problems of Internment Camps," *Journal of Abnormal and Social Psychology,* XXXVIII (October, 1943), 453–75.

[31] Cohen, *Human Behavior,* p. 177. Italics in original.

[32] Bettelheim, "Individual and Mass Behavior," p. 447.

[33] *Ibid.,* pp. 448–50. "Once, for instance, a guard on inspecting the prisoners' apparel found that the shoes of some of them were dirty on the inside. He ordered all prisoners to wash their shoes inside and out with water and soap. The heavy shoes treated this way became hard as stone. The order was never repeated, and many prisoners did not execute it when given. Nevertheless there were some old prisoners who not only continued to wash the inside of their shoes every day but cursed all others who did not do so as negligent and dirty. These prisoners firmly believed that the rules set down by the Gestapo were desirable standards of human behavior, at least in the camp situation." *Ibid.,* p. 450.

[34] *Ibid.* See also Cohen, *Human Behavior,* pp. 189–93, for a discussion of anti-Semitism among the Jews.

[35] Cohen, *Human Behavior,* pp. 176–77.

[36] *Ibid.,* p. 179. On this and other points I must also acknowledge my indebtedness to Mr. Ies Spetter, a former Dutch journalist now living in this country, who was imprisoned

for a time at Auschwitz during World War II. Mr. Spetter permitted me to see an unpublished paper, "Some Thoughts on Victims and Criminals in the German Concentration Camps," which he wrote in 1954 at the New School for Social Research; and this, together with a number of conversations I had with him, added much to my understanding of concentration-camp psychology.

³⁷ Kogon, *Theory and Practice*, p. 284.

³⁸ *The Other Kingdom*, p. 137.

³⁹ "In the preference camp Bergen Belsen, only four cases of attempted suicide were witnessed by Tas, three of which were saved with great effort, while in the Stammlager Auschwitz only one successful attempt came to my knowledge. This does not mean that there were not more, but their number was certainly small. Kaas, on the other hand, witnessed several attempted suicides in Buchenwald. He has remembered three that were successful (two by hanging, one by rushing into the electric fence). He also knows of prisoners who were known to be depressive cases, and who were shot down when during the night they had deliberately gone out of bounds. As compared with the large number of prisoners, the number of suicides, however, was very small." Cohen, *Human Behavior*, p. 158.

⁴⁰ Kogon, *Theory and Practice*, pp. 166–67. This occurred during fearful tortures at the quarry, where the Jews knew they were about to be killed anyway.

⁴¹ A. Hottinger, "Hunger Krankheit, Hunger Öden, Hungertuberkulose," p. 32, quoted in Cohen, *Human Behavior*, p. 197.

⁴² The experience of American prisoners taken by the Chinese during the Korean War seems to indicate that profound changes in behavior and values, if not in basic personality itself, can be effected without the use of physical torture or extreme deprivation. The Chinese were able to get large numbers of Americans to act as informers and to co-operate in numerous ways in the effort to indoctrinate all the prisoners with Communist propaganda. The technique contained two key elements. One was that all formal and informal authority structures within the group were systematically destroyed; this was done by isolating officers, non-commissioned officers, and any enlisted men who gave indications of leadership capacities. The other element involved the continual emphasizing of the captors' power and influence by judicious manipulation of petty rewards and punishments and by subtle hints of the greater rewards and more severe punishments (repatriation or non-repatriation) that rested with the pleasure of those in authority. See Edgar H. Schein, "Some Observations on Chinese Methods of Handling Prisoners of War," *Public Opinion Quarterly*, XX (Spring, 1956), 321–27.

⁴³ In a system as tightly closed as the plantation or the concentration camp, the slave's or prisoner's position of absolute dependence virtually compels him to see the authority-figure as somehow really "good." Indeed, all the evil in his life may flow from this man — but then so also must everything of any value. Here is the seat of the only "good" he knows, and to maintain his psychic balance he must persuade himself that the good is in some way dominant. A threat to this illusion is thus in a real sense a threat to his very existence. It is a common experience among social workers dealing with neglected and maltreated children to have a child desperately insist on his love for a cruel and brutal parent and beg that he be allowed to remain with that parent. The most dramatic feature of this situation is the cruelty which it involves, but the mechanism which inspires the devotion is not the cruelty of the parent but rather the abnormal dependency of the child. A classic example of this mechanism in operation may be seen in the case of Varvara Petrovna, mother of Ivan Turgenev. Mme Turgenev "ruled over her serfs with a rod of iron." She demanded utter obedience and total submission. The slightest infraction of her rules brought the most severe punishment: "A maid who did not offer her a cup of tea in the proper manner was sent off to some remote village and perhaps separated from her family forever; gardeners who failed to prevent the plucking of a tulip in one of the flower beds before the house were ordered to be flogged; a servant whom she suspected of a mutinous disposition was sent off to Siberia." Her family and her most devoted servants were treated in much the same manner. "Indeed," wrote Varvara Zhitova, the adopted daughter of Mme Turgenev, "those who loved her and were most devoted to her suffered most of all." Yet in spite of her brutality she was adored by the very people she tyrannized. David Magarshack describes how once when thrashing her eldest son she nearly

fainted with sadistic excitement, whereupon "little Nicholas, forgetting his punishment, bawled at the top of his voice: 'Water! Water for mummy!' " Mme Zhitova, who knew Mme Turgenev's cruelty intimately and was herself the constant victim of her tyranny, wrote: "In spite of this, I loved her passionately, and when I was, though rarely, separated from her, I felt lonely and unhappy." Even Mme Turgenev's maid Agatha, whose children were sent to another village, when still infants so that Agatha might devote all her time to her mistress, could say years later, "Yes, she caused me much grief. I suffered much from her, but all the same I loved her! She was a real lady!" V. Zhitova, *The Turgenev Family*, trans. A. S. Mills (London: Havill Press, 1954), p. 25; David Magarshack, *Turgenev: A Life* (New York: Grove, 1954), pp. 14, 16, 22.

[44] Bruno Bettelheim tells us of the fantastic efforts of the old prisoners to believe in the benevolence of the officers of the SS. "They insisted that these officers [hid] behind their rough surface a feeling of justice and propriety; he, or they, were supposed to be genuinely interested in the prisoners and even trying in a small way, to help them. Since nothing of these supposed feelings and efforts ever became apparent, it was explained that he hid them so effectively because otherwise he would not be able to help the prisoners. The eagerness of these prisoners to find reasons for their claims was pitiful. A whole legend was woven around the fact that of two officers inspecting a barrack one had cleaned his shoes from mud before entering. He probably did it automatically, but it was interpreted as a rebuff of the other officer and a clear demonstration of how he felt about the concentration camp." Bettelheim, "Individual and Mass Behavior," p. 451.

[45] Professor Stampp, in a chapter called "To Make Them Stand in Fear," describes the planter's resources for dealing with a recalcitrant slave. *Peculiar Institution*, pp. 141–91.

[46] Edward A. Pollard, *Black Diamonds Gathered in the Darkey Homes of the South* (New York: Pudney & Russel, 1859), p. 58.

[47] *Ibid.*, p. viii.

[48] John Pendleton Kennedy, *Swallow Barn* (Philadelphia: Carey & Lea, 1832).

[49] John Dollard, *Caste and Class in a Southern Town* (2d ed.; New York: Harper, 1949), p. 255. The lore of "accommodation," taken just in itself, is very rich and is, needless to say, morally very complex. It suggests a delicate psychological balance. On the one hand, as the Dollard citation above implies, accommodation is fraught with dangers for the personalities of those who engage in it. On the other hand, as Bruno Bettelheim has reminded me, this involves a principle that goes well beyond American Negro society and is to be found deeply imbedded in European traditions: the principle of how the powerless can manipulate the powerful through aggressive stupidity, literal-mindedness, servile fawning, and irresponsibility. In this sense the immovably stupid "Good Soldier Schweik" and the fawning Negro in Richard Wright's *Black Boy* who allowed the white man to kick him for a quarter partake of the same tradition. Each has a technique whereby he can in a real sense exploit his powerful superiors, feel contempt for them, and suffer in the process no great damage to his own pride. Jewish lore, as is well known, teems with this sort of thing. There was much of it also in the traditional relationships between peasants and nobles in central Europe.

Still, all this required the existence of some sort of alternative forces for moral and psychological orientation. The problem of the Negro in slavery times involved the virtual absence of such forces. It was with the end of slavery, presumably, that they would first begin to present themselves in generally usable form — a man's neighbors, the Loyal Leagues, white politicians, and so on. It would be in these circumstances that the essentially intermediate technique of accommodation could be used as a protective device beneath which a more independent personality might develop.

Chattel Slavery and Concentration Camps

Earle E. Thorpe

After criticizing the historical writings of Ulrich Bonnell Phillips as being strongly biased and based on faulty sources, Richard Hofstadter wrote in 1944:

Let the study of the Old South be undertaken by other (unbiased) scholars who have absorbed the viewpoint of modern cultural anthropology, who have a feeling for social psychology . . . , who will concentrate upon the neglected rural elements that formed the great majority of the Southern population, who will not rule out the testimony of more critical observers, and who will realize that any history of slavery must be written in large part from the standpoint of the slave — and then the possibilities of the Old South as a field of research and historical experience will loom larger than ever.[1]

In 1959 the University of Chicago Press published a book entitled *Slavery: A Problem in American Institutional and Intellectual Life*, which was written by a scholar who states that he accepted certain of the Hofstadter challenges as incentives for his study of the institution. This scholar, Stanley M. Elkins, in an opening chapter entitled, "Slavery as a Problem in Historiography," opines that studies of the Negro in American history made by Negroes themselves, as well as those by Ulrich Bonnell Phillips, James Ford Rhodes, Kenneth Stampp, Gunnar Myrdal, Herbert Aptheker, and just about everyone who has previously written on the subject have the serious defect of being biased, polemical, and overly dominated by moral considerations. Thus Professor Elkins clearly indicates that he is going to beware of the heavy hand of prejudice which he feels has done damage to previous writings about the Negro.

Elkins makes it clear that he does not believe the old charge that Negroes are biologically inferior. Although he shares the convictions that the slaves were indeed culturally inferior, this scholar goes to considerable length to disagree with U. B. Phillips and others who contended that plantation slaves in America were inferior because the African cultures from which they came were inferior. Unlike Phillips,

Earle E. Thorpe, "Chattel Slavery and Concentration Camps," *Negro History Bulletin*, XXV (May 1962), pp. 171–76. Reprinted by permission of the Association for the Study of Negro Life and History. © 1962 by the Association for the Study of Negro Life and History.

Melville J. Herskovits, and others, Elkins agrees with those scholars who believe that very little of the African heritage survived in North America.[2] "No true picture . . . of African culture," he concludes, "seems to throw any light at all on the origins of what would emerge in American plantation society as the stereotyped 'Sambo' personality."[3]

On one aspect of his own thesis, Elkins writes:

An examination of American slavery, checked at certain critical points against a very different slave system, that of Latin America, reveals that a major key to many of the contrasts between them was an institutional key: The presence or absence of other powerful institutions in society made an immense difference in the character of slavery itself. In Latin America, the very tension and balance among three kinds of organizational concerns — church, crown, and plantation agriculture — prevented slavery from being carried by the planting class to its ultimate logic. For the slave in terms of the space thus allowed for the development of men and women as moral beings, the result was an 'open system': a system of contact with free society through which ultimate absorption into society could and did occur with great frequency. The rights of personality implicit in the ancient traditions of slavery and in the church's most venerable assumptions on the nature of the human soul were thus in a vital sense conserved, whereas to a staggering extent the very opposite was true in North American slavery (which) operated as a 'closed system.'[4]

This scholar seeks to further buttress his conclusion with a contention that the impact of enslavement on the personality and character of Nazi concentration camp inmates was substantially identical with that which plantation slavery in North America had on the personality and character of Negroes. Utilizing the excellent and abundant literature which describes and analyzes the behavior of concentration camp inmates, Professor Elkins gives a concise but thorough picture of this behavior.[5] *Without any effort at all* to enumerate the *differences* between plantation slavery and the concentration camp, Elkins admits that there are differences but contends that this does not make comparison impossible.[6] He characterizes Negro slaves in North America as "a society of helpless dependents."[7] The dominant slave type, Elkins states, "corresponded in its major outlines to 'Sambo.' " This dominant type existed, he declares, because "there were elements in the very structure of the plantation system — its 'closed' character — that could sustain infantilism as a normal feature of behavior."[8] At the end of the volume, the author reminds us again, that in the analogy which he used, "the mechanism was the infantilizing tendencies of power."[9] Of what he feels was the dominant slave type, he writes:

Sambo, the typical plantation slave, was docile but irresponsible, loyal but lazy, humble but chronically given to lying and stealing; his behavior was full of infantile silliness and his talk inflated with childish exaggeration. His relationship with his master was one of utter dependence and childish attachment.[10]

Of his acceptance of this stereotype, Professor Elkins writes:

The picture has far too many circumstantial details, its hues have been stroked in by too many different brushes, for it to be denounced as counterfeit. Too much folk-knowledge, too much plantation literature, too much of the Negro's own lore, have gone into its making to entitle one in good conscience to condemn it as "conspiracy."[11]

"Why should it be, turning once more to Latin America," he continues, "that there one finds no Sambo, no social tradition, that is, in which slaves were defined by virtually complete consensus as children incapable of being treated with the full privileges of freedom and adulthood?" "There," he answers, "the system surely had its brutalities, (but) there . . . the system was not closed."[12]

The position taken in this article is that the Sambo stereotype was not the real Negro personality because, unlike the concentration camp, plantation slavery in North America had enough "elbow room" for the development of a more complex, better-rounded personality; that Sambo was often the side of his personality which the Negro chose to present to the white man; that although the child-posture is the one which whites generally sought to effect in their relationship with Negroes, because of the contradictions and "elbow room" in the system most bondsmen never internalized many of the planters' values. Elkins fails to recognize properly the complexity of slave personality. The bondsman wore many faces, of which Sambo usually was only his public and not his private one.[13]

With reference to the so-called Latin American contrast, it seems that there are at least three effective answers to the Elkins thesis. First, despite their differences, because of the high degree of similarity, it is erroneous to categorize Latin American slavery as an "open system" and the North American variety as the "closed system." A second point hinges on this scholar's often-repeated assertion that, "one searches in vain through the literature of the Latin-American slave systems for the 'Sambo' of our tradition — the perpetual child incapable of maturity."[14] This is so not because there were no slaves in Latin America who evidenced clear Sambo characteristics as one side of their personalities. Rather, the omission reflects Professor Elkins' own admission that in contrast to the situation in North America, Latin American culture *accepted the institution of slavery as a necessary evil,* Elkins fails to see that there was thus no need to create myths and stereotypes to justify the institution. In other words, the existence of the stereotype in North America is rooted not in a true estimate of slave personality but in the peculiar psychological needs of the slave owners. By their effort to convince themselves, and everyone else, that the institution was a positive good, the planters of North America were compelled to claim that Sambo was indeed the true slave personality.[15] Literature can be very misleading.

In addition to the objection that the personality differences are usually little more than mythical literary inventions created to satisfy the North American slave-

owner's conscience, one reviewer of the Elkins volume shows that when the capitalist system matured in Latin America, there was practically no difference between
treatment of slaves and freedmen there and the treatment meted out in North
America. The reviewer concludes:

The slave plantation . . . was a special, emergent capitalist form of industrial
organization, which appeared earlier, and with more intensity, in the colonies of
the north European powers than in the colonies of Spain. . . .
   The differentials in growth of slave plantations in different colonies are to be
understood as resulting from different ecologies, differential maturation of metropolitan markets and industries, and different political relationships between creole
governing bodies and the metropolitan authorities. The rate of growth of the slave
plantation . . . did not hinge on matters of race, civil liberties, protection of the
rights of individuals slave and free, or the presence or absence of one or several
religious codes.[16]

   As dark as the picture of chattel slavery in North America was, because the
theory, literature, law and actual practice were frequently at variance, the results
on personality development were not as extreme as Professor Elkins would have
us believe.[17]
   It is wrong to study in an institution or culture, as he does "the infantilizing
tendencies of power" without pointing out the countertendencies which were operative and which tended to minimize, negate, or eliminate many of the infantilizing
tendencies. This omission makes his conclusions about the personalities of plantation slaves in North America erroneous in their simplicity. Among the significant
omissions which would have to be included in a valid analogy are the following.

Differences

A major difference between the two systems is to be found in the extent of resistance
to enslavement. Many observers have noted the almost complete lack of resistance
among inmates of the concentration camps, pointing out that although guards were
usually few the prisoners walked meekly into the gas chambers or quietly dug their
graves and lined up beside them to be shot.[18] Bruno Bettelheim is severely critical
of the prisoners for what he feels was their unrealistic lack of resistance.[19] Elkins
agrees with this depiction of the behavior of camp inmates, but gives a similar
characterization of the plantation slaves, whom he calls "a society of helpless
dependents."[20] That he takes this statement literally can be seen in the disparaging
remarks which he makes about Herbert Aptheker's study of slave revolts,[21] and in
his own comparison of slave revolts in North and South America. Elkins does not

perceive that, despite the absence of protracted large scale slave revolts in North America, the many forms of persistent resistance by the bondsmen to their enslavement is dramatic evidence of the very significant difference between the two systems.

Professor Elkins offers as one proof that Negro slaves were a docile mass the statement that, "the revolts that actually did occur were in no instance planned by plantation laborers but rather by Negroes whose qualities of leadership were developed well outside the full coercions of the plantation authority-system."[22] So anxious is he to prove his thesis that he apparently discounts the possibility that this may be so not because of the lack of leadership qualities among plantation slaves but because the opportunity to plan revolts was greater in or near towns or cities. Furthermore, although, as Elkins points out, Denmark Vesey was a freed artisan, Nat Turner, a literate preacher, and Gabriel a blacksmith who lived near Richmond, their hundreds and thousands of co-conspirators were not of this category, but were mostly the plantation slaves whom Elkins describes as humble, lazy, silly, immoral, docile, and loyal. In other words, to Elkins the leaders of the plots and revolts were the unusual or exceptional individuals. This and similar arguments leads the present writer to the conviction that Professor Elkins is here utilizing a version of the old argument which attributed the intelligence and achievements of some light-skinned Negroes to the amount of so-called white blood in their veins, thereby eliminating them from the race.[23]

Several observers have written of the manner in which the Nazis thought of and sought to operate the concentration camps with the same organizational and administrative emphases as are found in the most modern factory.[24] Absence of the mid-twentieth century level of organizational knowledge and efficiency was a major factor which kept plantation slavery from being as dehumanizing as was the case with concentration camps. It is not without justification that modern man uses the word "totalitarianism" to describe this century's mass state. "Every single moment of their lives was strictly regulated and supervised," one critic says of the camp inmates, "They had no privacy whatsoever."[25] Even after the work day was over, the camp inmate lived in barracks-style quarters which did not afford anything like the amount of freedom from the surveillance and oppressions of the ruling elite that slave quarters on the plantation usually offered. It is because he was so constantly under surveillance and oppression, together with the chronic possibility and fear of momentary extermination, that the camp inmate presents the classic picture of the ever-regressed personality and character which Elkins mistakenly attributes to plantation slaves.

Many camp inmates were made the subject of barbarous medical experiments.[26] Plantation slaves were not so used as human guinea pigs. A highly literate former camp inmate states that at the peak of its development, "the . . . slave labor and extermination policy (of the concentration camps) did away with all considerations for the value of a life, even in terms of a slave society. . . . In the Hitler state slaves (did not even have an) investment value. That was the *great difference* between exploitation by private capitalists and exploitation by a state answering only to itself."[27] Are we to suppose, as Elkins does, that this "great difference" between the two systems made no difference where the personalities which they bred or allowed is concerned? Whereas the concentration camp inmate, in order to keep from becoming an elected candidate for the incinerators or gas chambers, always had to act and work as if he were physically able to be of some service to the Third Reich, the plantation slave was usually free from this daily and hourly threat of a death sentence. Because he represented economic capital, usually the worst that the plantation slave could expect for dissatisfying the ruling class on such matters was a lashing or being sold, but of the camp inmates, we are told, "Everybody was convinced that his chances for survival were very slim; therefore to preserve himself as an individual seemed pointless."[28] "The prisoner's lives were in such extreme danger," continues this observer, "that little energy or interest was left over" for anything except concern with the problem of sheer survival.[29]

In his 1947 Presidential Address before the American Historical Association, Professor William L. Langer discusses the great psychological impact which the Black Death had on the personality and character of Europeans of the late medieval and early modern periods. A study might well be made of the consciousness of death in Negro thought, but, apart from the horrors of the Middle Passage, there is nothing in the history of plantation slavery to match the impact of the Black Death or the omnipresent hand of death in the concentration camps. This fact is doubtless one of several which kept plantation slavery from being as dehumanizing as were the Nazis' internment camps.

Elkins, Victor Frankl, Bettelheim, and others have commented on the weakness and almost disappearance at times of the emotional life of the camp inmates.[30] This is a marked contrast to the emotional life of the plantation slaves, an emotionality often so variegated and strong that it has added an indelible heritage of dance, song, laughter, and pathos to the American way of life. In the literature on concentration camps, many pages are filled with discussions of the *Muselmanner,* or Moslems, persons who had completely given up all interest in life. To this the literature on chattel slavery stands in marked contrast. A number of scholars state that throughout the slave era, among other attributes Negroes manifested "childlike qualities of happiness and good nature."[31] Where were these qualities to be found in the concentration camps? In great contrast to the plantation system, with concentration camp inmates, *the other side of child behavior,* a side which Elkins ignores entirely — that of the happy child — is missing.

Bettelheim tells us that concentration camp inmates were deliberately kept on a starvation diet in order to make them easier to handle. "It is difficult," he writes, "to deeply terrorize a people that is well fed and well housed."[32] As inadequate as their diets usually were, plantation slaves were better fed than concentration camp inmates. Largely because of the poor quality and inadequate amounts of food given, after a few months of imprisonment, most of the latter were mere skin and bones suffering chronically from diarrhea and dysentery.[33]

The fact that most ante-bellum Negroes were *born into slavery,* while the concentration camp inmates were born and reared as free men and women must have considerable significance where the development of personality is concerned. Also, there were no state laws in Nazi Germany comparable to the "Black Codes" of the Old South. Although they were often honored more in the breach than in the observance, are we to suppose that the existence of laws setting limits to the cruelty which plantation slaves could be made the objects of, and actual court cases which resulted from the existence of these laws, had no effect on the personality and character development of the slave?

We are informed that "No prisoner was told why he was imprisoned, and never for how long."[34] In contrast to this, are we to suppose that the elaborate biblical, historical, and other justifications for his race's enslavement which were constantly presented to the plantation bondsman had no effect on the development of his personality and character? As ridiculous as these justifications now appear, may it not be that such rationalizations given to an enslaved race may affect their personality development in a more positive way than is the case with enslavement of selected members of a free populace, with no justification at all given?

Professor Elkins calls both the concentration camps and ante-bellum plantations highly similar "closed systems." Yet where in the concentration camps was there anything comparable to the ebony-hued slave women suckling white infants at their breasts, or free white children and slave children playing together, or planters paying high cash prices for colored mistresses and concubines? Where in Nazi Germany was there an Underground Railroad, or a geographically contiguous region rife with abolitionism, or anything even comparable to the colonization society? How many SS officers or Capos encouraged the camp inmates to sing while they worked as was the case with the Negro slaves? While the plantations produced the enchanting slave songs and tales, and eternally beautiful spirituals, what of comparable beauty has come out of the concentration camps?[35] And can we imagine inmates being in such physical and psychical condition so as to be considered for last-ditch military service in the manner of the Confederate Congress voting to enlist and arm Negro slaves? Because their fruits were so different, we must conclude that the personalities of slaves and camp inmates were different.

So absolute and unmitigated was the cruelty of the concentration camps that they were indeed the closed systems to which Elkins refers. In them it is true that prisoners had to make a total adjustment to enslavement, and for most dehumanization was well nigh complete. But in the United States even the slaves knew that the basic national creed as encouched in such documents as the Declaration of Independence and the Federal Constitution ran counter to the prospect of their remaining eternally in bondage. Where in Nazi Germany did a similar conflict exist between ideal and reality?

Professor Elkins' failure adequately to consider these differences means that his conclusion that the effect which the concentration camp had on its inmates is the same effect that plantation slavery in North America had on Negroes is in need of drastic revision. While he seems to understand fairly well the mind and personality of the camp inmate, his understanding of the mind of the Negro slaves leaves much to be desired.

Despite their similarities, the differences between the two systems are so significant that, for the development of a more healthy or adult personality, when compared to the concentration camps the plantation system in North America had considerably more "elbow room." It was not on the plantations of North America as Elkins claims, but in such products of Occidental efficiency and technology as Belsen, Sachsenhausen, Dachau, and Buchenwald that our Christian civilization first saw the institution of slavery "carried to its ultimate logic."[36]

It is not without significance that plantation slavery existed in a culture which was peace oriented, while the concentration camps were vital parts of a war-oriented culture. Just as the twentieth century has produced total war, in these camps it also has produced total enslavement. However, although the Nazis may be said to have perfected the institution of slavery, from the long record of North America's treatment of Africans and their descendants the Nazis could have and probably did learn much.

Because his own biases blurred his vision,[37] and because of the too-loose fashion in which Elkins handles his analogy, we must conclude that the challenge laid down for historical scholars in 1944 by Professor Hofstadter has not yet been met. Professor Elkins should have been more impressed with the words of Herbert J. Aptheker, written in 1943, which state — "The dominant historiography in the United States either omits the Negro people or presents them as a people without a past, as a people who have been docile, passive, parasitic, imitative."[38] "This picture," Aptheker declares, "is a lie." Elkins should have been more impressed with the words of a planter who wrote in 1837 —

The most general defect in the character of the Negro is hypocrisy: and this hypocrisy frequently makes him pretend to more ignorance than he possesses; and if his master treats him as a fool, he will be sure to act the fools part.[39]

Finally, Professor Elkins should have been more impressed with the work of the Association for the Study of Negro Life and History, which has devoted almost a half century of labor directed toward disproving the Sambo and similar stereotypes.

Notes

[1] Richard Hofstadter, "U. B. Phillips and the Plantation Legend," *Journal of Negro History,* XXIX (April, 1944) pp. 109–124.

[2] See Melville J. Herskovits, *The Myth of the Negro Past* (New York: Harpers, 1941), and E. Franklin Frazier, *The Negro in the United States* (New York: Macmillan, 1949).

[3] Elkins, *Slavery*, p. 97.

[4] *Ibid.*, p. 82.

[5] *Ibid.*, pp. 103 ff.

[6] *Ibid.*, p. 104.

[7] *Ibid.*, p. 89.

[8] When he holds that the Sambo stereotype is a factual representation of the plantation slave's personality, Elkins apparently fails to perceive that he may at the same time be ascribing this same personality to the masses of ante-bellum Southern whites. Bruno Bettelheim (see Chapter 7 of his *The Informed Heart: Autonomy in a Mass Age* [Glencoe, Illinois: The Free Press, 1960]), and other observers state that the same psychological forces operative within the concentration camps were the dominant ones operative on the German populace outside the camps, and the effect was the same, with the difference being largely one of degree. Wilbur Cash and other critics of southern culture have pointed out that the masses of southern whites were subjected to the same frontier forces, similar patterns of control, paternalism, general illiteracy, and exclusion from the political, social, and cultural mainstream as was the Negro slave, with the difference being one of degree. These same critics often have ascribed to southern whites, ante- and post-bellum, virtually the same negative personality traits and characteristics as those often attributed to the Negro.

It is doubtless true, as Professor Elkins writes, that certain situations or settings put premiums on certain types of behavior, while severely penalizing certain other types of behavior (*Slavery*, p. 228). In order for the rigid Sambo stereotype to emerge as the true slave personality, however, a high degree of constancy or consistency in behavior would have to be maintained. Such has never been the case where race relations in the South is concerned. The strange career of Jim Crow did not begin with Appomattox, as Elkins thinks (p. 133), but was a prominent feature of Old South culture.

Also, the rather common belief which Elkins appears to accept completely (pp. 82 ff) to the effect that the old South accepted the Negro only in the posture of a child is an erroneous over-simplification. Here again consistency was too lacking for the image to be true, for it is largely in the social relations or amenities that the child-posture was insisted on. At working time, which existed far more frequently and lasted much longer than the brief periods of what may be termed points of social contact, the white South sought to get the bondsman to give a very efficient and adult-like performance. The same is true where the matter of obeying the laws was concerned, for here the white South wanted not child-like irresponsibility, but adult-like respect for the law. The notion that the Old South always encouraged and wanted the child-posture from Negroes needs considerable revision.

[9] Elkins, *Slavery*, p. 225.

[10] *Ibid.*, p. 82.

[11] *Ibid.*, p. 84.

[12] *Ibid.*, p. 134.

[13] On the more positive side, it may be pointed out that Elkins' discussion of the role of guilt in liberal and reform movements is highly provocative. Too, unfortunately for the scholar who is interested in plantation slavery in America, there were no professional psychologists and psychiatrists among the Negro bondsmen. Therefore, if the student of this institution will avoid the pit-falls into which Elkins stumbled, from a careful study and comparison of the behavior of concentration camp inmates he may gain great insights into many aspects of this "problem in American institutional and intellectual life."

The growth of anthropology, psychoanalysis, social psychology and related disciplines, and the significance of the new insights into human behavior which they offer, means that the historian of the second half of the twentieth century will probably not be counted adequately literate who does not have an acquaintance with these disciplines. In calling for this broader approach to the study of the Negro in American history, Professors Hofstadter and Elkins are correct. In his December, 1957 address before the American Historical Association entitled, "The Next Assignment," William L. Langer had as his central concern "the directions which historical study might profitably take in the years to come" (in *American Historical*

Review, LXIII, No. 2, January, 1958, p. 284). Here he urged historians to cease to be "buried in their own conservatism" and to recognize "the urgently needed deepening of our historical understanding through exploitation of the concepts and findings of modern . . . psychoanalysis and its later developments and variations as included in the terms 'dynamic' or 'depth psychology.' " The whole of Professor Langer's Presidential address was an attack on what he called the "almost completely negative attitude toward the teachings of psychoanalysis" which historians have traditionally held together with some illustrations and suggestions as to specific applications of this knowledge which historians may make. The present writer believes that scholars who are interested in Afro-American studies would do well to take Professor Langer's suggestions seriously.

¹⁴ Elkins, *Slavery,* p. 84.

¹⁵ Any historian who denies that Sambo, *often feigned* but sometimes genuine, was *one side* of the bondsman's personality is probably guilty of being unrealistic. What is now known about both human behavior and totalitarian systems calls for a change in some aspects of the slave image which some Negro historians have favored. Since these were their immediate blood and cultural forebearers, and in view of the overly narrow image of them which the Slavocracy projected, it is understandable that they sometimes have given great stress to the neater side of the bondsman's personality and character. Thus in reacting against one stereotype, they have been in danger of creating another one, equally false.

Contemporary knowledge ought to have put beyond the bounds of controversy that slavery is generally debasing and degrading to human personality. Rather than fly in the face of this fact and deny the whole of the Slavocracy's propaganda, the truths that should be insisted upon are: (1) These negative behavior characteristics are not innate racial traits. (2) They indict the slave system and not the enslaved, and (3) They do not constitute the whole picture.

¹⁶ S. W. Mintz, in *American Anthropologist,* Vol. 63, No. 3 (June, 1961), p. 586. Professor Elkins appears to be essentially correct in his contention that in the case of plantation slavery and the concentration camps each became "a kind of grotesque patriarchy." (*Slavery,* pp. 104, 113). The present observer does not find this the startling discovery which Professor Elkins seems to think it is. There is a sense in which practically every highly authoritarian system is a grotesque patriarchy, and Elkins seems to miss Wilbur Cash's often repeated assertions in his volume, *The Mind of the South* (New York: A. Knopf, 1941), that the total southern culture, both ante- and post-bellum, has been essentially such a grotesque patriarchy. The present observer has even noticed that in several small colleges and universities the college president represents for a number of students and faculty members a father image and paternalism is the dominant basis of their relationships. This paternalistic factor is the major argument against highly authoritarian systems and, therefore, the major argument in favor of democracy as a way of life which does not treat adults as if they are children.

¹⁷ Apparently the only subject on which Professor Elkins is willing to accept the judgment of the slave-owners is their conclusion that Negroes constitute an inferior human type. As indicated, to be sure he does not accept the reasoning on which his conclusion rests, but he devotes one-half of his book in an effort to prove that the slave owners' conclusion was a correct one. Yet, near the end of his volume, when discussing, "Slavery, Consensus, and the Southern Intellect," he is well-nigh completely denunciatory of the southern intellect which he says, mainly because of its rigidity, single-mindedness, and hysterical fears (p. 207) was not able to think objectively about slavery. "At most," he writes, the southern intellect "thought in the vicinity of slavery" (*Ibid.*). On this point, Elkins further states:

"The existence of thoroughgoing consensus in a democratic community appears to create two sorts of conditions for the functioning of intellect. One is sternly coercive, the other, wildly permissive. On the one hand, consensus narrows the alternatives with which thought may deal; on the other, it removes all manner of limits — limits of discrimination, circumspection, and discipline — on the alternatives that remain. The former function is probably better understood than the latter; both, however, were fully at work in the intellectual life of the ante-bellum South" (pp. 212–213).

Elkins declares that the Southern intellect made "a general agreement" to stop "[objective] thinking about slavery altogether," and points up the ineffectiveness of pro-slavery propaganda by reminding us that though the slave's way of life was declared to be a better one than that of northern industrial workers, there was an absolute failure of "any free workers to present themselves for enslavement" (216). "In reality," he concludes, "the contour of this body of thought was governed by the fact that the South was talking no longer to the world, or even to the North, but to itself. It is this fact — the fact of internal consensus and the peculiar lack of true challenge-points at any level of Southern society — that gives the pro-slavery polemic its special distinction" (p. 217). In this chapter Elkins is clearly describing the southern mind as a diseased one and he rejects its conclusions on practically all points except one, this being the concept of Negro inferiority.

[18] See Otto Kurst, *Auschwitz,* Hillman Books (New York: Hillman Periodicals, 1960); Eugen Kogon, *The Theory and Practice of Hell,* tr. by Heinz Norden, Berkley Medallion Book (New York: Berkley Publishing Corp., 1960 ed.); Rudolf Hoess, *Commandant of Auschwitz,* tr. by Constantine FitzGibbon, Popular Library Book (New York: 1961); Victor Frankl, *From Death Camp to Existentialism,* tr. Ilse Lasch (Boston: Beacon Press, 1959).

[19] B. Bettelheim, *The Informed Heart,* see especially the last three chapters.

[20] Elkins, *Slavery,* p. 98.

[21] Aptheker's sources he calls "unsubstantiated rumors gleaned from rural Southern newspapers."

[22] Elkins, *Slavery,* p. 139.

[23] For other examples of the evidence of slave resistance which Elkins treats as of little significance see Harvey Wish, "American Slave Insurrections before 1861," *Journal of Negro History,* XXII (July, 1937), pp. 299–320; R. A. and A. H. Bauer, "Day to Day Resistance to Slavery," *Ibid.,* XXVII (October, 1942), pp. 388–419; Kenneth W. Porter, "Florida Slaves and Free Negroes in the Seminole War, 1825–1842," *Ibid.,* XXVIII (October, 1943), pp. 390–421; John Hope Franklin, *From Slavery to Freedom* (New York: A. Knopf, 1947); and Earle E. Thorpe, *The Mind of the Negro* (Baton Rouge, Louisiana: Harrington Publications, 1961), Chapters III, IV, and V.

Not only is Elkins' picture of what oppression did to the personality and character of plantation slaves overdrawn, the same is true of the picture which he paints of the results of oppression in the concentration camp. On this Victor Frankl has written:

"The sort of person the prisoner became was the result of an inner decision, and not the result of camp influences alone. Fundamentally, therefore, any man can, even under such circumstances, decide what shall become of him — mentally and spiritually. He may retain his human dignity even in a concentration camp" (in his *From Death Camp to Existentialism,* p. 66).

Of the changes in personality and character which took place, Bettelheim states — "Given the conditions of the camp, these changes were more often for the worse, but sometimes definitely for the better. So one and the same environment could bring about radical changes both for better and worse" (in his *The Informed Heart,* p. 14).

[24] See, for example, works already cited by Bruno Bettelheim, Otto Kurst, Eugen Kogon, Rudolf Hoess, and V. Frankl.

[25] B. Bettelheim, *op. cit.,* p. 108.

[26] See A. Mitscherlich and F. Mielke, *Doctors of Infamy* (New York: Henry Schuman, 1949).

[27] B. Bettelheim, *op. cit.,* p. 243. Italics supplied.

[28] *Ibid.,* p. 138.

[29] *Ibid.,* p. 203.

[30] *Ibid., passim;* S. M. Elkins, *op. cit.,* p. 115.

[31] Otto Klineberg, ed., *Characteristics of the American Negro* (New York: Harpers, 1944).

[32] B. Bettelheim, *op. cit.,* p. 297.

[33] Elkins states that in the concentration camps, because of chronic hunger due to the scanty meals, "even the sexual instincts no longer functioned" (*Slavery,* p. 107). Bettelheim

denies this and states that both homosexuality and masturbation were practiced in the camps, though often more because of anxiety as to whether one had lost his sexuality than for any other reason.

[34] Bettelheim, *op. cit.,* p. 108.

[35] There were, of course, similarities in the reactions of inmates of the concentration camps and the plantation slaves. Among those similarities, both groups tended to be highly interested in food and other bodily needs, to day-dream a lot as an escape from the harsh realities of their lives, and to internalize the values of the ruling class. Because of fear of the ruling elite, both tended to direct many of their aggressions against one another, and, as was the case with the camp prisoner-leaders known as Capos, sometimes Negroes put in positions of leadership outdid the Slavocracy in manifestations of anti-Negroism. Among both, stealing from or cheating the ruling elite was often considered as honorable as stealing from fellow slaves was thought despicable.

[36] A number of psychologists and psychiatrists have pointed out that the radical alterations in personality and character which occurred in concentration camps prove that some long-accepted Freudian concepts, valid under normal life-circumstances, are invalid where the behavior of man under extreme stress is concerned. Here is a situation roughly analogous to that of Newtonian physics, which twentieth-century scientists have shown to break down at both of the extreme ends of the matter and space continuities. It has been pointed out that much in Freudian psychology was peculiarly applicable to the nineteenth-century society in which Freud lived, "the stability of whose institutional and status relationships could always to a large extent be taken for granted," but less appropriate for a dynamic culture such as that long characteristic of the United States (Elkins, *Slavery,* p. 119). That Freud failed to perceive these particular limitations of his psychology, Elkins attributes in part to the fact that in modern occidental civilization, before the Nazi concentration camps chattel slavery in America was the only large-scale social laboratory which might have given Freud the evidence that he needed for a more inclusive psychology. Thus it seems that Freud might have benefited greatly from a close study of slavery in America. (For other comments on the changes in Freudian psychology wrought by the concentration camp experiences see Eli Cohen, *Human Behavior in the Concentration Camp,* New York: Norton, 1953; Bruno Bettelheim, *The Informed Heart: Autonomy in a Mass Age,* p. 14, passim; Leo Alexander, "War Crimes: Their Social-Psychological Aspects," *American Journal of Psychiatry,* CV (September, 1948) p. 173; and Victor Frankl, *From Death Camp to Existentialism,* passim.

On the subject of this paper, see also Kenneth Stampp, "The Historian and Southern Negro Slavery," *American Historical Review,* LXII (April, 1952).

[37] Although Professor Elkins usually has rejected the mood and methodology of the Slavocracy, he makes the mistake of accepting its conclusions about the nature of the bondsman's personality and character. Throughout the volume Professor Elkins reveals himself as a staunch elitist and conservative, in whose philosophy, like that of most conservatives, the word "gradualism" is sacrosanct. Further evidence of his biases in favor of the Slavocracy are evident in the strongly denunciatory tone which he takes where the American abolitionists are concerned. Calling them "Intellectuals without Responsibility," he writes as if they were all hate and guilt-ridden neurotics who should have been incarcerated for their own sake and for that of society (see pp. 140–192 of his *Slavery*). Elkins erroneously states that the "loftiest manifestation" of slave religion was "at about the level of Green Pastures" (p. 195), and he feels that had not irresponsible extremists, such as the abolitionists, had their way slavery would have been eliminated by a gradual, hence to him more adult, approach, This adult approach would have had as one step the insistence that each slave "be offered a spiritual life marked by dignity and be given instruction in Christian morality" (p. 195). That this would have involved a denial of the "positive good" argument of the South, or how a slave society can effectively teach Christian morality are points on which Elkins is silent.

Professor Elkins has great admiration for the English abolitionists and thinks that they were realistic, objective and dispassionate about their cause because they were men of wealth who operated through parliament and other well-established institutions, in contrast with the American abolitionists who were a displaced elite, anti-institutional, and each speaking for no one but himself. He ignores the fact that declining profits from slave produced products was a key factor in the success which English abolitionists had, while abolitionism in the United States was fighting a system which could boast of almost steadily rising prices from about 1810 to 1860. Too, he omits the fact that when England abolished slavery she had a diversity of economic interests while the Old South's economy rested almost exclusively on cotton culture. Finally, Elkins fails to consider another significant difference between the two abolitionist movements. "The United States alone, of all the great powers," comments one observer, "had to fight for the abolition of slavery within its own national territory. . . . The irreducible conflict, in the case of other nations, was fought by under-mining mercantilism, pushing free trade, and shifting power to the industrial capitalist . . . this was accomplished within the metropolis, far from the colonies themselves. The American South, however, was integrated with United States institutions in a way that the British West Indies never were, and never could be, with the institutions of Great Britain." (S. W. Mintz, *op. cit.*, p. 587.)

Professor Elkins repeatedly makes it clear that he detests uncompromising idealists, and has great admiration for "men with specific stakes in society, men attached to institutions and with a vested interest in one another's presence, men aware of being engaged with concrete problems of power." (pp. 146–47.) By his standards not only do Margaret Fuller, Ralph Waldo Emerson, William Ellery Channing, Orestes Browning, Theodore Parker, James Freeman Clark, Bronson Alcott, Henry David Thoreau and other persons mentioned flunk the course, but Socrates, Jesus Christ and similar nonpropertied idealists and reformers who worked largely outside of institutional frameworks also fail to pass. Elkins apparently fails to appreciate the fact that a dynamic society probably needs critics operating without as well as within the institutional framework, for if the man outside of institutions is liable to exaggerate the role of the individual, those who operate within institutions are liable to become organization and institution-bound and lose sight of human beings.

[38] Herbert J. Aptheker, *American Negro Slave Revolts* (New York: Columbia University Press), 1943.

[39] In Kenneth Stampp, *The Peculiar Institution* (New York: A. Knopf, 1956), p. 99, quoting *The Farmer's Register*, V (1837), p. 32.

Rebelliousness and Docility in the Negro Slave: A Critique of the Elkins Thesis

Eugene D. Genovese

Despite the hostile reception given by historians to Stanley M. Elkins' *Slavery: A Problem in American Institutional and Intellectual Life,*[1] it has established itself as one of the most influential historical essays of our generation. Although Elkins ranges widely, we may restrict ourselves to his most important contribution, the theory of slave personality, and bypass other questions, such as his dubious theory of uncontrolled capitalism in the South. His psychological model would fit comfortably into other social theories and may, up to a point, be analytically isolated.

Elkins asserts that the Sambo stereotype arose only in the United States. He attempts to explain this allegedly unique personality type by constructing a social analysis that contrasts a totalitarian plantation South with a feudal Latin America in which church, state, and plantation balanced one another. To relate this ostensible difference in social structure to the formation of slave personality he invokes an analogy to Nazi concentration camps to demonstrate the possibility of mass infantilization and proceeds to apply three theories of personality: (1) the Freudian, which relates the growth of a personality to the existence of a father figure and which accounts for the identification of a tyrannized child with a tyrannical father; (2) Sullivan's theory of "significant others," which relates the growth of a personality to its interaction with individuals who hold or seem to hold power over its fortunes; and (3) role theory, which relates the growth of a personality to the number and kinds of roles it can play.[2] Elkins assumes that Sambo existed only in the United States and that our task is to explain his unique appearance in the Old South. I propose to show, on the contrary, that Sambo existed wherever slavery existed, that he nonetheless could turn into a rebel, and that our main task is to discover the conditions under which the personality pattern could become inverted and a seem ingly docile slave could suddenly turn fierce.

Eugene D. Genovese, "Rebelliousness and Docility in the Negro Slave: A Critique of the Elkins Thesis," *Civil War History,* XIII (December 1967), pp. 293–314. Reprinted by permission of the publisher.

Elkins asserts that the United States alone produced the Sambo stereotype — "the perpetual child incapable of maturity." He does not, as so many of his critics insist, equate childishness with docility, although he carelessly gives such an impression. Rather, he equates it with dependence and, with a subtlety that seems to elude his detractors, skillfully accounts for most forms of day-to-day resistance. His thesis, as will be shown later, is objectionable not because it fails to account for hostile behavior, but because it proves too much and encompasses more forms of behavior than can usefully be managed under a single rubric.

Elkins' assumption that the existence of a stereotype proves the reality behind it will not stand critical examination either as psychological theory or as historical fact. As psychological theory, it is at least open to question. John Harding and his collaborators have argued that stereotypes, under certain conditions, may in fact be without foundation;[3] this side of the problem may be left to specialists and need not alter the main lines of the argument. Historically, Sambo was emerging in the United States at the same time he was emerging in the French colonies. Negroes, if we would believe the French planters, were childlike, docile, helpless creatures up until the very moment they rose and slaughtered the whites. Accordingly, I have a sporting proposition for Elkins. Let us substitute French Saint-Domingue for the United States and apply his logic. We find a Sambo stereotype and a weak tradition of rebellion. True, there was a century of maroon activity, but only the efforts of Mackandal constituted a genuine revolt. Those efforts were, in the words of C. L. R. James, "the only hint of an organized attempt at revolt during the hundred years preceding the French Revolution."[4] Boukman's revolt ought properly to be regarded as the first phase of the great revolution of 1791 rather than a separate action. In short, when the island suddenly exploded in the greatest slave revolution in history, nothing lay behind it but Sambo and a few hints. Now, let us rewrite history by having the French Jacobins take power and abolish slavery in 1790, instead of 1794. With the aid of that accident the slaves would have been freed as the result of the vicissitudes of Jacobin-Girondist factionalism and not by their own efforts. We would then today be reading a Haitian Elkins whose task would be to explain the extraordinary docility of the country's blacks. As the rewriting of history goes, this excursion requires little effort and ought to make us aware of how suddenly a seemingly docile, or at least adjusted, people can rise in violence. It would be much safer to assume that dangerous and strong currents run beneath that docility and adjustment.

Reaching further back into history, we find an identification of Negroes, including Africans, with a Sambo-like figure. As early as the fourteenth century — and there is no reason to believe that it began that late — so learned and sophisticated a scholar as Ibn Khaldun could write:

Negroes are in general characterized by levity, excitability, and great emotionalism. They are found eager to dance whenever they hear a melody. They are everywhere described as stupid. . . . The Negro nations are, as a rule, submissive to slavery, because (Negroes) have little (that is essentially) human and have attributes that are quite similar to those of dumb animals.[5]

In 1764, in Portugal, a pamphlet on the slavery question in the form of a dialogue has a Brazilian slaveowning mine operator say: "I have always observed that in Brazil the Negroes are treated worse than animals. . . . Yet, withal the blacks endure this." The conclusion drawn was that this submissiveness proved inferiority.[6]

Sambo appears throughout Brazilian history, especially during the nineteenth century. In the 1830's the ideologues of Brazilian slavery, significantly under strong French influence, assured planters that the black was a "man-child" with a maximum mental development equivalent to that of a white adolescent. This and similar views were widespread among planters, particularly in the highly commercialized southern coffee region.[7] Brazilian sociologists and historians accepted this stereotype well into the twentieth century. Euclides da Cunha, in his masterpiece, *Rebellion in the Backlands,* described the Negro as "a powerful organism, given to an extreme humility, without the Indian's rebelliousness."[8] Oliveira Lima, in his pioneering comparative history of Brazil and Spanish and Anglo-Saxon America, described the Negro as an especially subservient element.[9] Joao Pandígeras, in his long standard *History of Brazil,* wrote:

The Negro element in general revealed a perpetual good humor, a childish and expansive joy, a delight in the slightest incidentals of life. . . . Filled with the joy of youth, a ray of sunshine illumined his childlike soul. Sensitive, worthy of confidence, devoted to those who treated him well, capable of being led in any direction by affection and kind words, the Negro helped to temper the primitive harshness of the Portuguese colonists.[10]

One of the leading interpretations in Brazil today regards the blacks as having been subjected to a regime designed to produce alienation and the destruction of the personality by means of the exercise of the arbitrary power of the master. The account given in Kenneth M. Stampp's *The Peculiar Institution* of the efforts to produce a perfect slave has a close parallel in Octavio Ianni's *As Metamorfoses do Escravo,* which analyzes southern Brazil during the nineteenth century.[11]

Nor did Sambo absent himself from Spanish America. The traditional advocacy of Indian freedom often went together with a defense of Negro slavery based on an alleged inferiority that suggests a Sambo stereotype.[12] In 1816, Simón Bolívar wrote to General Jean Marión of Haiti:

I have proclaimed the absolute emancipation of the slaves. The tyranny of the Spaniards has reduced them to such a state of stupidity and instilled in their souls such a great sense of terror that they have lost even the desire to be free!! Many of them would have followed the Spaniards or have embarked on British vessels [whose owners] have sold them in neighboring colonies.[13]

Elkins cites evidence that the Spanish regarded the Indians as docile and the Negroes as difficult to control, but evidence also exists that shows the reverse. The view of the Indian or Negro as docile or rebellious varied greatly with time, place, and circumstance.[14] Sidney Mintz, with one eye on Cuba and Puerto Rico and the other eye on Brazil, has suggested that, regardless of institutional safeguards, the more commercialized the slave system the more it tended to produce dehumanization. This thesis needs considerable refinement but is at least as suggestive as Elkins' attempt to construct a purely institutional interpretation.[15]

On close inspection the Sambo personality turns out to be neither more nor less than the slavish personality; wherever slavery has existed, Sambo has also.[16] "Throughout history," David Brion Davis has written, "it has been said that slaves, though occasionally as loyal and faithful as good dogs, were for the most part lazy, irresponsible, cunning, rebellious, untrustworthy, and sexually promiscuous."[17] Only the element of rebelliousness does not seem to fit Sambo, but on reflection, even that does. Sambo, being a child, could be easily controlled but if not handled properly, would revert to barbarous ways. Davis demonstrates that by the fifth century B.C., many Greeks had come to regard the submission of barbarians to despotic and absolute rulers as proof of inferiority.[18] By the end of the eighteenth century, America and Europe widely accepted the image of the dehumanized black slave, and even Reynal believed that crime and indolence would inevitably follow emancipation.[19]

Sambo has a much longer pedigree and a much wider range than Elkins appreciates. Audrey I. Richards, in 1939, noted the widespread existence of "fatal resignation" among primitive peoples in Africa and suggested that their psychological and physical sluggishness might be attributable in a large part to poor diet and severe malnutrition.[20] Josué de Castro, former head of the United Nations Food and Agriculture Organization, has made the same point about Brazilian slaves and about people in underdeveloped countries in general.[21] As Jean-Paul Sartre has suggested, "Beaten, under-nourished, ill, terrified — but only up to a certain point — he has, whether he's black, yellow, or white, always the same traits of character: he's a sly-boots, a lazy-bones, and a thief, who lives on nothing and who understands only violence."[22] By constructing a single-factor analysis and erroneously isolating the personality structure of the southern slave, Elkins has obscured many other possible lines of inquiry. We do not as yet have a comparative analysis of slave diets in the United States, Brazil, and the West Indies, although it might tell us a great deal about personality patterns.

It is generally believed that Elkins merely repeated Tannenbaum when he declared Sambo to be a native of the Old South; in fact, the assertion is, for better or worse, entirely his own. I would not dwell on this point were it not that I cannot imagine Tannenbaum's taking so one-sided a view. I intend no disrespect to Elkins by this observation for, as a matter of fact, his single-mindedness, even when misguided has helped him to expose problems others have missed entirely. Elkins' greatest weakness, nonetheless, is his inability to accept the principle of contradiction, to realize that all historical phenomena must be regarded as constituting a process of becoming, and that, therefore, the other-sidedness of the most totalitarian conditions may be fact represent the unfolding of their negation. If Sambo were merely Sambo, then Elkins must explain how an overseer could publicly defend his class, without challenge, for having "to punish and keep in order the Negroes, at the risk of his life."[23]

Elkins recognizes a wide range of institutional factors as having contributed to the contrast between the Latin and Anglo-Saxon slave systems, but he places special emphasis on the system of law in relation to the structure and policies of Church and Crown.[24] Although in this way Elkins follows Tannenbaum, he necessarily must go well beyond him, and therein lies his greatest difficulty. Tannenbaum's well-known thesis need not be reviewed here, but we might profitably recall his suggestive comment on *Las Siete Partidas:*

Las Siete Partidas was formed within the Christian doctrine, and the slave had a body of law, protective of him as a human being, which was already there when the Negro arrived and had been elaborated long before he came upon the scene.[25]

The essential point of Tannenbaum's contrast between this legal tradition and that of the Anglo-Saxon lies in its bearing on the problem of emancipation. Whereas the Hispanic tradition favored and encouraged it, the Anglo-Saxon blocked it.[26] So long as a general contrast can be demonstrated, Tannenbaum's thesis obtains, for he is primarily concerned with the social setting into which the Negro plunged upon Emancipation. His thesis, therefore, can absorb criticism such as that of Arnold A. Sio, who argues that the Romans assimilated the rights of their slaves to property despite a legal code which respected the moral personality of the slave. Sio finds evidence of a similar tendency in Latin as well as Anglo-Saxon America.[27] Tannenbaum's thesis would fall only if the tendency were equally strong everywhere; but obviously it was not.[28] Elkins, however, cannot absorb such qualifications, for he necessarily must demonstrate the uniqueness of the southern pattern as well as the absoluteness of the contrast with Latin America. If the contrast could be reduced to a matter of degree, then we should be left with more American than Latin American Sambos, but Elkins' notion of a special American personality pattern and problem would fall.

Elkins, like Tannenbaum, ignores the French slave colonies, but nowhere was the gap between law and practice so startling. The *Code Noir* of 1685 set a high standard of humanity and attempted to guarantee the slaves certain minimal rights and protection. It was treated with contempt in the French West Indies, especially when the islands began to ride the sugar boom. It is enough to quote a governor of Martinique, one of the men charged with the enforcement of these laws: "I have reached the stage of believing firmly that one must treat the Negroes as one treats beasts."[29] On the eve of the Haitian Revolution probably not one of the protective articles of the *Code Noir* was being enforced.[30]

Elkins offers Brazil as a counterpoint to the Old South and invokes the Iberian legal tradition, together with the power of Church and Crown. Yet, even Gilberto Freyre, on whom Elkins relies so heavily, writes of the widespread murders of slaves by enraged masters.[31] As late as the nineteenth century, slaves were being whipped to death in the presence of all hands. The law might say what it would, but the *fazendeiros* controlled the police apparatus and supported the doctors who falsified the death certificates.[32] The measures designed to prevent wanton killing of slaves do not seem to have been better in Latin American than in Anglo-Saxon America.[33] If Brazilian slaves went to the police to complain about unjust or illegally excessive punishment, the police would, in Freyre's words, give them a double dose.[34] If the law mattered much, we need to know the reason for the repeated reenactment of legislation to protect slaves. The famous Rio Branco Law of 1871, for example, granted slaves rights they were supposed to have enjoyed for centuries, and these too remained largely unrespected.

The Portuguese Crown could legislate in any manner it wished, and so later could the Emperor of Brazil; local power resided with the *fazendeiros*, as the emissaries of the Crown learned soon enough. We may imagine conditions in the first three centuries of colonization from Freyre's succinct comment on conditions in the middle of the nineteenth century: "The power of the great planters was indeed feudalistic, their patriarchalism being hardly restricted by civil laws."[35] Not until that time did a strong central government arise to challenge effectively the great planters.[36] That the contrast with the Old South might have been the reverse of what Elkins thinks is suggested by the diary of an ex-Confederate who fled to Brazil after the war. George S. Barnsley, formerly a Georgia planter and Confederate army surgeon, complained as late as 1904 of the lack of government and the prevalence of virtually feudal conditions.[37]

Las Siete Partidas constituted a theoretical work and standard of values, the importance of which ought not to be minimized, but it had little to do with the actual practice on which Elkins' thesis depends.[38] The kind of protection that transcended the theoretical and might have conditioned decisively the personality development of the slave population as a whole probably did not appear until the *Real Cédula* of 1789. As Davis suggests, "There are many indications, moreover, that Spanish planters paid little attention to the law."[39]

Elkins assumes that the strongly centralized Spanish state could and did prevail over the planters. No doubt it did in matters of prime importance to its survival and income. In most matters, notwithstanding its best efforts at institutional control, the planters continued to have their way on their own estates. The Spanish court promulgated humane legislation to protect the natives of the Canary Islands, but attempts at enforcement so far from home proved futile. The problem swelled enormously when transferred to the West Indies, not to mention to the mainland.[40] The fate of the protective features of the Laws of Burgos (1512) and of similar legislation is well known.[41] The British and other foreigners who did business in Spanish America ridiculed the mass of laws and the clumsy administrative apparatus designed to enforce them. As the agent of the South Sea Company at Jamaica noted in 1736, he who wants to deal illegally with the Spanish officials needs only the cash necessary to bribe them.[42] The lot of the slaves could, under such conditions, hardly reflect other than the disposition of the masters. A case study by Jaime Jaramillo Uribe of the judicial system of New Grenada shows that even the reform laws of the eighteenth century could not reach down into the plantations to protect the slaves.[43]

Much of Elkins' treatment of Spanish law deals with Cuba and flows from the work of Herbert Klein.[44] Without attempting a close examination of the intricacies of the Cuban case, we ought to note that it presents a striking picture of a bitter struggle between planters and state officials. The planters, there too, usually won the day. The liberal Governor Concha finally admitted that the resistance of the slave-owners to government intervention was justified by the necessity for controlling the blacks and avoiding any ambiguity in authority. In 1845 the government did seriously challenge the masters' power, but the uproar proved so great that the militant officials had to be removed.[45]

The fate of the law during the sugar boom requires more attention than Elkins and Klein have given it. In its earlier phases Cuban slavery was exceptionally mild and fit much of Elkins' schema. When the Haitian Revolution removed the Caribbean's leading sugar producer from the world market, Cuba entered into a period of wild expansion and prosperity. The status of the slave declined accordingly. The old institutional arrangements did not disappear, but their bearing on the life of the great mass of slaves became minimal or nonexistent.[46]

The legal and political structure of Spanish America in general and of Cuba in particular helped ease the way to freedom by providing a setting in which the slave might be abused brutally but retained a significant degree of manhood in the eyes of society. For Tannenbaum's purpose, this distinction establishes the argument: the slave was abused as a slave but only incidentally as a Negro. The master might rule with absolute authority, but only because he could get away with it, not because it was, by the standards of his own class, church, and society, just and proper. Tannenbaum and Freyre do make too much of this argument. The persistence and depth of racial discrimination and prejudice in twentieth-century Brazil and Cuba ought to remind us that the enslavement of one race by another must generate racist doctrines among all social classes as well as the intelligentsia. Qualitative and quantitative distinctions nonetheless obtain, and Tannenbaum's argument requires correction and greater specificity, not rejection. For Elkins, Tannenbaum's distinction, however qualified, is not enough. If, as seems likely, the great majority of the slaves labored under such absolutism, theoretical or not, their personalities would have been shaped in response to conditions equivalent to those he describes for the United States.

In the United States, as in the British West Indies and everywhere else, custom and conventional moral standards had greater force than the law, as Ulrich B. Phillips long ago argued. Just as the vast range of rights granted the slaves in Latin

America usually proved unenforceable in a society in which power was largely concentrated in local planter oligarchies, so in Anglo-Saxon America the quasi-absolute power of the master was tempered by the prevailing ethos. Tannenbaum, and especially Elkins, go much too far in denying that English and American law recognized the moral personality of the slave. As Davis has demonstrated, the double nature of the slave as thing and man had to be, and in one way or another was, recognized in law and custom by every slave society since ancient times. As a result, every southern planter knew intuitively the limits of his power, as imposed by the prevailing standards of decency. If he exceeded those limits, he might not suffer punishment at law and might even be strong enough to prevent his being ostracized by disapproving neighbors. For these reasons historians have dismissed community pressure as a factor. In doing so, they err badly, for the point is not at all what happened to a violator of convention but the extent to which the overwhelming majority of slaveholders internalized conventional values. In this respect the legal structures of Brazil and the United States were important in conditioning those conventional values. Once again, the difference between the two cases suffices for Tannenbaum's thesis but not for Elkins' — which depends entirely on the experience of absolute power by the slave.

Elkins follows Tannenbaum in ascribing a special role to the Catholic Church in the development of Ibero-American slave societies. The Church defended the moral personality of the slave from a position of independent institutional strength, whereas in the Anglo-Saxon world the separation of church and state, the bourgeois notion of property rights, and the divisions within the religious community largely excluded the churches from the field of master-slave relations. The religious as well as the legal structure helped generate a particular climate of moral opinion into which the Negro could fit as a free man. The difference in structure and result satisfies Tannenbaum's argument; it does not satisfy Elkins' argument, which turns on the specific role played by the priesthood in the life of the slave.

Since Brazil, as the largest Catholic slaveholding country, ought properly to serve as a test case, we might profitably begin with a consideration of developments in Angola, which supplied a large part of its slaves. The clergy, including Jesuits and Dominicans, participated in every horror associated with the slave trade; there is little evidence of its having played a mediating role.[47] By the middle of the seventeenth century Catholic proselytism in the Congo and Angola had spent its force. Contemporary Catholic sources admitted that much of the failure was due to the greed of the clergy in pursuing slave-trade profits and to the generally venal character of priests, secular officials, and laymen.[48] The governor of Angola, the troops, the bishop, and the entire staff of civil and ecclesiastical officials drew their salaries from the direct and indirect proceeds of the slave trade. The Holy House of Mercy [*Misericordia*] at Luanda, as well as the Municipal Council [*Camara*] lived off the trade. Since the *Junta das missões,* the chief missionary agency, was supported by these proceeds we need not be surprised that it accomplished little.[49]

In Brazil itself the decisive questions concern the number, character, and relative independence of the priests.[50] We have little data on numbers, but in the mid-twentieth century, Brazil, with a population of fifty million, of whom 95 per cent were nominal Catholics, had, according to Vianna Moog, only six thousand priests.[51] We may, nonetheless, assume for a moment that a high ratio of priests to slaves existed. There is good reason to believe that a significant percentage of the priests who ventured to the colonies had questionable characters and that many of good character succumbed to the indolence, violence, and corruption that marked their isolated, quasi-frontier environment. It is no insult to the Church to affirm this state of affairs, for the Church has had to struggle for centuries to raise the quality of its priests and to maintain high standards of performance. Like other institutions of this world it has consisted of men with all the weaknesses of men, and in the difficult circumstances of colonial life the adherence of its men to the high standards of the Church Militant proved erratic and uncertain.

Even if we grant the Brazilian clergy a higher quality than it probably deserved, we confront the question of its relationship to the master class. The local chaplain depended on and deferred to the planter he served more than he depended on his bishop. The Brazilian Church never achieved the strength and cohesion of the Church in Spanish America. The typical sugar planter, in Freyre's words, "though a devout Catholic, was a sort of Philip II in regard to the Church: he considered himself more powerful than the bishops or abbots." Under these conditions the interposition of priest between master and slave was probably little more significant than the interposition of the mistress on a plantation in Mississippi. The analogy assumes particular force when we consider that, increasingly, the Brazilian priesthood was recruited from the local aristocracy.[52] In coffee-growing southern Brazil, in which slavery centered during the nineteenth century, few priests resided on plantations at all and visits were possibly less common than in the United States. The large number of Africans imported during 1830–1850 received little attention from the Church.[53]

The situation in Spanish America worked out more favorably for Elkins' argument because the Church there came much closer to that independence and crusading spirit which has been attributed to it. Even so, the ruthless exploitation of Indians and Negroes by large sections of the clergy is well documented. The position of the Church as a whole, taken over centuries, demonstrates its growing subservience to state and secular power in respects that were decisive for Elkins' purposes. The bulls of Popes and the decrees of kings proved inadequate to temper the rule of the great planters of the New World, although they did play a role in shaping their moral consciousness.[54] In Cuba the clergy acted more boldly and, according to Klein, had a numerical strength adequate to its tasks. However, the effective interposition of even the Cuban clergy during the sugar boom of the nineteenth century has yet to be demonstrated, and if it were to be, Cuba would stand as an exception to the rule.

That more Brazilian and Cuban slaves attended religious services than did southern is by no means certain, the law to the contrary notwithstanding. That the

Catholic clergy of Latin America interposed itself more often and more effectively than the Protestant clergy of the South cannot be denied. On balance, Tannenbaum's case is proven by the ability of the Catholic Church to help shape the ethos of slave society and the relative inability of the Protestant to do the same. But Elkins' case falls, for the difference in the potentialities for and especially the realities of personal interposition remained a matter of degree.

Despite the efforts of law and Church in Latin America it is quite possible that as high or higher a percentage of southern slaves lived in stable family units than did Latin American. The force of custom and sentiment generally prevailed over the force of law or institutional interference. In Brazil, as in the Caribbean, male slaves greatly outnumbered female; in the United States the sexes were numerically equal. This factor alone, which derived primarily from economic and technological conditions, encouraged greater family stability in the United States and therefore casts great doubt on Elkins' thesis. To the extent that participation in a stable family life encouraged the development of a mature personality, the slaves of the South probably fared no worse than others. Elkins argues that the Latin American families could not be broken up because of Church and state restrictions. In fact, they often were broken up in open defiance of both. The greatest guarantee against sale existed not where the law forbade it, but where economic conditions reduced the necessity.

The attendant argument that Latin American slaves could function in the roles of fathers and mothers, whereas southern slaves could not, is altogether arbitrary. The feeling of security within the family depended on custom and circumstance, not law, and a great number of southern slaves worked for masters whose economic position and paternalistic attitudes provided a reasonable guarantee against separate sales. In any case, all slaves in all societies faced similar problems. When a slave-owner beat or raped a slave woman in Brazil or Cuba, her husband was quite as helpless as any black man in Mississippi. The duties, responsibilities, and privileges of fatherhood were, in practice, little different from one place to another.

The point of Elkins' controversial concentration camp analogy is not altogether clear. Sometimes he seems to wish to demonstrate only the possibility of mass infantilization, but if this were all he intended, he could have done so briefly and without risking the hostile reaction he brought down on himself. At other times he seems to intend the analogy as a direct device. Although he denies saying that slavery was a concentration camp or even "like" a concentration camp, he does refer to concentration camps as perverted patriarchies and extreme forms of slavery; he finds in them the same total power he believes to have existed on the southern plantations. In the first, restricted, sense the analogy, used suggestively, has its point, for it suggests the ultimate limits of the slave experience. In the second, and broader, sense it offers little and is generally misleading. Unfortunately, Elkins sometimes exaggerates and confuses his device, which only demonstrates the limiting case, with the historical reality of slavery. His elaborate discussion of detachment offers clues but is dangerously misleading. The process did not differ for slaves bound for different parts of the New World; only the post-shock experience of the slave regimes differed, so that we are led right back to those regimes. No doubt Elkins makes a good point when he cites concentration camp and slave trade evidence to show that many participants were spiritually broken by the process, but he overlooks the contribution of newly imported Africans to slave disorders. Everywhere in the Americas a correlation existed between concentrations of African-born slaves and the outbreak of revolts. The evidence indicates that creole slaves were generally more adjusted to enslavement than those who had undergone the shock and detachment processes from Africa to America.[55]

The fundamental differences between the concentration camp and plantation experience may be gleaned from a brief consideration of some of the points made in Bruno Bettelheim's study, on which Elkins relies heavily.[56] Prisoners received inadequate clothing and food in order to test their reaction to extremities of inclement weather and their ability to work while acutely hungry. Slaves received clothing and food designed to provide at least minimum comfort. Slaves suffered from dietary deficiencies and hidden hungers, but rarely from outright malnutrition. In direct contrast to prisoners, slaves normally did not work outdoors in the rain or extreme cold; usually, they were deliberately ordered to stay indoors. Pneumonia and other diseases killed too many slaves every winter for planters not to take every precaution to guard their health. Therein lay the crucial differences: prisoners might be kept alive for experimental purposes, but slaves received treatment designed to grant them long life. Prisoners often did useless work as part of a deliberate program to destroy their personality; slaves did, and knew they did, the productive work necessary for their own sustenance. Prisoners were forbidden to talk to each other much of the day and had virtually no privacy and no social life. Slaves maintained a many-sided social life, which received considerable encouragement from their masters. The Gestapo deliberately set out to deny the individuality of prisoners or to distinguish among them. Planters and overseers made every effort to take full account of slave individuality and even to encourage it up to a point. Prisoners were deliberately subjected to torture and arbitrary punishment; those who followed orders endured the same indignities and blows as those who did not. Slaves, despite considerable arbitrariness in the system, generally had the option of currying favor and avoiding punishment. As Hannah Arendt has so perceptively observed: "Under conditions of total terror not even fear can any longer serve as an advisor of how to behave, because terror chooses its victims without reference to individual actions or thoughts, exclusively in accordance with the objective necessity of the natural or historical process."[57] Concentration camp prisoners changed work groups and barracks regularly and could not develop attachments. Slaves had families and friends, often for a lifetime. The Gestapo had no interest in indoctrinating prisoners. They demanded obedience, not loyalty. Masters wanted and took great pains to secure the loyalty and ideological adherence of their slaves. In general, the slave plantation was a social system, full of joys and sorrows and a fair degree of security, notwithstanding great harshness and even brutality, whereas the concentration camp was a particularly vicious death-cell. They shared a strong degree of authoritarianism, but so does the army or a revolutionary party, or even a family unit.

With these criticisms of data we may turn to Elkin's discussion of personality theory. His use of Sullivan's theory of "significant others" breaks down because of his erroneous notion of the absolute power of the master. In theory the master's power over the slave in the United States was close to absolute; so in theory was the power of Louis XIV over the French. In practice, the plantation represented a series of compromises between whites and blacks. Elkins' inability to see the slaves as active forces capable of tempering the authority of the master leads him into a one-sided appraisal.[58]

According to Elkins, the Latin American slave could relate meaningfully to the friar on the slave ship; the confessor who made the plantation rounds; the zealous Jesuit who especially defended the sanctity of the family; the local magistrate who had to contend with the Crown's official protector of the slaves; and any informer who could expect to collect one-third of the fines. In general, it would not be unfair to say that, notwithstanding all these institutional niceties, the Latin American slaveowners, especially the Brazilian, ruled their plantations as despotically as any southerner. Priest, magistrate, and anyone careless enough to risk his life to play the informer came under the iron grip of the plantation owners' enormous local power.

Various other persons did affect meaningfully the lives of slaves in all systems. The plantation mistress often acted to soften her husband's rule. The overseer did not always precisely reflect the master's temperament and wishes, and slaves demonstrated great skill in playing the one against the other. The Negro driver often affected their lives more directly than anyone else and had considerable authority to make their lives easy or miserable. Slaves who found it difficult to adjust to a master's whims or who feared punishment often ran to some other planter in the neighborhood to ask for his intercession, which they received more often than not. Elkins ignores these and other people because they had no lawful right to intervene; but they did have the power of persuasion in a world of human beings with human reactions. To the vast majority of slaves in all systems, the power of the master approached the absolute and yet was tempered by many human relationships and sensibilities. To the extent that slavery, in all societies, restricted the number of "significant others," it may well have contributed toward the formation of a slavish personality, but Latin America differed from the South only in permitting a somewhat larger minority to transcend that effect.

Similar objections may be made with reference to the application of role theory. The Latin American slave could ordinarily no more act the part of a husband or father than could the southern. The typical field hand had roughly the same degree of prestige and authority in his own cabin in all societies. Legal right to property did not make most Latin American slaves property owners in any meaningful sense, and many southern slaves were de facto property owners of the same kind. The theoretical right of the one and the mere privilege of the other did not present a great practical difference, for the attitude of the master was decisive in both cases.

For Tannenbaum's social analysis the significance of the difference stands; for Elkins' psychological analysis it does not.

The theory of personality that Elkins seems to slight, but uses to greatest advantage, is the Freudian, perhaps because it offers a simple direct insight quite apart from its more technical formulations. We do not need an elaborate psychological theory to help us understand the emergence of the slaveowner as a father figure. As the source of all privileges, gifts, and necessaries, he loomed as a great benefactor, even when he simultaneously functioned as a great oppressor. Slaves, forced into dependence on their master, viewed him with awe and identified their interests and even their wills with his. Elkins' analogy with concentration camp prisoners who began to imitate their SS guards indicates the extreme case of this tendency. All exploited classes manifest something of this tendency — the more servile the class the stronger the tendency. It is what many contemporary observers, including runaway slaves and abolitionists, meant when they spoke of the reduction of the slave to a groveling creature without initiative and a sense of self-reliance. Elkins, using Freudian insight, has transformed this observation into the politically relevant suggestion that the slave actually learned to see himself through his master's eyes.

Elkins has often been criticized for failing to realize that slaves usually acted as expected while they retained inner reservations, but he did recognize this possibility in his discussion of a "broad belt of indeterminacy" between playing a role and becoming the role you always play. The criticism seems to me to miss the point. The existence of such reservations might weaken the notion of total infantilization but would not touch the less extreme notion of a dependent, emasculated personality. The clever slave outwitted his master at least partly because he was supposed to. Masters enjoyed the game: it strengthened their sense of superiority, confirmed the slaves' dependence, and provided a sense of pride in having so clever a man-child. On the slave's side it made him a devilishly delightful fellow but hardly a man. The main point against Elkins here is the same as elsewhere — when he is sound he describes not a southern slave but a slave; not a distinctly southern Sambo personality but a slavish personality.[59]

Elkins' general argument contains a fundamental flaw, which, when uncovered, exposes all the empirical difficulties under review. In his model a regime of total power produces a Sambo personality. Confronted by the undeniable existence of exceptions, he pleads first things first and waives them aside as statistically insignificant. Even if we were to agree that they were statistically insignificant, we are left with a serious problem. Elkins did not construct a model to determine probabilities; he constructed a deterministic model, which he cannot drop suddenly to suit his convenience. The notion of "total power" loses force and usefulness and indeed approaches absurdity in a world of probabilities and alternatives. If Elkins were to retreat from this notion and consequently from his determinism, he could not simply make an adjustment in his model; he would have to begin, as we must, from different premises, although without necessarily sacrificing his remarkable insights and suggestions. If the basic personality pattern arose from the nature of the regime, so did the deviant patterns. It would be absurd to argue that a regime could be sufficiently complex to generate two or more such patterns and yet sufficiently simple to generate them in mutual isolation. The regime threw up all the patterns at once, whatever the proportions, and the root of every deviation lay in the same social structure that gave us Sambo.

This range of patterns arose from the disparity between the plantations and farms, between resident owners and absentees, and above all between the foibles and sensibilities of one master and another. They arose, too, within every slaveholding unit from the impossibility of absolute power — from the qualities, perhaps inherited, of the particular personalities of slaves as individuals; from the inconsistencies in the human behavior of the severest masters; from the room that even a slave plantation provides for breathing, laughing, crying, and combining acquiescence and protest in a single thought, expression, and action. Even modern totalitarian regimes, self-consciously armed with unprecedented weapons of terror, must face that opposition inherent in the human spirit to which Miss Arendt draws attention. The freedom of man cannot be denied even by totalitarian rulers, "for this freedom — irrelevant and arbitrary as they may deem it — is identical with the fact that men are being born and that therefore each of them *is* a new beginning, begins, in a sense, the world anew."[60] We need not pretend to understand adequately that remarkable process of spiritual regeneration which repeatedly unfolds before our eyes. The evidence extends throughout history, including the history of our own day; its special forms and content, not its existence, constitute our problem. Miss Arendt therefore concludes her analysis of terror wisely: "Every end in history necessarily contains a new beginning. . . . Beginning, before it becomes a historical event, is the supreme capacity of man; politically, it is identical with man's freedom. . . . This beginning is guaranteed by each new birth; it is indeed every man."[61]

Sambo himself had to be a product of a contradictory environment, all sides of which he necessarily internalized. Sambo, in short, was Sambo only up to the moment that the psychological balance was jarred from within or without; he might then well have become Nat Turner, for every element antithetical to his being a Sambo resided in his nature. "Total power" and "Sambo" may serve a useful purpose in a theoretical model as a rough approximation to a complex reality, provided that we do not confuse the model with the reality itself. Neither slavery nor slaves can be treated as pure categories, free of the contradictions, tensions, and potentialites that characterize all human experience.

Elkins, in committing himself to these absolutist notions, overlooks the evidence from his own concentration camp analogy. Bettelheim notes that even the most accommodating, servile, and broken-spirited prisoners sometimes suddenly defied the Gestapo with great courage. Eugen Kogon devotes considerable space in his *Theory and Practice of Hell* to the development and maintenance of resistance within the camps.[62] In a similar way the most docile field slaves or the most trusted house slaves might, and often did, suddenly rise up in some act of unprecedented violence. This transformation will surprise us only if we confuse our theoretical model with the reality it ought to help us to understand.

Elkins has not described to us the personality of the southern slave, nor, by contrast, of the Latin American slave; he has instead demonstrated the limiting case of the slavish personality. Every slave system contained a powerful tendency to generate Sambos, but every system generated countervailing forces. Elkins, following Tannenbaum, might properly argue that differences in tradition, religion, and law guaranteed differences in the strength of those countervailing forces; he cannot prove and dare not assume that any system lacked them.

Elkins accounts for such forms of deviant behavior as lying, stealing, and shirking by absorbing them within the general framework of childish response. He is by no means completely wrong in doing so, for very often the form of a particular act of hostility degraded the slave as much as it irritated the master. Elkins' approach is not so much wrong as it is of limited usefulness. Once we pass beyond the insight that the form of rebelliousness might itself reveal accommodation, we cannot go much further. If all behavior short of armed revolt can be subsumed within the framework of childishness and dependence, then that formulation clearly embraces too much. Our historical problem is to explain how and under what conditions accommodation yields to resistance, and we therefore need a framework sufficiently flexible to permit distinctions between accommodating behavior that, however slightly, suggests a process of transformation into opposite qualities; such a framework must, moreover, be able to account for both tendencies within a single human being and even within a single act.

It has become something of a fashion in the adolescent recesses of our profession to bury troublesome authors and their work under a heap of carping general and specific complaints; it is no part of my purpose to join in the fun. Elkins' book has raised the study of southern slavery to a far higher level than ever before, and it has done so at a moment when the subject seemed about to be drowned in a sea of moral indignation. It has demonstrated forcefully the remarkable uses to which psychology can be put in historical inquiry. It has brought to the surface the relationship between the slave past and wide range of current problems flowing from that past. These are extraordinary achievements. To advance in the direction Elkins has pointed out, however, we shall first have to abandon most of his ground. We cannot simply replace his psychological model with a better one; we must recognize that all psychological models may only be used suggestively for flashes of insight or as aids in forming hypotheses and that they cannot substitute for empirical investigation. As the distinguished anthropologist, Max Gluckman, has observed, respect for psychology as a discipline requiring a high degree of training in the acquisition and interpretation of data forces us to bypass psychological analyses whenever possible.[63] Or, to put it another way, if we are to profit fully from Elkins' boldness, we shall have to retreat from it and try to solve the problems he raises by the more orthodox procedures of historical research.

Notes

¹ Stanley M. Elkins, *Slavery: A Problem in American Institutional and Intellectual Life* (Chicago, 1959). For a brief critique of the book as a whole see Genovese, "Problems in Nineteenth-Century American History," *Science & Society,* XXV (1961). This present paper shall, so far as possible, be limited to questions of method and assumption. A much shorter version was read to the Association for the Study of Negro Life and History, Baltimore, Maryland, Oct., 1966, where it was incisively criticized by Professor Willie Lee Rose of the University of Virginia. Mrs. Rose was also kind enough to read and criticize the first draft of this longer version. I do not know whether or not my revisions will satisfy her, but I am certain that the paper is much better as a result of her efforts.

² Elkins, *Slavery,* pp. 115–133 and the literature cited therein.

³ John Harding, *et al.,* "Prejudice and Ethnic Relations," *Handbook of Social Psychology,* Gardner Lindzey (ed.) (Cambridge, 1954), II, 1021–1062, esp. 1024.

⁴ C. L. R. James, *The Black Jacobins: Toussaint L'Ouverture and the San Domingo Revolution* (Vintage ed., New York, 1963), p. 21.

⁵ Ibn Khaldun, *The Muqaddimah* (tr. Franz Rosenthal; New York, 1958), I, 174, 301; the parentheses were inserted by the translator for technical reasons. David Brion Davis maintains that as Muslims extended their hegemony over Africa, they came to regard black Africans as fit only for slavery: *The Problem of Slavery in Western Culture* (Ithaca, 1966), p. 50. Cf. Basil Davidson, *Black Mother* (Boston, 1961), pp. xvii, 7, 45, 92–93 for Sambo's appearance in Africa.

⁶ C. R. Boxer (ed.), "Negro Slavery in Brazil" [trans. of *Nova e Curiosa Relação* (*1764*)], *Race,* V (1964), 43.

⁷ Stanley J. Stein, *Vassouras: A Brazilian Coffee County, 1850–1900* (Cambridge, Mass., 1957), p. 133.

⁸ Euclides da Cunha, *Rebellion in the Backlands* (*Os Sertoes*) (trans. Samuel Putnam; Chicago, 1944), p. 71; for a critical review of some of this literature see Arthur Ramos, *The Negro in Brazil* (Washington, 1939), pp. 22–24.

⁹ Manoel de Oliveira Lima, *The Evolution of Brazil Compared with That of Spanish and Anglo-Saxon America* (Stanford, 1914), p. 122.

¹⁰ João Pandía Calógeras, *A History of Brazil* (Chapel Hill, 1939), p. 29. Even today, when Negroes face discrimination in Brazil, whites insist that it is a result of their own incapacities and sense of inferiority. See Fernando Henrique Cardoso and Octavio Ianni, *Côr e mobilidade em Florianópolis* (São Paulo, 1964), p. 231.

¹¹ Kenneth M. Stampp, *The Peculiar Institution* (New York, 1956), p. 148: "Here, then, was the way to produce the perfect slave: accustom him to rigid discipline, demand from him unconditional submission, impress upon him his innate inferiority, develop in him a paralyzing fear of white men, train him to adopt the master's code of good behavior, and instill in him a sense of complete dependence. This at least was the goal."

Octavio Ianni, *As Metamorfoses do Escravo* (São Paulo, 1962), pp. 134–135: "Essential to the full functioning of the regime [was] a rigorous, drastic system of control over the social behavior of the enslaved laborer; . . . mechanisms of socialization appropriate to the dominant social strata . . . ; the impossibility of vertical social mobility; . . . rules of conduct ordered according to a standard of rigid obedience of the Negroes in front of white men, whether masters or not."

See also Fernando Henrique Cardoso, *Capitalismo e Escravidão no Brasil Meridional* (São Paulo, 1962), pp. 312–313. Davis follows Ianni and others and speaks of Brazilian slaves as having been reduced "to a state of psychic shock, of flat apathy and depression, which was common enough in Brazil to acquire the special name of *banzo.*" *Problem of Slavery,* p. 238; cf. Ramos, *Negro in Brazil,* pp. 22, 135–136.

[12] Davis, *Problem of Slavery*, p. 171.

[13] *Selected Writings of Bolivar* (New York, 1951), I, 131.

[14] For an interpretation of the Spanish slave law as holding Negroes to be an especially revolutionary people see Augustín Alcalá y Henke, *Esclavitud de los negros en la América espanola* (Madrid, 1919), p. 51. For a view of Brazilian Indians that sounds much like Sambo see the comments of the famous Dutch sea captain, Dierck de Ruiter, as reported in C. R. Boxer, *Salvador de Sá and the Struggle for Brazil and Angola* (London, 1952), p. 20.

[15] Sidney Mintz, review of Elkins' *Slavery, American Anthropologist*, LXIII (1961), 585.

[16] "Slavery is determined 'pas par l'obéissance, ni par rudesse des labeurs, mais par le statu d'instrument et la réduction de l'homme à l'état de chose.'" *François Perrous, La Coexistence pacifique*, as quoted by Herbert Marcuse, *One-Dimensional Man: Studies in the Ideology of Advanced Industrial Society* (Boston, 1964), pp. 32–33.

[17] Davis, *Problem of Slavery*, pp. 59–60.

[18] *Ibid.*, pp. 66–67.

[19] *Ibid.*, p. 420.

[20] Audrey I. Richards, *Land, Labour and Diet in Northern Rhodesia: Economic Study of the Bemba Tribe* (London, 1939), p. 400.

[21] Josué de Castro, *The Geography of Hunger* (Boston, 1952), *passim*.

[22] Jean-Paul Sartre, preface to Frantz Fanon, *The Wretched of the Earth* (New York, 1965), p. 14.

[23] Quoted from the *Southern Cultivator*, VII (Sept., 1849), by William K. Scarborough, "The Southern Plantation Overseer: A Re-evaluation," *Agricultural History*, XXXVIII (1964), 16.

[24] See his explicit summary statement, "Culture Contacts and Negro Slavery," *Proceedings of the American Philosophical Society*, CVII (1963), 107–110, esp. p. 107.

[25] Frank Tannenbaum, *Slave & Citizen: The Negro in the Americas* (New York, 1946), p. 48.

[26] *Ibid.*, pp. 65, 69, and *passim*.

[27] Arnold A. Sio, "Interpretations of Slavery: The Slave Status in the Americas," *Comparative Studies in Society and History*, VII (1965), 303, 308. For a fresh consideration of the problem of slave law in the islands see Elsa V. Goveia, "The West Indian Slave Laws in the Eighteenth Century," *Revista de Ciencias Sociales* (1960), 75–105.

[28] Marvin Harris has counterposed an economic viewpoint to Tannenbaum's. Despite considerable exaggeration and one-sidedness, he does demonstrate the partial applicability of an institutional approach. For a critical analysis of Harris' polemic and the literature it touches see Genovese, "Materialism and Idealism in the History of Negro Slavery in the Americas," *Journal of Social History*, forthcoming.
The experience of the Dutch demonstrates how much religious and national attitudes gave way before the necessities of colonial life. The Dutch experience in Surinam, New Netherland, Brazil, etc. varied enormously. See, e.g., C. R. Boxer, *The Dutch in Brazil* (Oxford, 1957), esp. p. 75; Edgar J. McManus, *A History of Negro Slavery in New York* (New York, 1966), Ch. I.

[29] Quoted by James, *Black Jacobins*, p. 17.

[30] *Ibid.*, p. 56; Davis, *Problem of Slavery*, p. 254 and the literature cited therein.

[31] Gilberto Freyre, *The Masters and the Slaves: A Study in the Development of Brazilian Civilization* (2nd English Language ed., rev.; New York, 1956), p. xxxix.

[32] Stein, *Vassouras*, p. 136.

[33] See, e.g., the discussion of the law of 1797 in Antigua in Elsa V. Goveia, *Slave Society in the British Leeward Islands at the End of the Eighteenth Century* (New Haven, 1966), p. 191.

[34] Gilberto Freyre, *The Mansions and the Shanties: The Making of Modern Brazil* (New York, 1963), p. 226.

[35] Gilberto Freyre, "Social Life in Brazil in the Middle of the Nineteenth Century," *Hispanic American Historical Review* V (1922), 597–628; see also, Freyre, *Masters,* pp. xxxiii, 24, 42; *New World in the Tropics: The Culture of Modern Brazil* (New York; Vintage ed., 1963), p. 69.

[36] Alan A. Manchester describes 1848 as the turning point. See *British Pre-Eminence in Brazil* (Chapel Hill, 1933), pp. 261–262.

[37] George S. Barnsley MS Notebook in the Southern Historical Collection, University of North Carolina, Chapel Hill.

[38] For a penetrating discussion of these two sides of *Las Siete Partidas* see Davis, *Problem of Slavery,* pp. 102–105.

[39] *Ibid.,* p. 240.

[40] Arthur Percival Newton, *The European Nations in the West Indies, 1493–1688* (London, 1933), p. 3.

[41] For a useful recent summary discussion of the literature see Harris, *Patterns of Race,* pp. 18–20.

[42] Cf., Arthur S. Aiton, "The Asiento Treaty as Reflected in the Papers of Lord Shelburne," *Hispanic American Historical Review,* VIII (1928), 167–177, esp. p. 167.

[43] Jaime Jaramillo Uribe, "Esclavos y Senores en la sociedad colombiana del siglo XVIII," *Anuario colombiano de historia social y de cultura,* I (1963), 1–22.

[44] Herbert Klein, "Anglicanism, Catholicism and the Negro," *Comparative Studies in Society and History,* VIII (1966), 295–327; *Slavery in the Americas: A Comparative Study of Cuba and Virginia* (Chicago, 1967).

[45] See H. H. S. Aimes, *A History of Slavery in Cuba, 1511 to 1868* (New York, 1907), pp. 150–151, 175–177.

[46] On this point see Sidney Mintz foreword to Ramiro Guerra y Sánchez, *Sugar and Society in the Caribbean* (New Haven, 1964), and his review of Elkins' book in the *American Anthropologist,* LXIII (1961), 579-587. Klein, Tannenbaum and Elkins make much of the practice of *coartación.* For a critical assessment see Davis, *Problem of Slavery,* pp. 266–267.

[47] Boxer, *Salvador de Sá,* p. 279.

[48] C. R. Boxer, *Race Relations in the Portuguese Colonial Empire, 1415–1825* (Oxford, 1963), pp. 7–8, 11–12, 21.

[49] C. R. Boxer, *Portuguese Society in the Tropics: The Municipal Councils of Goa, Macao, Bahia, and Luanda, 1510–1800* (1965), pp. 131–132, Davidson, *Black Mother,* p. 158.

[50] Elkins certainly errs in ascribing a protective role to the Jesuits, whose efforts on behalf of the Indians were not repeated with the Negroes. Jesuit treatment of those Negroes within their reach does not constitute one of the more glorious chapters in the history of the order. The literature is extensive; for a good, brief discussion see Joao Dornas Filho, *A Recravidao no Brasil* (Rio de Janeiro, 1939), p. 105.

[51] Vianna Moog, *Bandeirantes and Pioneers* (New York, 1964), p. 209. Cf., Percy Alvin Martin, "Slavery and Abolition in Brazil," *Hispanic American Historical Review,* XIII (1933), 168: "On most plantations the spiritual life of the slaves received scant attention. Priests were found only on the larger estates."

[52] Freyre, *New World in the Tropics,* pp. 70–71, 87–88; *Mansions,* p. 244.

[53] Stein, *Vassouras,* pp. 196–199.

[54] Cf., Rene Maunier, *The Sociology of Colonies* (London, n.d.), I, 293–294.

[55] Elkins seems troubled by this — see p. 102 — but he does not pursue it. K. Onwuka Dike points out that Guineans brought to the trading depots of the Niger Delta had already been prepared psychologically for slavery by the religious indoctrination accompanying the cult of the Aro oracle. See "The Question of Sambo: A Report of the Ninth Newberry Library Conference on American Studies, *Newberry Library Bulletin,* V (1958), 27 and Dike's *Trade and Politics in the Niger Delta, 1830–1885* (Oxford, 1956), Ch. II.

[56] Bruno Bettelheim, "Individual and Mass Behavior in Extreme Situations," *Journal of*

Abnormal and Social Psychology, XXXVIII (1943), 417–452. On the general problem of the concentration camp analogy see the remarks of Daniel Boorstin as reported in the *Newberry Library Bulletin,* V (1958), 14–40 and Earle E. Thorpe, "Chattel Slavery & Concentration Camps," *Negro History Bulletin,* XXV (1962), 171–176. Unfortunately, Mr. Thorpe's thoughtful piece is marred by a clumsy discussion of the problem of wearing a mask before white men.

[57] Hannah Arendt, "Ideology and Terror: A Novel Form of Government," *Review of Politics,* XV (1953), 314. I am indebted to Professor Daniel Walden of the Pennsylvania State University for calling this illuminating article to my attention and for suggesting its relevance to the subject at hand.

[58] For a perceptive and well-balanced discussion of this side of plantation life see Clement Eaton, *The Growth of Southern Civilization* (New York, 1961), p. 74 and *passim.*

[59] Brazilian slaves saw their masters as patriarchs and, in Freyre's words, "almighty figures." Freyre, *Mansions,* p. 234. See also Celso Furtado, *The Economic Growth of Brazil* (Berkeley, 1963), pp. 153–154.

[60] Arendt, *Review of Politics,* XV (1953), 312.

[61] *Ibid.,* 327.

[62] Bettelheim, *Journal of Abnormal and Social Psychology,* XXXVIII (1943), 451; Eugen Kogon, *The Theory and Practice of Hell* (New York, 1950), esp. Chs. XX, XXXI.

[63] Max Gluckman, *Order and Rebellion in Tribal Africa* (New York, 1963), pp. 2–3.

The Vesey Plot: Conflicting Interpretations

3

On Denmark Vesey

Herbert Aptheker

Depression-ridden Charleston, South Carolina, whose census of 1820 showed an actual decline in the number of its white inhabitants, and a rise in that of the Negroes until the latter comprised four-sevenths of its residents,[1] was the scene in 1822 of one of the most serious, widespread, and carefully planned conspiracies.[2] Since the leader of this plot, Denmark Vesey (born, it is reported, in Africa, and serving for several years aboard a slave-trader) had succeeded in purchasing his freedom in 1800 and thus was a member of the free Negro[3] group, it is especially interesting to observe that the rapid increase in that class of people[4] had aroused concern which several times found expression just prior to the discovery of the conspiracy, and which resulted in legislation aimed against the group.[5]

Vesey seems, however, to have been the only non-slave directly implicated in the plot. He and several other leaders, such as Peter Poyas and Mingo Harth, were urban artisans — carpenters, harness-makers, mechanics, and blacksmiths; they were literate, and Vesey was master of several languages. He was the oldest of the plotters, being apparently in his late fifties.[6] Until the betrayal of the conspiracy, he wore a beard, but further than this little is known concerning his personal appearance.

Active organizational work was begun by Vesey in December, 1821, when he selected the leaders mentioned above. According to the *Official Report* of the trials:

In the selection of his leaders, Vesey showed great penetration and sound judgment. Rolla [slave of Governor Thomas Bennett] was plausible and possessed uncommon self-possession; bold and ardent he was not to be deterred from his purpose by danger. Ned's [owned by the same person] appearance indicated that he was a man of firm nerves and desperate courage. Peter [slave of James Poyas] was intrepid and resolute, true to his engagements, and cautious in observing secrecy where it was necessary; he was not to be daunted nor impeded by difficulties, and though confident of success, was careful in providing against any obstacles or casualties which might arise, and intent upon discovering every means which might be in their favor if thought of before hand. Gullah [slave of P. Pritchard] was

From Herbert Aptheker, *American Negro Slave Revolts* (New York: International Publishers, 1943), pp. 267–76. Copyright © 1943 by International Publishers Co., Inc. Reprinted by permission of International Publishers.

regarded as a Sorcerer, and as such feared by the natives of Africa, who believe in witchcraft. He was not only considered invulnerable, but that he could make others so by his charms; and that he could and certainly would provide all his followers with arms. He was artful, cruel, bloody; his disposition in short was diabolical. His influence amongst the Africans was inconceivable. Monday [slave of John Gell] was firm, resolute, discreet and intelligent.

Appeals to the rights of man, couched in both theological and secular terms, were used by Vesey. Thus, he would read to the Negroes "from the bible how *the children of Israel were delivered out of Egypt from bondage,*" or if his companion were to bow "to a white person he would rebuke him, and observe that all men were born equal, and that he was surprised that any one would degrade himself by such conduct; that he would never cringe to the whites, nor ought any who had the feelings of a man." Affairs relating to enslavement were noted by him and called to the attention of the slaves, as the bitter debates in Congress over the Missouri question, or the success of the Haitians[7] in establishing and maintaining their independence.

Personal motives did not remain unexpressed. Thus, a slave reported that, "Vesey said the negroes were living such an abominable life, they ought to rise. I said I was living well — he said though I was others were not." He had not heeded the urgings of the slaveowners for free Negroes to go to Africa, *"because he had not the will, he wanted to stay and see what he could do* for his fellow creatures," including his own children who were slaves. Another slave reported of Peter Poyas: "I met him the next day according to appointment, when he said to me, we intend to see if we can't do something for ourselves, we can't live so."

Most of the other Negroes felt as did Poyas and Vesey. Two of the rebels said, "They never spoke to any person of color on the subject, or knew of any who had been spoken to by the other leaders, who had withheld his assent." The fear of betrayal, however, was great, so that, "In enlisting men the great caution observed by the leaders was remarkable. Few if any domestic servants were spoken to, as *they* were distrusted; . . . and Peter whilst he urged one of his agents to speak to others and solicit them to join, at the same time gave him this charge, 'but take care and don't mention it to those waiting men who receive presents of old coats, etc. from their masters, or they'll betray us; *I will speak to* them.' " One agent did not receive, or did not benefit from, such advice and, on May 25, attempted to interest a favorite slave of Colonel Prioleau in the scheme. He immediately disclosed[8] the plan to a free Negro named Pencell who advised that he inform his master. This he did, and on May 30 the authorities took the first steps towards crushing the conspiracy by arresting Peter Poyas and Mingo Harth.

Vesey had set the date for the outbreak on the second Sunday in July, the Sabbath being selected since it was customary for many slaves to enter the city on that day, and the summer month because many whites would then be vacationing outside Charleston. The betrayal led him to put the date ahead one month, but Vesey could not communicate this to his country confederates, some of whom were as many as eighty miles outside the city. The two leaders, Peter and Mingo, though arrested, behaved "with so much composure and coolness" that "the wardens were completely deceived." Both were freed on May 31, but spies were detailed to watch their movements.

Another slave, William, now turned informer, and more arrests followed, the most damaging of which was that of Charles, slave of John Drayton, who agreed to act as a spy. This quickly led to complete exposure. One hundred and thirty-one Negroes of Charles were arrested and forty-nine were condemned to die. Twelve of these were pardoned and transported, while thirty-seven were hanged, the executions taking place from June 18 to August 9.[9]

Although the leaders had kept lists of their comrades, only one list and part of another were found. Moreover, most of them followed the admonition of Peter Poyas, "Die silent, as you shall see me do," and so it is difficult to say how many Negroes were involved. One witness said sixty-six hundred outside of Charleston, another said nine thousand altogether were implicated. The plan of revolt, involving simultaneous attacks from five points and a sixth force on horseback to patrol the streets, further indicated a very considerable number of conspirators. The *Official Report* declared, "enough has been disclosed to satisfy every reasonable mind, that considerable numbers were involved . . . it extended to the North of Charleston many miles towards Santee, and unquestionably into St. John's Parish; to the South to James' and John's Islands; and to the West beyond Bacon's Bridge over Ashley River."

The preparations had been thorough. By the middle of June the Negroes had made about two hundred and fifty pike heads and bayonets and over three hundred daggers. They had noted every store containing any arms and had given instructions to all slaves who tended or could get horses as to when and where to bring the animals. Even a barber had assisted by making wigs and whiskers to hide the identities of the rebels. Vesey had also written twice to St. Domingo telling of his plans and asking for aid. All who opposed were to be killed for the creed of the Negroes was "he that is not with me is against me."

Following the arrests there was formulated a plan for the rescue of the prisoners; and, on the day of Vesey's execution, according to one source:[10] "Another attempt at insurrection was made but the State troops held the slaves in check. So determined, however, were they to strike a blow for liberty that it was found necessary for the federal government to send soldiers to maintain order." Contemporary evidence establishing the truth of the second point, that referring to federal reinforcements, has been seen.[11]

While the executions were proceeding in Charleston, activity among armed runaway Negroes was reported from Jacksonborough (now Jacksonboro), South Carolina, forty miles to the west. Three were captured, and hanged July 19. In August Governor Bennett offered a reward of two hundred dollars for the capture of about twenty maroons in the same region.[12] It is possible that these people had

had some connection with Vesey's farflung plot. A laconic press item of late September reports another possible link in the scheme:[13] "It appears that an insurrection of the blacks was contemplated at Beaufort, South Carolina, and that ten negroes belonging to the most respectable families were arrested. The town council was in secret session. Particulars had not transpired."

The pattern of recommendations, and the enactments of new measures of restriction and repression following serious rebellious activity was copied in this case. Post-conspiracy literature stressed the wisdom of keeping down the number of free Negroes, and of making their lives more difficult. For [14]

the superior condition of the free persons of color, excites discontent among our slaves, who continually have before their eyes, persons of the same color, many of whom they have known in slavery, and with all of whom they associate on terms of equality — free from the controls of masters, working when they please, going whither they please, and expending their money how they please — the slave seeing this, finds his labor irksome; he becomes dissatisfied with his state, he pants for liberty!

Or more briefly put, the slaves seeing the free Negroes,[15] "naturally become dissatisfied with their lot, until the feverish restlessness of this disposition foments itself into insurrection."

Specific proposals called for ceasing to hire out slaves, keeping them out of cities, forbidding their instruction, and strengthening the military prowess of the community.[16] And, significantly, one influential commentator found dangerous and therefore lamentable the "indiscreet zeal in favor of universal liberty" that existed and found frequent expression in the United States.[17]

Action was taken. During the year following Vesey's conspiracy, laws were passed forbidding the hiring out of slaves, providing that every free Negro over fifteen years of age was to have a guardian whose function would be to serve as a control on his behavior, the congregating of slaves was forbidden, the instructing of Negroes in the arts of reading and writing was made a crime, slaves were ordered not to converge on Charleston every Sunday, and patrol regulations were made more severe.[18] It was, moreover, forbidden for any Negro from Mexico, the West Indies or South America to enter the State, and Negro crew members of any ship entering any harbor of South Carolina, were not to leave their boat on penalty of imprisonment, with the necessity of the captain paying the State the charges of his confinement, if he wished the seaman released.[19] In addition two extra-legal steps were taken when a volunteer military organization, under the leadership of Robert J. Turnbull, was formed July, 1823 in Charleston; and a Negro religious leader, Bishop Moses Brown, whose African Methodist Church in Charleston had three thousand members in 1822, was forced to leave the State.[20]

Of additional interest as an aftermath of the Vesey plot and its suppression is the fact that not a few Northern newspapers, like the New York *Daily Advertiser,* the Philadelphia *Gazette,* and the Boston *Recorder,* published articles in a deprecating tone to both the institution of slavery and the uprisings and bloody repressions it called forth.[21] Even in South Carolina itself there is evidence of such a feeling,[22] and publicists in that State did not hesitate to rush to the defense of its action in repressing the conspiracy, and to the defense, *per se,* of the system of chattel slavery.[23]. . .

Notes

[1] In his legislative message of December, 1821, Governor Bennett, whose own slaves were to be prominent rebel leaders, called attention to this disproportionate population trend. — T. D. Jervey, *Robert Y. Hayne,* p. 130.

[2] All material, unless otherwise indicated, on the Vesey plot comes from two contemporary pamphlet accounts: [James Hamilton, Jr., Intendant of Charleston] *Negro Plot an Account of the Late Intended Insurrection among a Portion of the Blacks of the City of Charleston, South Carolina;* Lionel H. Kennedy and Thomas Parker, members of the Charleston bar, and the presiding magistrates of the Court; *An Official Report of the Trials of Sundry Negroes Charged with an Attempt to raise an Insurrection in the State of South-Carolina.*

[3] Although often referred to by later writers as a mulatto, contemporary sources mention him as a "negro" or a "black" — Kennedy and Parker, *op. cit.,* p. 17; *Washington National Intelligencer,* July 6, 1822.

[4] In 1790 there were 1,801 free Negroes in South Carolina; in 1820 there were 6,826. An important source of this marked increase was Quaker manumissions — H. M. Henry, *Police Control of the Slave in S.C.,* p. 177.

[5] In 1820 and 1821, largely through the efforts of Col. John C. Prioleau, a member of the legislature whose favorite slave was to betray Vesey's plot, laws were passed forbidding manumission except with the legislature's approval, and prohibiting the immigration of free Negroes or the return of native free Negroes who left the State. And, in 1820, it was provided that anyone convicted of spreading anti-slavery ideas was to pay a fine of one thousand dollars. See Charleston *Courier,* Dec. 12, 1820; *Acts and Resolutions . . . of S.C. passed Dec. 1820,* pp. 22–24; Henry, *op. cit.,* p. 155.

[6] Kennedy and Parker, *op. cit.,* p. 85, describe Vesey as an "old man." According to *Harper's Encyclopaedia of United States History,* X, p. 53, he was born abut 1767, which agrees with A. H. Grimke's remark that, when exeuted, July 2, 1822, he was not over fifty-six years of age. — *Right on the Scaffold,* p. 10.

[7] *Ante,* pp. 81, 98. Note Thomas Jefferson's comment on the Missouri debates: "If Congress has the power to regulate the conditions of the inhabitants of the States, it will be but another exercise of that power to declare that all shall be free. Are we then to see again Athenian and Lacedemonian confederacies? To wage another Pelopeneasian war to settle the ascendency between them? Or is this the tocsin of merely a servile war? That remains to be seen; but not, I hope, by you or me." To John Adams, January 21, 1822, quoted by Gilbert Chinard, *Thomas Jefferson the Apostle of Americanism* p. 503.

[8] The official report refers to the informer as Devany, but in the act granting him a reward he is called Peter; in both cases Col. J. C. Prioleau is given as the owner. The legislature freed him and gave him an annual pension of $50. He was living in 1857 when the yearly payment

was raised to $200. The free Negro, Pencell, was given $1,000. — J. C. Brevard, *Statutes at Large of South Carolina,* VI, p. 194; XII, p. 562; Henry, *op. cit.,* p. 17; J. C. Carroll, *Slave Insurrections in the United States, 1800–1865,* p. 102.

⁹ Washington *Daily National Intelligencer,* August 10, 13, 16, 1822. It may also be noted that Charles, the slave of John Drayton who had aided the State, was hanged on July 12. This adds credence to the charge made in Peter Neilson, ed., *The Life and Adventures of Zamba,* p. 238, where it is said that Negroes were induced to talk by promises of reprieves, but were executed anyway. Vernon Loggins, however, doubts the authenticity of this work. — *The Negro Author,* p. 231.

¹⁰ *Harper's Encyclopaedia of United States History,* pp. 53–55.

¹¹ Charleston *Courier,* n.d., in Richmond *Enquirer,* August 3, 1822; Charleston *City Gazette,* n.d., in *ibid.,* August 23, 1822.

¹² Washington *Daily National Intelligencer,* July 23, August 24, 1822.

¹³ *Niles' Weekly Register,* Baltimore, September 28, 1822, XXIII, p. 64. John H. Russell in *The Free Negro in Virginia, 1619–1865,* p. 169 declares: "Moses, a free negro of Goochland County, revealed a conspiracy of slaves in 1822." The cited source, a petition (dated December 18, 1822, Goochland, no. A7086) does not contain the information Russell gives. Moses, formerly the slave of a Mr. Peers, had purchased his own freedom in 1820 and petitioned for permission to remain in Virginia. To support his request he stated he was self-supporting and hard working. A statement to the same effect is made by Mr. Peers' son, who adds that Moses, as a slave, had "made communications . . . concerning insurrection." On this last point the petition of Moses reads: "In times when there were frequent alarms of insurrections of the Blacks, in the neighborhood, where there [sic] number was great being near large estates and extensive coal mines your Petitioner has more than once secretly made known to his Mistress the whispers of such Plots being agitated and concerning them he was always distressed and anxious to make discoveries." — Archives, Virginia State Library, Richmond.

¹⁴ Memorial of the citizens of Charleston to the Senate and House of Representatives of the State of South Carolina, 1822, in U. B. Phillips, ed., *Plantation and Frontier Documents,* II, pp. 108–109.

¹⁵ [E. C. Holland] *op. cit.,* p. 83. These statements vividly contrast with those to come about ten years later and to last until the Civil War as an important part of the pro-slavery argument, concerning the supposedly awful conditions of the free Negroes, North and South, so that, it was alleged, they were worse off than slaves.

¹⁶ As note 27; South Carolina *State Gazette,* October and November, 1822; Charleston Grand Jury report in Charleston *Courier,* June 21, 1823; H. Henry, *op. cit.,* pp. 101, 167.

¹⁷ "Achates" [General Thomas Pinckney] *Reflections Occasioned by the Late Disturbances in Charleston,* pp. 6–7. An anonymous pamphleteer, probably the Reverend Frederick Dalcho, suggested that Negroes be kept away from Fourth of July celebrations! — *Practical Considerations Founded on the Scriptures Relative to the Slave Population of South-Carolina,* pp. 33 n.

¹⁸ A special city guard of one hundred and fifty men was also provided for Charleston. *Acts and Resolutions of the General Assembly of the State of South-Carolina passed in December, 1822,* Columbia, 1822, pp. 9–11; David J. McCord, *The Statutes at Large of South Carolina, 1814–1838,* VI, pp. 179, 220.

¹⁹ The Negro Seamen's Act had interstate and international repercussions. But South Carolina, basing itself on its rights as a sovereign state, refused to modify or repeal the law. Other Southern states later passed such acts. The argument aroused by this law influenced the thinking of Thomas Cooper. See, Dumas Malone, *The Public Life of Thomas Cooper,* p. 285; H. Henry, *op. cit.,* pp. 124 ff.; Jervey, *Hayne, loc. cit.,* pp. 178–85; J. B. McMaster, *A History of the People of the United States,* V, pp. 200–205; Louis B. Boudin, *Government by Judiciary,* I, p. 310.

²⁰ U. B. Phillips, *The Course of the South to Secession,* p. 102; C. G. Woodson, *The History of the Negro Church,* p. 78.

²¹ See J. C. Carroll, *op. cit.,* pp. 109–111.

²² William Johnson, a South Carolinian and a justice of the United States Supreme Court, adopted such an attitude and was, therefore, denounced by Thomas Cooper; see D. Malone, *op. cit.,* p. 269.

²³ Charleston *City Gazette,* August 14–15, September 22, 1822; Charleston *Courier,* November 15, 1822. . . .

The Vesey Plot:
A Reconsideration

Richard C. Wade

On May 25, 1822, two slaves stood alongside the fish wharf in Charleston harbor chatting idly about the ships that lay at anchor nearby. William Paul asked Devany Prioleau if he knew that "something serious is about to take place." Then, more precisely, he said that "many of us are determined to right ourselves" and "shake off our bondage." Devany had not heard of the plot. "Astonished and horror struck," he quickly broke off the conversation and hurried away.[1] After a few agitated days he confided the news to a free Negro, George Pencil, and asked what to do. Pencil told him to tell his owner. On May 30 at three o'clock Devany gave the fateful information to Mrs. Prioleau.[2]

Two hours later the Mayor of Charleston called the city council into extraordinary session. The police picked up both Devany and William; officials began an intensive inquiry. For a week they kept William in solitary confinement in the "black hole of the Work-House," interrogating him every day. Finally he gave them the names of Mingo Harth and Peter Poyas. These Negroes were questioned but disclosed nothing. In fact, they "behaved with so much composure and coolness, and treated the charges . . . with so much levity" that the officials were "completely deceived" and released them both.[3] Later William implicated others, but they too claimed no knowledge. The authorities were further baffled when Ned Bennett, a slave of Governor Thomas Bennett of South Carolina, came in voluntarily to clear himself of suspicion.[4]

Having turned up nothing — but suspicious of everything — the Mayor strengthened his patrols, armed his men for extensive action, and waited. On June 14 the break came. Another slave corroborated William Paul's testimony, disclosing that the uprising originally set for July 2 was now moved up to June 16. For the first time the public knew that danger threatened. A strong guard surrounded the city; the police appeared in force. Still nothing happened. On June 16, ten slaves were arrested; and, two days later, a hastily assembled court of freeholders began hearing secret testimony. On June 21 the police brought in Denmark Vesey. And eleven days later, on July 2, the bodies of Vesey and five other Negroes swung from the gallows at the edge of town.

Richard C. Wade, "The Vesey Plot: A Reconsideration," *Journal of Southern History,* XXX (May 1964), pp. 143–61. Copyright 1964 by the Southern Historical Association. Reprinted by permission of the publisher.

The uprising now seemed quashed. But, as word of it spread in the city, public shock turned into hysteria. No master could be sure his bondsmen were not involved; whites who owned no slaves had little more assurance. Every Negro became a possible enemy, indeed assassin; every action by a black could be construed as a prelude to violence. Since slaves lived in the same yard with their masters, it was not even possible to lock out the intruder.

As the terror spread, so too did the presumed magnitude of the conspiracy. The letters of Ana Hayes Johnson, daughter of a respected judge and a niece of the Governor, describe the fears and rumors that were current. "Their plans were simply these," she wrote late in June: "They were to set fire to the town and while the whites were endeavoring to put it out they were to commence their horrid depredations." Then in more detail: "It seems that the Governor, Intendant [i.e. Mayor], and my poor father were to have been the first victims — the men and Black women were to have been indiscriminately murdered — & we poor devils were to have been removed to fill their — Harams — horrible — I have a very beautiful cousin who was set apart for the wife or more properly, the 'light of the Haram' of one of their chiefs."[5]

Panic gripped the colored community, too, after the execution. As more and more blacks disappeared into prison, as rumors widened, and as the newspapers announced new arrests, the alarm deepened. Was someone informing on his neighbor? Had the police picked up so many that some had to be housed in a nearby county? Were white irregulars about to take things in their own hands because the court was too slow? In the awful uncertainty the Negroes found an uneasy unity. Most of those questioned by municipal officials professed no knowledge of any plot; others wore armbands of crepe in mourning for the dead until officials forbade demonstrations of sympathy.[6]

Outwardly, the normal deference to whites increased. "There was a wonderful degree of politeness shown to us," a white recalled, "bows and politeness, and — give way for the gentlemen and ladies, met you at every turn and corner."[7] Before long the crisis waned. The first six executions seemed to have ripped the heart out of the rebellion. "We thought it was ended," Miss Johnson wrote on July 18; "the court had been dismissed and the town was again sinking into its wonted security when information was given that another attempt would be made." The tip came from a Negro who later became a key witness. The court reassembled, the patrol returned to its stations, and more Negroes were jailed.

A new excitement swept the city, and the court, working rapidly, ordered more executions. "In all probability the executed will not end under 100," Miss Johnson estimated, and others asserted that "even should there be 500 executed there would still be enough" conspirators to pull off the scheme. "How far the mischief has extended heaven only knows," she lamented fearfully.[8] A later letter reported morbid details: "22 unfortunate wretches were at one fatal moment sent to render their account, 29 had been sentenced but 7 had their sentences commuted to perpetual banishment — but on Tuesday 6 more are to be executed ... . gracious heavens to what will all this lead . . . and I am told that there are an awful number yet to be tried." Miss Johnson had more knowledge than most, but she could observe on the street that "there is a look of horror in every countenance." "I wish I could act for myself," she added; "I would not stay in this city another day . . . my feelings have been so lacerated of late that I can hardly speak or act."[9]

From the beginning municipal authorities had been no less frightened, but they were compelled to act. The five freeholders who comprised the court appointed on June 18 were chosen because they possessed "in an eminent degree the confidence of the community." The tribunal quickly drew up its rules: no slave could be tried without the presence of his owner or the owner's counsel; "the testimony of one witness unsupported by additional evidence or by circumstances, should lead to no conviction of a *capital* nature"; witnesses would confront the accused except "where testimony was given under a solemn pledge that the name . . . would not be divulged" because the judges feared the informant might be "murdered by the blacks"; a master or free Negro could have counsel if asked for, and "the statements of defenses of the accused should be heard, in every case, and they be permitted themselves to examine any witness they thought proper."[10] The freeholders worked in complete secrecy because of the "peculiar nature of the investigations" and because "it was also morally certain that no coloured witness would have ventured to incur the resentment of his comrades, by voluntarily disclosing his testimony in a public court."[11]

During its sittings, from the first outbreak in June until July 26, the court heard over 130 cases.[12] It divided the conspirators into two groups. The first comprised those "who exhibited energy and activity"; they were executed. The other included those "who did little (if any more) than yield their acquiescence to the proposal to enter the plot"; they were deported. The judges later confided to the Governor that the distinction did not wholly meet the facts, but "the terror of example we thought would be sufficiently operative by the number of criminals sentenced to death" that "without any injury to the community . . . a measure might be adopted . . . which would save the necessity of more numerous executions than policy required."[13]

The court found it difficult to get conclusive evidence. Vesey and the first five went to the gallows without confessing — indeed asserting their innocence. During the second trial, however, three men under the sentence of death implicated, under a promise of leniency, scores of other blacks. In asking the Governor to pardon Monday Gell, Charles Drayton, and Harry Haig, the judges described the conditions of their testimony: "Under the impression that they could ultimately have their lives spared they made . . . disclosures not only important in the detection of the general plan of the conspiracy but enabling the court to convict a number of principal offenders." Like "the terror of example," the officials wanted deportation in place of the hangman so that "negroes should know that even their principal advisers and ringleaders cannot be confided in and that under the temptations of exemption from capital punishment they will betray the common cause."[14]

Despite the difficulty of acquiring sufficient evidence, the court moved energetically and decisively. Of the 131 picked up, 35 were executed, 31 transported, 27 tried and acquitted, and 38 questioned but discharged.[15] Throughout July the gallows was kept busy. On "the Line," which separated the city from the Neck, the neighborhood numbly watched the public display.

Most of the condemned died without admitting guilt, and some with almost defiant contempt. Bacchus Hammett, who had "confessed," "went to the gallows, *laughing and bidding his acquaintances in the streets* 'good bye;' on being hung, owing to some mismanagement in the fall of the trap, he was not thrown off, but the board canted, he slipped; yet he was so hardened that he *threw himself forward, and as he swung back he lifted his feet, so that he might not touch the board!*"[16] Others were dispatched more expertly, and the bodies left to dangle for hours to make certain that no colored resident could mistake the point of the punishment.

Constable Belknap, the executioner, later complained that the frequency of the hangings had caused him great "personal inconvenience" and had "deranged" his "private business." At the height of the crisis he had spent "all his time and services" in the "call of the public, both by night and by day, in assisting at the preparation of the Gallows, the digging of the graves and various other offices connected with the execution."[17] The city's budget too felt the strain. In December the council asked the state to reimburse it for the unusual expenses surrounding the plot and trial. The bill came to $2,284.84¼, including costs of confinement, a payment of $200 to "Col. Prioleau's man peter for secret services rendered," and the expenses of "erecting a Gallows" and procuring "carts to carry the criminals to the place of execution."[18]

A second court, which included Robert Y. Hayne and Joel Poinsett, was appointed August 1 "for the trial of sundry persons of color, apprehended for attempting to raise an insurrection."[19] Though it sat only a week, it sentenced one man to death and directed six others to be transported out of the state. These new cases, however, were connected with the events of May and June.[20]

As the court wound up its grim business, the city tried to recover something of its old composure. In the second week of August the *Courier* closed the books on the episode. "The legal investigations of crime have ceased. The melancholy requisitions of Justice, as painful to those who inflicted, as to those who suffered them, have been complied with; and an awful but a necessary, and, it is hoped, an effectual example has been afforded to deter from further occasions of offense and punishment."[21] The editor then called on the council for a day of thanksgiving to God for "his preserving care" and because "he has watched and guarded the tranquillity of our city" and "endowed our magistrates with firmness and wisdom, rendered necessary by an alarming crisis."[22]

This brief narrative includes the essential facts about the Vesey uprising generally accepted by historians today. The standard source is a long pamphlet containing the court's record of the trial, published by the city in 1822 under the title of *An Official Report of the Trials of Sundry Negroes* and edited by two members of the court. This document conveyed a special authenticity because the testimony and confessions purported to be as "originally taken, without even changing the phraseology, which was generally in the very words and by the witnesses." Indeed, the court had instructed the editors *"not to suppress any part of it.*"[23] Scholars had few other sources to turn to. Charleston newspapers imposed a nearly perfect blackout on the details of the episode throughout the summer, confining themselves to a simple recording of sentences and executions. And contemporaries left only a few scattered items to help fill out the slight skeleton provided by the council's publication.

Hence, historians accepted the only facts available and drew their accounts from the official record. They did not question the court's findings but rather dwelt on certain aspects of the episode. Some, like Carter G. Woodson and Ulrich B. Phillips, emphasized the extent and precision of the planning.[24] Others centered on the extraordinary quality of the rebels, especially their leader. Dwight Dumond found Denmark Vesey a "brilliant man," familiar with the Bible, and acquainted with the debates in Congress over the admission of Missouri to the Union. He concluded that "few men were better informed . . . in the history of race relations." John Hope Franklin characterized Vesey as "a sensitive, liberty-loving person" who "believed in equality for everyone and resolved to do something for his slave brothers." Still others were impressed with the unity of the Negroes which made the plot possible. Herbert Aptheker, for example, quoted the report of two Negroes who said they "never spoke to any person of color on the subject, or knew of any who had been spoken to by the other leaders, who had withheld his assent."[25]

More important was the broader meaning of the conspiracy. Most authors viewed it in the context of the resistance of Negroes to the institution of slavery. Along with Nat Turner, they placed Denmark Vesey at the head of the list of colored rebels. For some his plot demonstrated the latent urge for freedom that lay beneath the regime of bondage; for others it revealed an ugly layer of hatred and revenge contained only by stringent laws and alert policemen.

But all accepted the official version: that a widespread conspiracy existed and only a last-minute betrayal rescued the city from insurrection and civil war. Whether the author was Negro or white, Northerner or Southerner, opponent of or apologist for slavery, there was no quarrel on this point. Historians who otherwise disagreed on many issues did not question the conventional story. Hence there was little incentive for reappraisal.[26]

Yet, in spite of the apparent agreement of most contemporaries and the consensus of subsequent historians, there is persuasive evidence that no conspiracy in fact existed, or at most that it was a vague and unformulated plan in the minds or on the tongues of a few colored townsmen. No elaborate network had been established in the countryside; no cache of arms lay hidden about the city; no date for an uprising had been set; no underground apparatus, carefully organized and secretly maintained, awaited a signal to fire Charleston and murder the whites. What did exist were strong grievances on one side and deep fears on the other. Combined with a number of somewhat unrelated circumstances, they made it possible for many people, both white and Negro, to believe in the existence of a widespread scheme to overturn the institution of slavery.

The first note of skepticism came from a respected judge, a long-time resident of Charleston. Watching the mounting excitement in June, and privy to the proceedings of the court, he warned in a newspaper letter against the "Melancholy Effect of Popular Excitement." In an oblique parable he recounted an episode "within the recollection of thousands" when a freeholders' court had hastily hanged a slave, Billy, for sounding a false alarm to the patrols by blowing a horn. Although "no evidence was given whatever as to a motive for sounding the horn, and the horn was actually found covered and even filled with cobwebs, they condemned that man to die the next day!" The only testimony had been provided by another slave who "was first whipped severely to extort a confession, and then, with his eyes bound, commanded to prepare for instant death from a sabre" if he would not divulge the needed information. Many of the worthiest men in the area protested and asked for "a more deliberate hearing." It did no good, however. "Billy was hung amidst crowds of execrating spectators," the "popular demand for a victim" being so great that it was doubtful whether even a Governor's pardon could have saved him.[27]

The letter was unsigned, but everyone knew its author was of "commanding authority." Moreover, published at the time of the newspaper blackout, it obviously came from someone close to those involved in the trial. In fact, its author was William Johnson, a judge and brother-in-law of the Governor. His daughter observed that when the article appeared, the freeholders "took up the cudgels, supposing it was a slur at them — guilty conscience you know" and "threatened their anathemas at him." Johnson responded with a pamphlet, which his daughter characterized as asserting the "entire innocence of the slaves" and in which he pointed out that the charge against Billy had been "an attempt to raise an insurrection."[28] The moral could hardly be clearer: he feared the court would bend to the popular hysteria and find guilt where there was none.[29]

His daughter, too, soon took this view. Her letters spanning the two months of the crisis moved from frenzy to skepticism. At the beginning of the trouble she wrote that the conspirators spoke of "rapine and murder" with "the coolness of demons" and that "the plot is computed to be about 30,000 — the children were to have been spiked and murdered &c."[30] A few weeks later the tone became more measured, the numbers involved much fewer, and she could "thank God none of our slaves have been found in the plot, though there are twenty of them in the yard."[31]

Still later some deeper doubts crept in. "You know," Miss Johnson wrote, "that the leading characteristic of our state is our impetuosity and ardency of feeling which unavoidably lays them [the people] open to deception and consequently leads them on to error in action." Not much, however, could be done about it: "you might as well attempt to 'fetter tides with silken bands' as to make them listen to reason when under this excitement." Yet she concluded that in a few days "the unfortunate creatures are to be hung — it is most horrible — it makes my blood curdle when I think of it, but they are guilty most certainly."[32] Her final letter mentions no plot at all and is obsessed with "the most awful tragedy in this . . . city that comes within the recollection of man" — the mass executions. "Certainly," she added, the whole affair "will throw our city back at least ten years."[33] By the end, Miss Johnson, if she believed a conspiracy existed at all, thought it surely had not extended far enough to justify the massive retaliation of the courts.

The criticism by Governor Thomas Bennett was much more precise. The court should not have "closed its doors upon the community" in its secret proceedings and "shut out those accidental rays which occasionally illuminate the obscurity." Moreover, he found the testimony gathered by the judges "equivocal, the offspring of treachery or revenge, and the hope of immunity." "Nor should it be less a source of embarrassment and concern," he continued, contesting the official version of the city, "that the testimony should be received under pledges of inviolable secrecy" and "that the accused should be convicted, and sentenced to death, without seeing the persons, or hearing the voices of those who testified to their guilt."[34]

The Governor noted particularly that the decisive information came from three witnesses "while they were under the impression that they would have their life spared." Their testimony not only facilitated "the detection of the general plan of conspiracy, but enabled the court to convict a number of the principal offenders." While questioned "two of them were sometimes closeted together," achieving a uniformity of evidence. In one case William, "the slave of Mr. Palmer," was convicted "exclusively on the testimony of two of the persons under sentence of death." He protested his innocence, claimed he had attended no meetings and had never talked about a plot, and demonstrated his high reputation in many ways. Worse still, Charles Drayton "predicated his claim of escape [from the gallows] on the number of convictions he could make" with his story. "Nothing," Governor Bennett asserted, "could exceed the chilling depravity of this man."

Though the Governor probably believed in a plot of some kind, he could not take the one described by the city very seriously. "It is scarcely possible to imagine one, more crude or imperfect," he said. "They were unprovided with arms," and except for a few pennies that had been subscribed, "no effort was used to procure them." The leaders showed "no confidence in each other"; in fact, they were "in many instances unknown to each other." They had "no definite plans of attack concerted; nor place of rendezvous fixed." Yet the city represented the danger as "mature and within a few hours of consummation."

He went on to say that the idea of an insurrection itself seemed unlikely, although some of the reasons he gave are less convincing. "The liberal and enlightened humanity of our Fellow Citizens, produce many attachments, that operate as checks on the spirit of insubordination." Indeed, there were "unsurmountable obstacles" — the "habitual respect" of the slaves "for an obedience to the authority of their owners; their natural indolence, and want of means and opportunities to form combinations; their characteristic cowardice and treachery, excited by a knowledge of the positive ability of the state to crush in an instant their boldest enterprise." The Governor's view of the episode was plain. "The public mind had been raised to a pitch of excitement" over the rumor of a slave revolt and "sought relief in an exhibition of truth."[35] Instead, the action of the city created further panic and confusion.

A close examination of the published record of the trial tends to confirm the Governor's doubts. Though the testimony seems at first reading to suggest a ripe plan, the important evidence is missing at the critical points. For example, the transcript stated that "the whole numbers engaged" were 9,000, "partly from the country and partly from the city." But, it added, "it is true that the witness who had made these assertions did not see the lists [of accomplices] himself; but he heard from one who was in daily communication with Peter, . . . and as Peter wrote a good hand and was active throughout the whole affair, it is impossible to doubt that he had such lists." To be sure, the judges then contended that the larger figure was "greatly exaggerated, and perhaps designedly so."[36] Yet not a single roster of names ever turned up.

If the numbers were conjectural, the extent of the conspiracy was even more so. The report estimated the infected area covered not only the regions around the city but neighboring parishes as well. All through the crisis, however, no one detected any activity in the rural sections.[37] The charge that some of the central figures had acquaintances in the surrounding area was not accompanied by any evidence of complicity. Indeed, one black testified that Pierre Lewis told him "something serious would happen" but that "I was country born, and he was afraid to trust me."[38]

On the matter of weapons the official record reveals the same ambivalence. A blacksmith was supposed to have made some long pikes, six of which a few witnesses claimed existed. But the pikes were never located, thereby forcing the court into a curious logic: "as those six pike heads have not been found, there is no reason for disbelieving the testimony of there hav[ing] been many more made." Later the transcript mentions that "one hundred (pike heads and bayonets) were said to have been made at an early day, and by the 16th of June, as many as two or three hundred, and between three and four hundred daggers." And there was still more. "Besides the above mentioned, it was proved that Peter had a sword; that Charles Drayton had a gun & sword; that John Henry had a sword; that Pharo Thompson had a scythe converted into a sword; that Adam Yates had a knife . . . that Monday had a sword"; and that Bacchus Hammett gave a sword and a gun to others. Yet, except for these few individual weapons, no arms cache was uncovered. "To presume that the Insurgents had no arms because none were seized," the judges concluded, "would be drawing an inference in direct opposition to the whole of the evidence."[39] Since the city published the full text of the trial to allay suspicions both in Charleston and in the North that some injustice had been done the inconclusiveness of the case at the crucial points is significant.[40]

Equally important is the fact that the printed transcript is at odds in both wording and substance with manuscript records of the witnesses. For example, the confessions of Bacchus Hammett and John Enslow, among the few surviving original documents, have been carefully edited in the authorized version. Some passages were omitted; facts not mentioned in the original interrogation were added; even the tone of the narrative was changed with the alterations.[41]

For example, while Bacchus Hammett is reported to have testified: "At Vesey's they wanted to make a collection to make pikes for the country people, but the men had no money,"[42] the manuscript suggests something different: "Denmark told me in March, he was getting arms fast, about 150 to 200 pikes made, and there was a great deal of money placed in his hands for the purpose."[43] Again the *Official Report* lists names of accomplices. "Bellisle Yates I have seen at meetings, and Adam Yates and Napham Yates and Dean Mitchell, and Caesar Smith, and George a Stevidore [*sic*]." It also includes Jack McNeil, Prince Righton, Jerry Cohen. None appear in the original confession.[44]

At some points the manuscript included material not found at all in the printed version. to use but a single instance, the confession of Bacchus is quite explicit on a rebellion in Georgetown which would precede the Charleston uprising. "I also heard them say that they were well informed in Georgetown. That they would let the principal Men know the time of the attack, being a short distance from Charleston, would commence a day or two before." The plan was simple. "Kill all the whites between there and Charleston, make their way through the woods and be in time to assist these people in town. It is also said by them that the Population in Georgetown could be killed in one half hour." Yet the city's account contains no mention of this extraordinary dimension of the plot.

The discrepancies seem deliberate since the preface of the pamphlet went to great pains to say that "the whole evidence has been given in each particular case, in the order of its trial, and wherever any additional, or incidental testimony has been disclosed against any criminal subsequently to his conviction, sentence or execution, it has been noticed." "In most cases," the judges contended, "it was as originally taken, without even changing the phraseology" and using "the very words" of the witnesses.[45] Yet these two depositions indicate that little confidence can be placed in the authenticity of the official account.[46]

Strangely, historians have received it less skeptically than some contemporaries. While many newspapers outside the state approved the silence of the Charleston press during the trial, some also looked forward to "a succinct account of the whole transaction" that had been promised by the court. When it arrived, however, there was disappointment. "We doubt the policy of the present publication," wrote a reader of the Boston *Daily Advertiser*. "If intended to awe the blacks, it would seem the executions and banishments *silently* made, would be more terrible, but if really designed as an appeal, and a justification to the American people and to the world, as to the justice of the sentences, it appears either too much or too little." The "historical part," he concluded, "is too loose."[47]

In fact, the explanation of the whole episode lay in the "historical part." If a genuine conspiracy was lacking, tension between the races was not. In the years before the "plot," several developments had worsened relations that always were uneasy. The census figures conveniently summed up white fears. Officially Negroes outnumbered whites 14,127 to 10,653.[48] During the summer when many families left the city to escape the heat, the colored majority was even larger. Thomas Pinckney, in an extended post-mortem on the grim event, expressed the consequent anxiety. He called the imbalance "the principal encouragement to the late attempt, for without it, mad and wild as they appear to have been, they would not have dared to venture on a contest of force." In a word, numerical superiority was the *"sine qua non* of insurrection."[49]

Numbers alone, however, would not have produced panic. Some rural areas had a higher percentage of slaves than the city without the same alarm. It was the kind of colored population, not its mere predominance, that frightened white leaders. Charleston's Negroes, like urban blacks elsewhere, were a far different lot than their country brothers. They were more advanced, engaged in higher tasks, more literate, more independent, and less servile than those on plantations. Not confined to the field or the big house, many found employment as draymen, porters, fishermen, hucksters, butchers, barbers, carpenters, and even as clerks and bookkeepers. Their work took these slaves away from the constant surveillance of their masters and generated a measure of self-reliance not usually found in the "peculiar institution." Added to this was an urban environment that provided churches, livery stables, cook houses, and grog shops as centers of informal community life.

Even the domestics who comprised the bulk of urban bondsmen in Charleston afforded slight comfort, though they were popularly believed to be loyally attached to the families of their owners.[50] In fact, Pinckney thought them "certainly the most dangerous" because they had an "intimate acquaintance with all circumstances relating to the interior of the dwellings," because of "the confidence reposed in them," and because of "information they unavoidably obtain, from hearing the conversation, and observing the habitual transactions of their owners." Having "the amplest means for treacherous bloodshed and devastation," this group would comprise the core of a conspiracy. Yet these slaves, he complained, had been "so pampered" by "indulgencies," even "being taught to read and write," that the "considerable control" embodied in ordinances and state laws had been frustrated by the "weakness of many proprietors."[51]

Nearly all those believed to be ringleaders by the court came from one or another of these areas of colored life. Denmark Vesey, who "stood at the head of this conspiracy" according to the court's report, was a successful carpenter who had bought his freedom with money won in a lottery in 1801. Since he was the only free Negro executed (six others were questioned and dismissed), officials assumed "the idea undoubtedly originated with him" and that he concocted the plot. His house and shop became the rendezvous of the rebels and he the moving genius. For several years before he "disclosed his intentions to anyone," the court declared, "he appears to have been constantly and assiduously engaged in endeavoring to embitter the minds of the coloured population against the white." He "rendered himself perfectly familiar" with the Bible and used whatever parts "he could pervert to his purpose; and would readily quote them, to prove that slavery was contrary to the laws of God." Moreover, he distributed "inflammatory pamphlets" among the bondsmen. He even "sought every opportunity" to "introduce some bold remark on slavery" into conversations with whites while in the presence of other Negroes.[52]

His associates were no less impressive. Monday Gell not only hired his own time but kept a shop on Meeting Street where he made harness; his owner entrusted arms as well as money to him. Governor Bennett once called him "the projector of the plot" and its "most active partisan."[53] Peter Poyas was a "first rate ship carpenter" who had an excellent reputation and the implicit confidence of his master. Two others belonged to the Governor of the state, and one of 'hem tended the family's business when his owner was at the capital. Only Gullah Jack, who claimed to be a sorcerer with mysterious powers, seemed irregular.

White fears fixed on this colored urban elite, on those who managed to "succeed" a little in bondage. To the whites of Charleston, the character of the city's Negro population made an uprising seem possible, indeed, reasonable. The Negroes were, as a group of residents put it, the "most condensed and most intelligent."[54] Moreover, the extent of literacy brought the "powerful operation of the Press" on "their uninformed and easily deluded minds" and, more precisely, made them privy to events outside the city and the South. The example of Santo Domingo, where the blacks had risen successfully against the whites, and the debate over the Missouri Compromise were thought to have "directly or indirectly" heightened the unrest and encouraged insurrectionary activity.[55] In sum, both the quality and the quantity of Charleston slaves rendered the whites uneasy.

The Negroes, too, were edgy, for things had not gone well for them in the preceding months. New state legislation had made manumission more difficult, nearly closing the door on those who hoped to get their freedom either by purchase or the generosity of their masters.[56] Such "uncivilized laws," "A Colored American" recalled, were "a great and intolerable hindrance" to the slaves' "peace and happiness," since some had already made arrangements to buy their liberty.[57]

Another cause of controversy was the closing of an independent Methodist church established for colored people. In this sanctuary many blacks had found both spiritual consolation and brief relief from servitude. When it was closed down in 1821, the Negro community became embittered. Bible-class leaders especially felt aggrieved because it deprived them of one of the few positions of modest status open to bondsmen. The resentment of this articulate group was scarcely a secret. In fact, the city later charged that almost all the ringleaders were connected with this church.[58]

The atmosphere, then, was charged with fears and grievances. No doubt conversations among whites turned often, if hesitantly, to the topic; and certainly in the grog shops, in Negro quarters, and on the job, the slaves talked about their difficulties. The gap between the races was great, calculatedly so, and was quickly filled by gossip and rumor. Blacks heard the whites were going to "thin out" the colored population, that a false alarm would bring out the militia and volunteers to butcher the slaves on the spot, that new restraints were under consideration in city hall and the state legislature. Circulating among the whites were equally hair-raising notions: a servile uprising, the seizure of the city, the carrying off of women after all males had been exterminated.

Under these circumstances anything specific — names, places, target dates — seemed to give substance to the rumor, suggesting that a plot not only existed but was ripe. Prudence dictated preventive action and a withering show of force by the city. Not only the ringleaders but even those remotely connected had to be swiftly seized, tried, and punished. Hence, the chance encounter of Devany Prioleau with William Paul on the wharf on May 25, 1822, with its garbled but ominous portent, set off a chain of events that did not end until thirty-five had been executed, still more deported, and a town frozen in terror for almost a summer.

Thus Charleston stumbled into tragedy. The "plot" was probably never more than loose talk by aggrieved and embittered men. Curiously, its reputation as a full-scale revolt has endured, in part, because both sides in the slavery controversy believed insurrections to be essential to their broader argument. Apologists for the "peculiar institution" contended that the stringent laws against Negroes in the South were needed to protect whites from violence; opponents of slavery asserted that the urge for freedom was so embedded in human nature that none would passively remain enchained. In either event the Denmark Vesey uprising became a convenient illustration of a larger view of bondage. No closer examination seemed necessary. What *both* Aptheker and Phillips could accept as fact, it was assumed, must necessarily be true.

But the very agreement tended to obscure the important reality. For a concerted revolt against slavery was actually less likely in a city than in the countryside. The chances for success anywhere, of course, were never very good, but ordinary circumstances favored a Nat Turner over a Denmark Vesey. The reasons for this are clear. Nowhere, not even in Charleston, did the blacks have the great numerical superiority that was present on many plantations. Moreover, police forces in the towns, large and well organized, constituted a more powerful deterrent than the vigilante patrol system characteristic of places with scattered populations. And ironically, the urban environment proved inhospitable to conspiracies because it provided a wider latitude to the slave, a measure of independence within bondage, and some relief from the constant surveillance of the master. This comparative freedom deflected the discontent, leading Negroes to try to exploit their modest advantages rather than to organize for desperate measures.

The white community, however, could see only the dangers. The Negroes in Charleston were not only numerous but quite different from the imbruted field hands of the cane and cotton country. Many mastered skills, learned to read and write, joined churches and in every way tried to comport themselves as free men. This was the source of the fear. They seemed capable both of resenting their bondage and organizing an insurrection against it. It was not difficult to translate a few rumors into a widespread conspiracy. Indeed, it was so easy that historians, too, have done so for nearly a century and a half.

Notes

---

¹ Lionel H. Kennedy and Thomas Parker, *An Official Report of the Trials of Sundry Negroes, Charged with an Attempt to Raise an Insurrection in the State of South-Carolina: Preceded by an Introduction and Narrative; and in an Appendix, a Report of the Trials of Four White Persons, on Indictments for Attempting to Excite the Slaves to Insurrection, Prepared and Published at the Request of the Court* (Charleston, 1822), 50.

² A postscript to the publication revised this original version slightly, asserting that Devany told his young master before he did Pencil, but the free Negro advised him to go directly to his master. Since Mr. Prioleau was not available he told Mrs. Prioleau. The editor concluded that this added information "places the fidelity of the slave . . . on much higher ground." *Official Report,* "Extracts," 4. The state rewarded both Devany and Pencil with a $50 annuity for life. In 1837, when Devany turned seventy, the state raised it to $150. Memorial of the City Council of Charleston to the Senate of South Carolina, 1822 (South Carolina Archives Division); Petition of Peter Devany for Increase of Annual Bounty Conferred upon Him by the Act of Assembly, Anno Domini, 1822 for Meritorious Services in the Disturbances of That Year, October, 1837 (South Carolina Archives Division). Devany had also been manumitted for his role in uncovering the plot.

³ *Official Report,* 51.

⁴ *Ibid.,* 3 ff.

⁵ Ana Hayes Johnson to Elizabeth E. W. Haywood, Charleston, June 23, 1822, in Ernest Haywood Papers (Southern Historical Collection, University of North Carolina Library).

⁶ A Colored American, *The Late Contemplated Insurrection in Charleston, S. C., with the Execution of Thirty-Six of the Patriots, Etc.* (New York, 1850), 7.

⁷ Charleston *Southern Patriot and Commercial Advertiser,* September 12, 1822.

⁸ Ana Hayes Johnson to Elizabeth E. W. Haywood, Charleston, July 18, 1822, in Ernest Haywood Papers.

⁹ Ana Hayes Johnson to Elizabeth E. W. Haywood, Charleston, July 27, 1822, *ibid.*

¹⁰ *Official Report,* vi.

¹¹ *Ibid.,* iii, vii.

¹² The court sat in "arduous session for five weeks and three days" and probably had some contact with more than this number. *Southern Patriot and Commercial Advertiser,* July 27, 1822.

¹³ L. Kennedy, Thomas Parker, William Drayton, Nathaniel Heyward, J. R. Pringle, H. Deos, and Robert J. Turnbull to Governor Thomas Bennett, July 24, 1822 (South Carolina Archives Division).

¹⁴ Petition for the Pardon of Monday Gell, Charles Drayton, and Harry Haig to the Governor of South Carolina, July 24, 1822 (South Carolina Archives Division).

¹⁵ *Official Report,* 183.

¹⁶ Bacchus, the Slave of Benjamin Hammett, Confession, in William and Benjamin Hammett Papers (Duke University Library).

¹⁷ Petition of B. Belknap of the City of Charleston to the Senate and House of Representatives, November 14, 1822 (South Carolina Archives Division).

[18] Report of the Committee on the Memorial of the City of Charleston, Senate Committee, December 14, 1822 (South Carolina Archives Division).

[19] *Southern Patriot and Commercial Advertiser,* August 2, 1822.

[20] *Ibid.,* August 8, 1822. The prisoner who was executed, William Garner, had earlier escaped from the city. His death brought the total to thirty-six and explains the confusion in secondary sources concerning the precise number of executions. H. M. Henry, *The Police Control of the Slave in South Carolina* (Emory, Va., 1914), 152.

[21] Charleston *Courier,* August 12, 1822.

[22] *Ibid.,* August 24, 1822.

[23] *Official Report,* iii.

[24] Carter G. Woodson, *The Negro in Our History* (Washington, 1927), 180; Ulrich B. Phillips, "The Slave Labor Problem in the Charleston District," *Political Science Quarterly,* XXII (September 1907), 429–30.

[25] Dwight Lowell Dumond, *Antislavery: The Crusade for Freedom in America* (Ann Arbor, Mich., 1961), 114; John Hope Franklin, *From Slavery to Freedom: A History of American Negroes* (New York, 1956), 210; Herbert Aptheker, *American Negro Slave Revolts* (New York, 1943), 270.

[26] In a paper delivered to the Southern Historical Association meeting in 1957 Thomas T. Hamilton of the University of Wichita evidently developed some doubts about the case from "irregularities in the trials and testimony." Presumably this skepticism stemmed from a close reading of the text. *Journal of Southern History,* XXIV (February 1958), 71. Standard accounts of the Vesey plot include Anne King Gregorie, "Denmark Vesey," *Dictionary of American Biography,* XIX, 258–59; John Lofton, "Negro Insurrectionist," *Antioch Review,* XVIII (Summer 1958), 183–96; and John M. Lofton Jr., "Denmark Vesey's Call to Arms," *Journal of Negro History,* XXXIII (October 1948), 395–417.

[27] Charleston *Courier,* June 21, 1822.

[28] Ana Hayes Johnson to Elizabeth E. W. Haywood, Charleston, July 24, 1822, in Ernest Haywood Papers. For the court's reply see Charleston *Courier,* June 29, 1822.

[29] "If it was intended as it would seem to be to make this moral, and the story which accompanies applicable to a supposed existing state of things in our community, . . . " wrote the Mayor [Intendant], "I have only to remark that the *discretion* of the writer is altogether equal to the unjust libel he has insinuated against his Fellow Citizens." The Mayor contended that the measures adopted were taken "in a spirit of the most perfect justice and moderation." *Southern Patriot and Commercial Advertiser,* June 22, 1822.

[30] Ana Hayes Johnson to Elizabeth E. W. Haywood, Charleston, June 23, 1822, in Ernest Haywood Papers.

[31] Ana Hayes Johnson to Elizabeth E. W. Haywood, Charleston, July 18, 1822, *ibid.*

[32] Ana Hayes Johnson to Elizabeth E. W. Haywood, Charleston, July 24, 1822, *ibid.*

[33] Ana Hayes Johnson to Elizabeth E. W. Haywood, Charleston, July 27, 1822, *ibid.*

[34] Message of Governor Thomas Bennett to the Senate and House of Representatives of the State of South Carolina, November 28, 1822 (South Carolina Archives Division). The Charleston delegation thought the Governor's message too harsh on the city's handling of the episode. Charleston *Mercury,* December 18, 1822.

[35] Message of Governor Thomas Bennett.

[36] *Official Report,* 25–26.

[37] Nonetheless, a prominent planter explained "the orderly conduct of the negroes in any district within 40 miles of Charleston, is no evidence that they were ignorant of the intended attempt. A more orderly gang than my own is not to be found in this state — and one of Denmark Vesey's directives was, that they should assume the most implicit obedience." *Official Report,* 28n–31n. The plot presumably stretched as far as 70 or 80 miles from the city. *Ibid.,* 31.

[38] *Ibid.,* 159.

[39] *Ibid.*, 32.

[40] The Washington *Daily National Intelligencer* of August 3, 1822, noted that the Charleston *City Gazette* promised that "a succinct account of the whole transaction shall be given to the world. It will bring to view a scheme of wildness and of wickedness, enough to make us smile at the folly, did we not shudder at the indiscriminate mischief of the plan and its objects. Those (they were but few) who at first thought we had no cause for alarm, must be overwhelmed with conviction to the contrary."

[41] Bacchus, the Slave of Benjamin Hammett, Confession, and The Confession of Mr. Enslow's Boy John, 1822, in William and Benjamin Hammett Papers.

[42] *Official Report*, 146.

[43] Bacchus, the Slave of Benjamin Hammett, Confession, and The Confession of Mr. Enslow's Boy John.

[44] *Official Report*, 146, 7.

[45] *Ibid.*, iii.

[46] Indeed, a close reading of the report suggests that the object of the trials was not to discover the extent of the plot but rather to awe the Negroes by a show of force. "The object of punishment being effectually attained by these examples, and the ring leaders being convicted," the court explained, "the arrests stopped here." *Ibid.*, 48, 59.

[47] Boston *Daily Advertiser*, October 8, 1822.

[48] *Census for 1820, Published by Authority of an Act of Congress, Under the Direction of the Secretary of State* (Washington, 1821), 26.

[49] Achates [Thomas Pinckney], *Reflections Occasioned by the Late Disturbances in Charleston* (Charleston, 1822), 10.

[50] The *Official Report* contained the conventional view. "Few if any domestic servants were spoken to [by the leaders], as *they* were distrusted." *Ibid.*, 26. Pinckney's appraisal of the domestics suggests that he did not wholly trust the analysis of the court even though he believed in the existence of the plot.

[51] Pinckney, *Reflections,* 6–9.

[52] *Official Report,* 17–19. Later in the testimony, however, the court contended that Vesey "enjoyed so much the confidence of the whites, that when he was accused, the charge was not only discredited, but he was not even arrested for several days after, and not until proof of his guilt had become too strong to be doubted." This does not square well with the previous description of years of agitation and bold confrontation with whites.

[53] Message of Governor Thomas Bennett.

[54] *Southern Patriot and Commercial Advertiser,* August 21, 1822.

[55] Pinckney, *Reflections,* 9.

[56] *Acts and Resolutions of the General Assembly of the State of South-Carolina Passed in December, 1820* (Columbia, 1821), 22–24.

[57] A Colored American, *Late Contemplated Insurrection,* 5.

[58] The church included both slaves and free blacks. Though some accounts emphasize the petition of free Negroes to the legislature for the privilege of conducting their own worship, the report of the trial asserts that nearly all the bondsmen involved also belonged to the African church and that many were class leaders.

Denmark Vesey's Slave Conspiracy of 1822: A Study in Rebellion and Repression

Robert S. Starobin

Black people have resisted their white oppressors throughout American history — the most spectacular forms of black resistance being the conspiracies and rebellions which have surfaced from one generation to another. In 1822, the Denmark Vesey slave conspiracy was uncovered in Charleston, South Carolina;[1] one of the most extensive plots of all, it is still revered today by black militants. This reexamination of the Vesey affair focuses on the occupational backgrounds of the rebel participants and their leadership, the influence on the revolt of African cultural identity and the black revolution in Saint-Domingue, the position of white collaborators, the role of the house servant group, the complexity of the rebels' ideology, and the nature of the white reaction to the plot. In addition, the thesis recently put forward by Richard Wade, that "no conspiracy in fact existed," is critically analyzed.

South Carolina society seemed serene in the spring of 1822, yet beneath the surface there were signs of discontent. The 260,000 slaves who worked in the upcountry cotton fields and coastal rice swamps, a majority of the population, had long protested their enslavement, with a conspiracy in Camden, S.C., broken up as recently as 1816. The presence in Charleston of a free black community of 1475 persons was a bad example and a potential source of leadership for the slaves, who outnumbered whites by 12,652 to 10,653 in the city.[2] Beginning in 1815, several thousand free blacks and slaves had separated from the white Methodist church and established their own African Methodist Episcopal organization. This unprecedented act of religious self-determination outraged white officials, who arrested several hundred black leaders for illegally instructing slaves and in 1820 passed a new code prohibiting free blacks from entering the state, proscribing the manumission of slaves, and taxing and licensing black tradesmen generally.[3] Altogether, then, Charleston blacks — both free and slave — found themselves under considerable pressure.

In the winter of 1821–22, if the official sources are to be believed, Denmark Vesey — a free black carpenter — began organizing a slave uprising. He recruited lieutenants, established an urban organization, and travelled to outlying plantation districts to muster further support. Together with Monday Gell and Peter Poyas (two other important leaders) Vesey allegedly kept lists of the several hundred slaves recruited; and a slave blacksmith was employed to make bayonets and pikes (some of which were later found). Other rebels obtained daggers, swords, fuses, powder, and a few firearms. Painted disguises, wigs, and false whiskers were to be used. The city's draymen, carters, butchers, and liverymen were in charge of the horses for the rebel cavalry. The plantation slaves, hundreds of whom came to Charleston in canoes on weekends, were supposed to bring weapons. Vesey then wrote two letters asking assistance to Saint-Domingue, which were carried to a departing vessel by Gell and Perault Strohecker. In May 1822, Vesey set July 14, the darkest night of the month, for the commencement of the revolt. The plans were to capture arms, seize Charleston with a seven-pronged assault, kill most of the whites, and if necessary escape to the Caribbean or Africa. The rebels followed the Biblical dictum, "he that is not with me is against me."[4]

On May 25, William Paul, a slave of J. and D. Paul, attempted to recruit Peter Devany, the elderly personal servant of Colonel J. C. Prioleau, into the rebel group. However, Peter informed his mistress, her son, and a free black named William Pencil, who urged Peter to confide to his master the insurgents' plans. On May 30, Peter informed Colonel Prioleau of the suspected plot and was interrogated by Charleston authorities, led by Intendant James Hamilton, Jr., who immediately arrested the Paul slaves. The next day, William Paul implicated Peter Poyas and Mingo Harth, two slave artisans, who were arrested and questioned. However, they "behaved with so much composure and coolness, and treated the charge alleged against them with so much levity," according to the authorities, "that the Wardens were completely deceived and had these men discharged." Vesey now advanced the time for the rebellion to midnight June 16, and the leaders destroyed all records. In order further to deceive the whites, Ned Bennett, a personal servant of Governor Thomas Bennett, went "voluntarily to the Intendant, and solicited an examination, if he was an object of suspicion." He was also released.[5]

On June 8, William Paul made further disclosures, and on June 14, George Wilson, a slave used as a spy by the Charleston officials, learned the exact date of the uprising and that the African Church was one center of the plot. On June 15 and 16, whites deployed military forces at strategic points in the city, while Vesey and his lieutenants tried, unsuccessfully, to communicate with their rural supporters, and then went into hiding. The uprising never materialized, but between June 17 and 27, about two dozen more slaves were tried before a special court of magistrates and freeholders, and sentenced to death. On June 22, Vesey was captured at his wife's house, and tried and convicted the next day. He defended himself ably in court, challenging witnesses and disputing the charges against him, while Peter Poyas responded to the courts interrogation with only a "cryptic smile," and strengthened a fellow prisoner in jail, who was being tortured for information, by urging him to "Die like a man." Dignified and composed, Vesey was executed on July 2, along with Peter Poyas, Ned and Batteau Bennett, Jesse Blackwood, and Rolla Bennett, the last of whom confessed under coercion. From the gallows Poyas stated to black onlookers: "Do not open your lips; die silent, as you shall see me do!"[6]

Gullah Jack, an important African religious leader, was captured on July 5, after planning to rescue the imprisoned leaders to continue the revolt, and was executed a week later. Meanwhile, on July 10, Monday Gell and Perault Strohecker confessed under torture, and further arrests followed. The trials continued until July 26, when twenty-two more slaves were hanged — one of whom reportedly "went to the gallows laughing and bidding his acquaintances in the streets 'good bye.' " That brought the number of trials so far to well over a hundred, with a total of thirty-four executions. From August 3 through 8, another court held several trials, and William Garner, a rebel cavalry commander, was put to death. Then, in October, four white men were convicted of the misdemeanor of inciting slaves to rebellion, and were sentenced to prison terms and stiff fines.[7]

Concerning the participants, rebel recruits came mostly from the slave workers of Charleston and its environs. The conspirators were, according to the *Official Report of the Trials,* "principally confined to Negroes hired or working out, such as Carters, Draymen, Sawyers, Porters, Labourers, Stevidores, Mechanics, those employed in lumberyards, and in short to those who had certain alloted hours at their disposal." Others joined from the waterfront ricemills, one of which was owned by the Governor himself, while slaves from rice and cotton plantations adjoining the city and in a seventy-mile radius therefrom allegedly had been contacted.[8] That recruits came mainly from the urban, industrial slaves of Charleston casts great doubt on the assertion by some historians (like Richard Wade, whose findings will be criticized further below) that urban bondsmen and slave hirelings were more content and less rebellious than rural, plantation bondsmen.[9] Indeed, the evidence suggests that urban slaves were, despite their supposedly greater privileges and higher standard of living, at least as discontented as rural slaves.[10] No wonder whites were horrified when even their most trusted servants and apparently contented bondsmen were implicated in the plot.

In contrast to the common-laborer participants stood the rebel leadership, which consisted mainly of skilled urban slave artisans and religious leaders in the African Church. Peter Poyas, for example, "was a slave of great value, and for his colour, a first rate ship carpenter." Poyas enjoyed the "confidence of his master, in a remarkable degree, and had been treated with indulgence, liberality and kindness." Mingo Harth was a "mechanic," Tom Russell and Perault Strohecker were blacksmiths, while William Garner and Smart Anderson were draymen. Monday Gell was "a most excellent harness-maker," with his shop on Meeting Street. He could read and write "with great and equal facility." Gell was allegedly "much indulged and trusted by his master, his time and a large proportion of the profits of his labour were at his own disposal. He even kept his master's *arms* and sometimes his money." Other leaders were religious figures or deacons in the African Church. For instance, Gullah Jack — "a little man . . . with small hands and feet and large [black] whiskers" — was a "conjurer" who kept alive African religious traditions. "A decided majority of the Insurgents," according to the Court, "either did or had belonged to the African Congregation; amongst whom the inlistments were principally and successfully carried on."[11] Undoubtedly, slave artisans had through their work gained more spare time and geographical mobility, a greater sense of independence, and more education than most common workers, while religious figures were greatly respected by the black community. Moreover, artisans and preachers could articulate shared grievances more easily than most ordinary workers, whose rage at oppression was expressed mainly through action.[12]

Vesey himself was born either in Africa or the Caribbean around 1767. At the age of 14 he was transported and sold along with 390 other slaves from St. Thomas in the Virgin Islands to Cap Francois in Saint-Domingue by Captain Joseph Vesey, a Bermuda slavetrader. In 1782, Captain Vesey reacquired Denmark after he was declared "unsound and subject to epileptic fits;" the young slave worked on board Vesey's slave ship as a personal servant. The next year, Captain Vesey settled in Charleston, South Carolina, as a ship merchandiser and slave broker, with Denmark as his assistant. Then, in 1800, Denmark Vesey won a lottery jackpot of $1500, with which he purchased his freedom from his master for $600 and established himself as a carpenter with the rest of the money. By 1817, Denmark Vesey had several slave wives and children, was a member of the newly organized African Church, spoke a number of languages, and had become an artisan, with his carpentry shop near the center of Charleston. Vesey was "distinguished for great strength and activity. Among his colour he was always looked up to with awe and respect. His temper," according to whites, "was impetuous and domineering in the extreme."[13]

Combining an acute consciousness of the wrongness of slavery with charismatic organizational qualities, Vesey would rebuke blacks who acted submissively before whites, observing that all men were born equal. When answered by blacks that they were, after all, slaves, Vesey would sarcastically reply: "Then you deserve to remain slaves." He once had the opportunity to return to Africa with a colonizationist group, but he rejected it, according to one rebel, "because he wanted to stay and see what he could do for his fellow-creatures." Another conspirator reported that "Vesey said he was satisfied with his own condition, being free, but as all of his children were slaves, he wished to see what could be done for them."[14]

Like Vesey, many of the other leaders and followers could easily trace their heritage to their former African or Caribbean homelands. Since the overseas slave trade remained legal until 1808 and a great deal of illicit importing occurred thereafter, many of the participants were either native-born Africans or only first-generation Americans. Leaders like Monday Gell, an Ebo, Gullah Jack, an Angolan, and Mingo Harth, a Mandingo, hailed from Africa or the Caribbean. Similarly, the rebel Perault Strohecker "was born at Jumba in Africa, about a weeks travel from Goree. . . . Perault was engaged in three battles against the people of Hassou [and]

. . . also fought twice against the people of Darrah, but in the second battle he was taken prisoner and . . . brought to Charleston in a Brig. . . . He is very tenacious," noted his master, "whenever he conceives that he is right."[15] Certainly, these Africans had not been as acculturated to South Carolina society as those born in the United States, and their consciousness of previous cultural identity and national independence was a source of dissidence.

The extent of white involvement is an interesting aspect of the Vesey plot, for whites were — as in other revolts, like Gabriel's and Turner's — suspected of collaboration with blacks. The Charleston authorities never proved that whites actually engaged in the planning of the insurrection, but once rumors about the revolt began to spread, some whites apparently encouraged blacks to rebel. Eventually, four white men were tried for the misdemeanor of "inciting slaves to insurrection," a non-capital offense.[16] Three of these four whites were poor, European immigrants (among whom were a Scottish sailor, a Spanish seaman, and a German peddler) — suggestive of the depths of South Carolina's xenophobia — while the fourth man was not a native of the state. However, though the blacks were condemned to death or deportation, the whites received only prison terms and fines, which in two cases may have amounted to life imprisonment, since they were too poor to pay the fines. William Allen was the most interesting of the whites, for when he conspired with the blacks he declared, according to the Court, "that there ought to be an indiscriminate destruction of all the whites, men, women, and children." However, the blacks "objected . . . that he (Allen) being a white man, could not be safely trusted by them." To this charge, Allen replied that "though he had a white face, he was a negro in heart."[17]

The surviving evidence also reveals somewhat unexpected information about those blacks who informed against conspiracies. Though popular mythology holds that the so-called "house nigger" group usually betrayed revolts, in this instance the informers came from various backgrounds. To be sure, Peter Devany, the elderly slave of John C. Prioleau, William, the slave of J. and D. Paul, and Rolla Bennett, who later confessed, were trusted domestic servants. But William Pencil, another informer, was a skilled, free-black tin-plate worker; George, the spy belonging to the Wilson family, was a blacksmith and religious leader in the African Church; and Monday Cell and Perault Strohecker, both of whom turned state's evidence, were skilled artisans.[18] It is also true that one rebel leader warned recruits not to reveal plans "to those waiting men who receive presents of old coats, etc., from their masters, or they'll betray us." But other leaders seemed willing to rely on trustworthy house servants to steal arms, slit their masters' throats, or to poison the city's water wells; and even some of the Governor's personal servants were involved. So incendiary did whites regard these individual acts of sabotage by house servants that references to poisoning wells were deleted from printed records.[19] Perhaps a revision of the treacherous role assigned to house servants is in order, since they suffered, despite their privileges, a special oppression which could sometimes result in rebellion.

Compared to other insurrections the Vesey Plot achieved an extraordinarily rich ideology. Beyond a general hatred of whites, Vesey combined the Old Testament's harsh morality and the story of the Israelites with African religious customs, knowledge of the Haitian Revolution of 1793–1804, and readings from antislavery speeches from the debates in Congress during 1819–21 over the admission of Missouri as a slave state. According to one conspirator, Vesey "read to us from the Bible how the Children of Israel were delivered out of Egypt from bondage." Vesey's favorite Biblical verses were apparently from Exodus, Zachariah, and Joshua: "Behold the day of the Lord cometh, and thy spoil shall be divided in the midst of thee. For I shall gather all nations against Jerusalem to battle; and the city shall be taken. . . . And they utterly destroyed all that was in the city, both man and woman, young and old, and ox, and sheep, and ass, with the edge of the sword." Concerning Vesey's recruiting methods, another rebel testified that "he was in the habit of reading to me all the passages in the newspapers that related to St. Domingo, and apparently every pamphlet he could lay his hands on that had any connection with slavery. He one day brought me," the black continued, "a speech which he told me had been delivered in Congress by a Mr. King on the subject of slavery [referring to Rufus King, antislavery congressman from New York]; he told me this Mr. King was the black man's friend, that he, Mr. King, had declared that slavery was a great disgrace to the country." Several rebels testified "that Congress had made us free," and believed — with an internationalist perspective — "that St. Domingo and Africa would come over and cut up the white people if only we made the motion here first." Gullah Jack provided recruits with African religious symbols, such as crab claws ("cullahs"), parched corn, and ground nuts, which would guarantee safety and victory. Blacks believed that they would be invulnerable if they retained these charms, and that Gullah Jack himself could neither be "killed, shot or taken." Monday Gell may have written twice to the Haitians in order to obtain assistance or refuge, for it was "unhesitatingly stated to Monday's face, that he had written two letters to St. Domingo, and [given] them in charge of a black cook on board of a schooner bound to that island." After this accusation, Gell "confessed that the fact was so." It is also possible that Vesey planned, if the need arose, to escape to Haiti or to Africa. Consciousness of the African homeland was certainly revealed when Vesey chose not to return there several years before the revolt and when one rebel after his conviction "at his own request was transported to Africa on board of a vessel which sailed from Charleston."[20] Indeed, few other slave revolts, except for the Haitian Revolution itself, developed such a high level of political and cultural consciousness as a revolutionary impetus.[21]

The repression of the conspiracy by white authorities was, of course, severe. The trials took place in a small room in the same building where the prisoners were confined. The public was barred from the courtroom and blacks were not allowed within two blocks of the building. Troops guarded the prison and court day and night to prevent blacks from freeing prisoners and continuing the conspiracy. The trial procedure was far from equitable: owners and counsel were present, but defendants could not confront those witnesses who gave testimony under a pledge of secrecy. Thus, four out of five witnesses against Rolla Bennett were anonymous, and the fifth was a slaveowner. The court permitted hearsay evidence without objection, and attorneys often did not bother to cross-examine those witnesses who testified openly. There was no jury; only a majority of the magistrates was necessary for conviction. Little evidence bears on the extent of the torture of prisoners, but even Governor Bennett admitted publicly that "no means which experience or ingenuity could devise were left unessayed, to eviscerate the plot."[22] Bennett and Johnson objected that these procedures were so unfair as to endanger valuable slave property, and the court later admitted that it had departed "in many essential features, from the principles of common law, and some of the settled rules of evidence."[23] However, since blacks were involved, Attorney General Robert Y. Hayne ruled that the procedures were justified. So the trials continued.

Moreover, the purpose of the trials clearly was not only to ferret out and punish slave conspirators but also to terrorize and pacify the rest of the black community. "The terror of example we thought would be sufficiently operative by the number of criminals sentenced to death," explained the magistrates. Governor Bennett conceded that the death sentences were intended "to produce a salutary terror."[24] Altogether thirty-five blacks were executed, many in a mass hanging toward the end of July; more than forty others were deported from the state. Many awaiting deportation were still incarcerated in the workhouse as late as the beginning of 1823; others received public whippings. Those sentenced to death were hung publicly before crowds of spectators, and reportedly "their bodies [were] to be delivered to the surgeons for dissection, if requested." To complete the "terror of example," the black community was prevented from dressing in black or wearing dark crêpe to mourn its dead.[25]

In order to promote "proper" behavior by blacks in the future, the original informers received substantial rewards from the state legislature in the fall of 1822. The owners of Peter Devany and George Wilson were authorized to emancipate their slaves. The betrayers received life-time annuities and exemption from taxation. The assembly then granted William Pencil, the free black who had counseled Peter to inform, $1,000 outright. Scott, a free black who had implicated a white man, received a $500 award. Of course, the owners of banished slaves also gained compensation for the loss of their human chattel.[26]

In repressing the Vesey plot virtually all white Charlestonians reacted with almost uncontrolled hysteria, indicating the pathological dimensions of the "mind of the Old South." The white community seemed gripped by fear for over two months, no one doubted at the time that the blacks actually intended to rebel, and the panic persisted through the fall legislative session and beyond. Even Governor Bennett and his brother-in-law, United States Supreme Court Justice William Johnson, both of whom deplored the panic and criticized the repressive procedures of the authorities, believed that a plot did in fact exist and became somewhat hysterical themselves.[27] Bennett secretly communicated with Secretary of War John C. Cal-

houn to request federal reinforcements for local garrisons; Calhoun complied by
shifting troops from Savannah and St. Augustine to the Charleston area.[28] Thus,
the military preparations; the numbers of arrests, deportations, and executions; the
harsh punishments; and the fears expressed privately by many whites — all indicate
the magnitude of the hysteria.

The fear of servile retribution and of so-called sexual "transgressions" were
prominent themes in both private and public utterances during the Vesey affair, just
as they had been in earlier crises. Most of all, slaveowners feared their "indiscriminate slaughter" and the rape and "prostitution" of white women by the black
insurgents. A Charleston businessman, for example, disclosed that "the females
were to be reserved for *worse than death*," while a Baltimore newsweekly reported
that a slave of Governor Bennett "was to have had his daughter, a beautiful young
lady, as part of his share of the spoils."[29] Even young Anna Johnson (whose father
was urging public calm) believed that "we poor devils were to have been reserved
to fill their Harams — horrible — I have a very beautiful cousin," she added, repeating the rumor abut Bennett's daughter, "who was set apart for the wife or more
properly the 'light of the Haram' of one of their Chiefts. . . ."[30]

Though some had already achieved notoriety, politicians manipulated the hysteria (which they had also created and promoted) for their own political purposes.
By the fall of 1822, James Hamilton, Jr., the zealous mayor-prosecutor, was elected
to the United States House of Representatives. Robert Y. Hayne, commander of
the troops and attorney general, was chosen United States Senator. And John L.
Wilson, owner of a slave informer, became Governor. By comparison, Bennett left
the Governor's office in disrepute, and had his report on the conspiracy tabled by
a legislature hostile to criticism of the means used to repress blacks. Justice Johnson
was denounced throughout the state for his dissenting view that the hysteria was
unwarranted; eventually he was hounded from the state because of his opposition
to nullification in 1833.[31] In general, the policies of the fanatical racists triumphed
over those of the liberal politicians in the suppression of the Vesey Conspiracy.

After an event with such awesome implications for the future of slavery, it was
natural for whites to search for the causes of the plot and to enact "reforms" to
forestall further insurrections and preserve the "domestic tranquility" of the state.
Most whites blamed the Vesey Conspiracy on the Haitian Revolution, the antislavery movement, black religion and education, the influence of free blacks and slave
artisans, and the indulgence of urban slaves by naïve masters. One Charleston
businessman, for example, attributed the plot to black meetings "held under the
perfidious cover of religion. . . aided by black missionaries" from the North.
"When your kind and tender-hearted Philadelphians, as well as Quakers, preach
up emancipation," he warned, "let them *ponder* on the deeds of darkness and misery
that would have taken place had this plot even in part succeeded." Similarly, a
Savannah woman blamed the black societies for the "wildest plans engendered by
religious enthusiasm and a wrong conception of the Bible." Congressman Joel R.
Poinsett's personal belief that the Missouri debates "produced" the plot and the

Charleston *City Gazette's* fear of "the Missouri poison" were supported by the Columbia *South Carolina State Gazette's* conclusion that "extracts of speeches on the Missouri question were calculated to promote insurrection." Chancellor Henry W. Desaussure feared, along with others, that South Carolina's "vicinity to the West Indian Islands, and the great intercourse with them, must introduce among our people many of those who have been engaged in scenes of blood in the West Indies, who will beguile our slaves into rebellion with false hopes and idle expectations."[32]

Many reform-minded whites were concerned that masters had indulged their slaves and had been lax in discipline. Charleston Intendant James Hamilton, Jr., noted that Vesey's followers, "without scarcely an exception, had no individual hardship to complain of, and were among the most humanely treated negroes in our city." The Court reported that the rebels not only had time at their disposal, but had been "indulged in every comfort, and allowed every privilege compatible with their situation in the community [and] *not one [was] of bad character.*" Hamilton attributed Vesey's actions to "a malignant hatred of the whites, and inordinate lust of power and booty." But, the New York *National Advocate* and *Niles' Weekly Register* repeated the charges of overindulgence. The latter journal "admitted" that "the slaves have a *natural right* to obtain their liberty, if they can, . . . and the *necessity* of the whites to prevent them from obtaining it." Significantly, no Southerner could admit that slavery, even in its most privileged form, was an oppressive institution which inevitably led to rebellion. Only the New York *Advertiser* condemned bondage on humanitarian grounds and approached an understanding of the actual reasons for insurrection. "It ought to excite no astonishment with those who boast of freedom themselves, if they should occasionally hear of plots and desertion among those who are held in perpetual bondage," remarked the northern editor. "Human beings, who once breathed the air of freedom in their own mountains and in their own valleys, but who have been kidnapped by white men and dragged into endless slavery, cannot be expected to be contented with their situation."[33]

After analyzing the causes of the conspiracy, Carolinians proposed several reforms intended to control blacks more effectively. While Governor Bennett urged whites to comply with the patrol laws, Chancellor Desaussure favored having the slave codes made more "humane" and strictly enforced. Slaves should be confined to agricultural pursuits, black artisans should be prohibited from cities, and bondsmen should be kept in ignorance and denied separate places for worship. Desaussure's proposal to teach both masters and slaves the "mild doctrines of the Gospel" was supported by the Reverend Richard Furman, a leading southern Baptist, who argued that the Scriptures were not inherently subversive. "Instead of taking away the Bible from blacks, and abridging the truly religious Privileges they have been used to enjoy, to avoid Danger," Furman advised Bennett, "the better Way would be to take Measures for bringing them to a more full and just acquaintance with the former; and secure to them the latter, under Regulations the least liable to abuse." One Savannahan's proposal to banish to the countryside "Huxters, day labourers, draymen, and all that useless class of servants who are only a tax to their owners and a nuisance to the city" was seconded by the editor of the Charleston *Times* who branded blacks "the *Jacobins* of the country. . . the *anarchists* and the *domestic* enemy; the *common enemy of civilized society,* and the barbarians who would, if they could, become the destroyers of *our race.*" In addition to banishing free blacks — "the greatest and most deplorable evil" — Charleston petitioners urged the legislature to restrict the practice of hiring out, require supervision of slave mechanics by their masters, regulate the mode of black dress, forbid the teaching of reading and writing to slaves, and control the holding of real property, living arrangements, and the importing of slaves from the middle Atlantic states. A regular military force for Charleston and stronger penalties for white involvement in slave plots were also demanded.[34]

In December of 1822, the state legislature responded to these proposals by strengthening the black code. It forbade blacks leaving the state ever to return, placed a stiff fifty-dollar-a-year tax on free blacks and required them and mulattoes to have guardians, prohibited slave self-hiring, made white participation in insurrections a capital felony, and provided for the detention in jail of black seamen while in South Carolina ports. In effect, therefore, the reform of the black code meant heavier repression of the black community, for as Intendant Hamilton reported: "There can be no harm in the salutary inculcation of one lesson among a *certain* portion of our population, that there is nothing they are bad enough to do, that we are not powerful enough to punish."[35]

In 1964, Richard Wade published an analysis of the Vesey affair which reached the major conclusion that "no conspiracy in fact existed." On the basis of an appraisal of the trial record Wade argued that there were serious inconsistencies and "deliberate" discrepancies in the rebel testimony so that "little confidence can be placed in the authenticity of the official account." Wade concluded that the plot was "at most . . . a vague and unformulated plan in the minds or on the tongues of a few colored townsmen." But, "no elaborate network had been established in the countryside; no cache of arms lay hidden about the city; no date for an uprising had been set; [and] no underground apparatus, carefully organized and secretly maintained, awaited a signal to fire Charleston and murder the whites." A general urban insurrection was less likely than a rural one, according to Wade, because city blacks enjoyed greater freedom than plantation hands. Moreover, Wade stressed the skepticism about the extent of the conspiracy on the part of whites like the Johnson family and Governor Bennett; their disbelief contrasted with the hysterical reaction by other Charlestonians, suggesting that the conspiracy really existed more in white minds than in black planning. "What did exist," according to Wade, "were strong grievances on one side and deep fears on the other. . . . But as word of [the plot's] scope spread, public shock turned into hysteria. . . . Thus Charleston stumbled into tragedy. The 'Plot' was probably never more than loose talk by aggrieved and embittered men."[36] However, it is possible seriously to criticize Wade's use of evidence and to refute his conclusions.

Methodological problems do arise in assessing the reliability of the evidence surviving from the plot — all of which derives either from terrorized blacks or fearful whites. The trial testimony came largely from several witnesses who desired to escape death, to direct attention away from themselves, or only confessed under extreme duress. William Paul, for example, was kept in solitary confinement for nine days until he incriminated other slaves, while other suspects were chained in separate cells to prevent communication among them. Monday Gell, Charles Drayton, and Harry Haig confessed only after being sentenced to death and then promised clemency if they cooperated; they implicated and testified against other rebels, and were deported instead of executed as a reward. Such commutation was denied, however, to other confessors like Rolla Bennett.[37] Given the savagery of white retaliation against the rebels, therefore, the trial testimony must be used cautiously.

Concerning the printed trial record, the Court stated that "the evidence [was] in most cases preserved as it was originally taken, without even changing the phraseology, which was generally in the very words used by the witnesses. . . . it was thought adviseable to lay before the public the whole narrative, as it was given by the witnesses, *and not to suppress any part of it.*" Even though the whole trial record was edited by the magistrates before publication, a line-by-line comparison between the manuscript version of the trials (in the South Carolina Department of Archives and History) and the printed account reveals that the Court's statement was accurate. Some reorganization of evidence occurred, but the Court did not change any testimony, contrary to Wade's thesis, except for the deletion of a few sentences referring to the poisoning of water wells.[38] Wade notes discrepancies between the manuscript confessions by Bacchus Hammett and John Enslow and the printed version of their testimony. However, these manuscript confessions need not be identical to the printed record (or to the manuscript version for that matter), since the confessions were taken in jail before they were reiterated or read in court for the record.[39] In any event, Wade is not entitled to dismiss the authenticity of the trial record entirely, just because it disparages the conspirators and contains minor inconsistencies.

Concerning Wade's charge about lack of rebel planning, the caliber of the leadership and their discipline of silence over their recruits suggests that there is no reason why the rebels should have disclosed their full plan of action to the court, even under coercion. Since the magistrates admitted that only a minority of participants had been detected,[40] why should those arrested have revealed the whole scheme when there was still a possibility of those at large beginning the revolt? Besides, the complete plans were probably known only to a few top leaders, most of whom denied complicity or died without disclosing any information. Even the "vague" plans uncovered were sufficient to seize the city had the revolt actually occurred.

Though Vesey may have been unable to create an "elaborate" rural network, where communications were difficult, he probably had mustered enough plantation support to carry out the plans.[41] Regarding the urban underground, where communications were easier, the fact that several score of blacks were convicted points to a city organization adequate to begin a rebellion, not counting those recruits who remained undetected by the authorities and those blacks who might have joined in once the uprising began.

The absence of a cache of arms may be explained by the refusal of defendants to divulge such information or by the fact that there were places to conceal arms in the black community where whites would never find them. Also, the rebels intended to capture the necessary arms by surprise attacks on homes, stores, and arsenals. The lack of rosters of names can be explained on similar grounds, as well as by the fact that each leader was supposed to keep track of his own recruits — a point further verified when many of the accused denied knowing each other.[42] Such organizing-by-groups suggests, moreover, the extensiveness of the plot rather than, as Wade maintains, its non-existence, and, in any event, the rebel leadership had sufficient time to destroy their records and secrete their arms, since Peter Poyas and Mingo Harth were temporarily released, while Vesey and Gullah Jack remained at large for several days.

Since several blacks testified that Vesey had set July 14 for the commencement of the insurrection and then advanced it to June 16 after the initial arrests, Wade's argument that no date had been set seems to be a misreading of the evidence; he certainly errs when he mentions July 2 as the date for the plot, when the testimony clearly states it was the *second* Monday in July. Indeed, what is most striking about the trial testimony as a whole is the wealth of detail about the rebels' plans, the coincidence of names disclosed, and the correspondence of places, times, numbers, dates, and other specific information divulged by different witnesses. All of this testimony therefore points more to common knowledge by blacks of the reality of a conspiracy than to evidence deliberately manufactured by whites caught up in an unfounded panic.[43]

The skepticism about the plot, the fear of uncontrolled white hysteria, and the concern about illiberal persecution of blacks expressed publicly and privately by Justice Johnson, Anna Johnson, and Governor Bennett proves exactly the opposite of Wade's contentions. Such evidence demonstrates that, like other whites, the Johnsons and Bennett emphatically believed that a conspiracy existed, even though they questioned its extent and the court's means of uncovering it.[44] In other words, contrary to Wade's assertions, no white Charlestonian at the time, including those with a vested interest in skepticism, thought that the conspiracy was just "loose talk." Wade himself even concedes that Bennett "probably believed in a plot of some kind," and according to William Freehling, who carefully examined all of the sources,

Bennett believed that a serious conspiracy was afoot, but he doubted that it involved more than eighty Negroes and questioned whether it ever came close to being consummated. . . . "In my judgment," concludes Freehling, "Bennett's position, but not Wade's, is consistent with all the evidence. While the terrorized community exaggerated the extent of the danger, there was, in fact, a conspiracy worth getting excited about."[45]

Wade's final claims — that "a concerted revolt against slavery was actually less likely in a city than in the country," because urban blacks enjoyed (relative to plantation slaves) better treatment, higher living standards, "modest advantages," "a measure of independence within bondage," and "comparative freedom," while they lacked "great numerical superiority," all of which "deflected their discontent" — can be criticized on several grounds. Many urban rebellions or conspiracies occurred before Vesey's attempt; the New York City insurrection of 1712 and the Gabriel Plot near Richmond, Virginia, in 1800, for example, suggest that urban uprisings were as "likely" as rural ones. Though blacks only slightly outnumbered whites in the city of Charleston, in the surrounding plantation districts the black-white ratio of about ten to one was favorable to slaves overpowering their masters. White urban guards may have been a better deterrent than rural patrols, but for black rebels communication and organization were less difficult in cities than between outlying plantations. The living conditions and treatment of urban house servants and slave artisans may have been superior to those for rural field hands,[46] but the bulk of urban day-laborers and factory slaves were, according to my own research on "industrial slavery," no more comfortable in terms of food, clothing, shelter, and working conditions than plantation bondsmen. Since urban slaves attempted to escape as frequently (proportional to their numbers) as rural slaves, city slaves seemed to feel as oppressed as their rural counterparts.[47] Even if some urban slaves received comparatively greater privileges, as Wade contends, they did not necessarily feel less oppressed, for as the fugitive slave Peter Randolph recalled, urban slavery "as seen here by the casual observer might be supposed not to be so hard as one would imagine. . . . But Slavery is *Slavery,* wherever it is found." This slave's explanation seems sufficient reason for a conspiracy to develop which has been termed "one of the most courageous ever to threaten the racist foundations of America."[48]

Notes

[1] Previous discussions of the Vesey Conspiracy include: Thomas Wentworth Higginson, "Denmark Vesey," *Atlantic Monthly,* 7 (June 1861), 728–744; Joseph C. Carroll, *Slave Insurrections in the United States, 1800–1865* (Boston, 1938); Herbert Aptheker, *American Negro Slave Revolts* (New York, 1943); John M. Lofton, *Insurrection in South Carolina* (Yellow Springs, Ohio, 1964); Richard Wade, "The Vesey Plot: A Reconsideration," *Journal of Southern History,* 30 (May 1964), 143–161; William W. Freehling, *Prelude to Civil War* (New York,

1966), 53–61; Sterling Stuckey, "Remembering Denmark Vesey," *Negro Digest,* 15 (Feb. 1966), 28–41.

² Richard Wade, *Slavery in the Cities* (New York, 1964), appendix.

³ Lofton, *Insurrection in South Carolina,* pp. 81–94, 133. Act of 1820, in *House Reports,* #80, 27 U.S. Congress, 3 session, Jan. 20, 1843.

⁴ Lionel H. Kennedy and Thomas Parker, eds., *An Official Report of the Trials of Sundry Negroes, Charged with an Attempt to Raise an Insurrection in the State of South-Carolina* (Charleston, Oct. 22, 1822), pp. 17–60, 82, which follows in most respects a manuscript version of the trial record in the South Carolina Department of Archives and History, Columbia, S.C. (SCA, hereafter).

⁵ *Ibid.*

⁶ *Ibid.*

⁷ *Ibid.*

⁸ *Ibid.*

⁹ Wade, "Vesey Plot," pp. 157–161.

¹⁰ Robert Starobin, *Industrial Slavery in the Old South, 1790–1861* (New York, Oxford Univ. Press, 1970), ch. 3.

¹¹ *Official Report,* pp. 41–44, 104; James Hamilton, Jr., *An Account of the Late Intended Insurrection Among a Portion of the Blacks of This City. . . .* (Charleston, August 16, 1822), p. 21.

¹² Robert Starobin, ed., *Slavery As It Was: The Testimony of the Slaves Themselves While in Bondage* (Chicago, Quadrangle Books, 1971), part I.

¹³ *Official Report,* pp. 19, 42–43, 87–88, 95.

¹⁴ *Ibid.*

¹⁵ *Ibid.,* p. 110 and *passim.* This is in contrast to Gerry Mullin's finding that the leaders of the Gabriel Plot near Richmond in 1800 were apparently highly assimilated to Virginia society; however, the character of the leaders of the Vesey episode confirms Melville Herskovits' conclusion in *The Myth of the Negro Past* (Boston, 1941, 1958), ch. 4 and 5 that the African heritage contributed to New World slave protests.

¹⁶ *Official Report,* appendix.

¹⁷ *Ibid.,* appendix, p. iv.

¹⁸ *Ibid., passim.*

¹⁹ *Ibid.,* pp. 75, 107, compared to manuscript version of the trial record in the SCA. On the oppression of domestic servants, see Albert Memmi, *Dominated Man* (Boston, 1969), ch. 13.

²⁰ *Official Report,* pp. 18, 62, 64, 67, 75, 87–88, 96, 103, 118, 163; Hamilton, *An Account,* p. 41.

²¹ C. L. R. James, *The Black Jacobins* (New York, 1963).

²² Lofton, *Insurrection in South Carolina, passim; Official Report, passim;* Bennett letter in Washington, D.C., *Daily National Intelligencer,* August 24, 1822.

²³ Thomas Bennett to L. H. Kennedy and Thos. Parker, Charleston, July 1, 1822, in *Official Report,* pp. 70–71; Charleston *Courier,* June 21, 1822; *Official Report,* p. vi.

²⁴ Lionel H. Kennedy, *et al.,* to Governor Thomas Bennett, Charleston, July 24, 1822, in Governor's Message #2, November 28, 1822, Document F, page 2; Thomas Bennett, Message #2 to the state legislature, November 28, 1822 (SCA).

²⁵ Charleston *Courier,* July 27, 1822; Charleston *Mercury,* December 25, 1822; "A Colored American," *The Late Contemplated Insurrection in Charleston, S.C.* (New York, 1850).

²⁶ Charleston *Mercury,* December 25, 1822.

²⁷ Hamilton, *An Account,* preface; public letter by Governor Thomas Bennett, Charleston, S.C., August 10, 1822, in Washington, D.C., *Daily National Intelligencer,* August 24, 1822; Governor Bennett's unpublished Message #2, November 28, 1822, to the state legisla-

156   The Vesey Plot: Conflicting Interpretations

ture (SCA). [William Johnson], "The Melancholy Effect of Popular Excitement," Charleston *Courier,* June 21, 1822; William Johnson, *To the Public of Charleston* (Charleston, July 4, 1822).

[28] Governor Thomas Bennett to Secretary of War John C. Calhoun, Charleston, S.C., July 15 and 30, 1822; Secretary of War John C. Calhoun to Colonel A. Eustis, and to Major James Bankhead, Washington, D.C., July 22, 1822, Secretary of War Papers (National Archives, Washington, D.C.).

[29] John Potter to Langdon Cheves, Charleston, July 10, 1822, Cheves Papers (South Carolina Historical Society, Charleston, S.C.); cf. letters of June 29, July 5, 16, and 20, 1822. *Niles' Weekly Register,* 22 (July 13, 1822), 320, and 23 (Sept. 14, 1822), 18. cf. Winthrop Jordan, *White Over Black: American Attitudes Toward the Negro, 1550–1812* (Baltimore, 1969).

[30] Anna Hayes Johnson to Elizabeth Haywood, Charleston, S.C., June 23, 1822, Haywood Papers; cf. letters of July 18, 24, and 27, 1822, and Martha P. Richardson to James P. Screven, Savannah, Ga., July 6, Aug. 7, and Sept. 16, 1822, Arnold-Screven Papers (University of North Carolina Library, Chapel Hill, N.C.).

[31] Charleston *Mercury,* Dec. 4, 10, 11, 1822; Donald G. Morgan, *Justice William Johnson* (Columbia, S.C., 1954).

[32] John Potter to Langdon Cheves, Charleston, June 29 and July 10, 1822, Cheves Papers (South Carolina Historical Society); Martha P. Richardson to nephew, Savannah, Ga., July 6 and Aug. 7, 1822, Arnold-Screven Papers (University of North Carolina Library); Joel R. Poinsett to James Monroe, Charleston, August 13, 1822, Monroe Papers (Library of Congress); Columbia *South Carolina State Gazette,* Sept. 7, 1822; Charleston *City Gazette,* Aug. 14, 1822; Henry W. Desaussure to Joel R. Poinsett, Columbia, S.C., July 6, 1822, Poinsett Papers (Historical Society of Pennsylvania, Philadelphia); Anna Johnson to cousin, Charleston, July 18, 1822, Haywood Papers (University of North Carolina Library).

[33] Hamilton, *An Account,* p. 2; *Official Report,* p. 41; New York *National Advocate,* quoted in Washington *National Intelligencer,* July 20, 1822; *Niles' Register,* 23 (Sept. 14, 1822), 18; Salem, Mass., *Gazette,* Jan. 10, 1823; New York *Daily Advertiser,* July 31, Aug. 6, 1822.

[34] Public Letter by Governor Bennett, August 10, 1822; "A Columbian" [Chancellor Henry W. Desaussure], *A Series of Numbers Addressed to the Public on the Subject of the Slaves and Free People of Colour* (Columbia, Sept.–Oct. 1822); the Reverend Richard Furman to Governor Thomas Bennett, n.d., [ca. Autumn 1822]; Furman Papers (South Carolinian Library, University of South Carolina, Columbia); cf. *The Reverend Richard Furman's Exposition of the Views of the Baptists, Relative to the Coloured Population of the United States* (Charleston, 1823); Martha P. Richardson to nephew, Savannah, Aug. 7, 1822, Arnold-Screven Papers; E. C. Holland, *A Refutation of the Calumnies Circulated Against the Southern and Western States* (Charleston, Oct. 29, 1822); Memorial of the Citizens of Charleston to the Senate and House of Representatives of the State of South Carolina, Nov. 1822, in U. B. Phillips, ed., *Plantation and Frontier Documents* (Cleveland, 1909), vol. II, pp. 103–116; cf. [Thomas Pinckney], *Reflections, Occasioned by the Late Disturbances in Charleston. By Achates* (Charleston, Nov. 4, 1822); the Reverend Frederick Dalcho, *Practical Considerations Founded on the Scriptures Relative to the Slave Population of South Carolina* (Charleston, 1823).

[35] An Act for the Better Regulation and Government of Free Negroes and Persons of Color, in *House Reports,* #80, 27 U.S. Congress, 3 session, Jan. 20, 1843, pp. 21–23; Hamilton, *An Account,* p. 1.

[36] Wade, "Vesey Plot," pp. 143–161; Wade, *Slavery in the Cities,* 228–241.

[37] *Official Report, passim.*

[38] *Ibid.,* pp. iii–iv; original manuscript version of the trial in the SCA.

[39] Wade, "Vesey Plot," 155–156; Confessions of Bacchus Hammet and John Enslow, Hammett Papers (Duke University Library Durham, N.C.) compared to *Official Report* and original manuscript version of the trial record in the SCA.

[40] *Official Report,* pp. 25, 27, 48, 59.

[41] *Ibid.,* pp. 27–31.

[42] *Ibid., passim.*

[43] Robert Starobin, ed., *Denmark Vesey: The Slave Conspiracy of 1822* (Englewood Cliffs, N.J., Prentice-Hall, Inc., 1970), introduction and afterword.

[44] Charleston *Courier,* June 21, 1822; Washington D.C., *Daily National Intelligencer,* August 24, 1822; Anna Hayes Johnson to Elizabeth Haywood, June 23, July 18, 24, 27, 1822, Haywood Papers (University of North Carolina Library); Governor's Message #2, Nov. 28, 1822, to state legislature (SCA); William Johnson to Secretary of State John Quincy Adams, Charleston, July 3, 1824, in *House Reports,* #80, 27 U.S. Congress, 3 session, 1843, pp. 14–15.

[45] Wade, "Vesey Plot," pp. 150, 160, 153; Freehling, *Prelude to Civil War,* pp. 53–54, note 6.

[46] Robert Starobin, "Privileged Bondsmen and the Process of Accommodation," unpublished paper, 1969.

[47] Starobin, *Industrial Slavery,* ch. 2 and 3.

[48] Peter Randolph, *Sketches of Slave Life* (Boston, 1855), 58–59. Stuckey, "Remembering Denmark Vesey," p. 41.

New Approaches

4

Religion, Acculturation, and American Negro Slave Rebellions: Gabriel's Insurrection

Gerry Mullin

In the summer of 1800 a group of slave artisans organized an attack on Richmond.[1] Because their plan was essentially an expression of their class and its understanding of the values and norms of the American Revolutionary era, the rebellion was exceptionally political in character. Gabriel's Insurrection never took place. The following essay is divided into a narrative conveying the conspiracy's meaning for its participants, and an examination of its preconditions and setting, in order to illuminate the sources of its failure.[2]

"A Society to Fight the White People for [Our] Freedom "

At the gallows in Richmond, Friday noon, 12 September 1800, Colonel John Mayo questioned the slaves who were awaiting execution for their part in Gabriel's Rebellion. Mayo asked about his own slave George, a fugitive and a waitingman, who was implicated in the conspiracy. This man was a very special type of slave whose most distinguishing physical and psychological characteristics had been described in a newspaper advertisement:

One Hundred and Fifty Doll[ar]s

R E W A R D
For stopping the Villain ! ! !
RAN-AWAY on the 25th of July last from the subscriber, near this city

GEORGE

A likely stout made mulatto man, 24 or 25 years of age, five feet eight or nine inches, with a conspicuous [sc]ar under his left jaw, occasioned b[y] a defective tooth, a large scar on the back of his right hand from the cut of a knife — and a small one inclining obliquely downwards, in the middle of his forehead, occasioned by some accident when a child — stutters a little when about to speak, a bushy head of hair, — legs rather small from the constant use of boots, and of sulky looks and temper, except when he chooses to force a deceitful smile —— He has served an apprenticeship to the barber's trade, — knows a little of shoemaking, and is, when he pleases, a very complete domestic servant.

—— As he has several times travelle[d] with me into the Northern states, it is possible he may obtain a forged certificate of freedom, and endeavour to go that way.

As a fugitive and insurrectionist, Mayo's George typifies the men who participated in Gabriel's Rebellion — born in Virginia, not Africa; highly assimilated, well-traveled, and versatile in a variety of skilled tasks.

Mayo also asked about his friend and neighbor William Young, whose slaves instigated the rebellion. Although Young was merely negligent (it was necessary for him to publicly defend himself in the Richmond newspapers), his actions called in question the practices of other slaveowners, who on this count were equally as guilty. This carelessness was indicative of the permissive, confused, and disordered state of slavery in Virginia in the final years of the eighteenth century: careless and permissive because whites usually ignored such critical features of the slave code as the system of written passes for slaves who traveled, prohibitions against selling to slaves, and the supervision of their gatherings. Slavery was also in a confused and indecisive state, because in this period of revolutionary and religious idealism reform ameliorated the slave's condition, but seldom made him a free man. Such examples of "humanitarianism" as the liberalized manumission procedure, a restricted slave trade, and the encouragement of the sale of slaves in families (mothers and their children only) did not placate some slaves. Governor James Monroe's remarks to the Governor of South Carolina were representative of the slaveowners' misconceptions about the effects of liberalizing slavery without abolishing it outright. "It seemed strange that the slaves should embark in this novel and unexampled enterprise," Monroe reported, "for their treatment has been more favorable since the revolution." Indeed the most puzzling and ominous development for whites was that the conspirators were the same type of relatively highly advantaged men who in the past had seen slavery as an individual problem and typically resisted it as solitary fugitives passing as free men. With this avenue of escape and freedom as accessible as ever before, why, they asked, did this class of slaves turn, organize, and fight for their freedom in 1800? As John Mayo rode slowly back into Richmond pondering this "strange" and "novel enterprise" of a few very unusual slaves, we can imagine that he was preoccupied with questions such as these.

Six miles northeast of the city, two months earlier, late evening 10 July, one of these slaves stood before a woodpile, axe in hand. He was Ben Woolfolk, a shrewdly intelligent man, hired out to William Young. George Smith, one of the conspiracy's most active recruiters, stepped from the scrubby pine woods and asked Woolfolk:

Would you join a free Mason society?
All free Masons would go to hell.
It [is] not a free mason society I have in mind [but] a society to fight the white people for [our] freedom.

Woolfolk hesitated; he said he would give "the idea" some thought. Smith persisted, inviting him to a meeting at a neighboring plantation.

Within the next few weeks Woolfolk, who was to become the state's principal witness, met several conspirators including Jack Bowler, a proud and physically overpowering man, who ultimately placed the rebellion above his own personal ambitions. Bowler, who was also hired out (his owner, a widow, lived in Urbanna, a small, decaying tobacco port on the lower Rappahannock River), was 28, 6 feet 5 inches tall, scarred above one eye, with long hair worn in a queue and twisted at the sides. He was described by one official as "stra[i]ght made and perhaps as Strong a man as any in the State."

The process of enlisting slaves like Woolfolk intensified the conspiracy's confused beginnings and its search for form and direction. Leadership positions presumably were open to anyone. But only those who were sufficiently resourceful and persuasive in obtaining men and arms came to be leaders; and for a while no one was in charge. No plans were made, few arms were collected, and organizers and recruitment were uncoordinated. Gabriel, for example, who operated independently of Smith and Bowler, once mentioned to his brother that he first heard about the conspiracy from Bowler, who, another slave testified, was "determined to raise and Enlist Men and Contend for Command with Gabriel." To this end Bowler engaged in a bit of psychological warfare; he frequently visited the blacksmith shop where Gabriel and his brothers worked, and "repeatedly" challenged them with stories of his accomplishments: seven pounds of gunpowder, and the names of two Frenchmen who were allegedly his contacts. The issue of overall command for a time was unresolved because several recruiters, including Bowler, Smith, and Gabriel, were adept at converting slaves to conspirators by temporarily overcoming their caution and conservatism.

Opportunities for recruiting men were numerous. Slaves late in the century had a rich fraternal and religious life; and recruiters were sufficiently free of any kind of meaningful supervision to travel extensively, and to meet slaves at barbecues, at Sunday afternoon drinking sessions beneath well-known bridges, at meeting-houses, and at outdoor "preachings."

Recruitment was widespread. The organizers, spreading out from the James River basin through virtually the entire southern half of the state, depended on the extensive river system and numerous black watermen. Stepney, a waterman whose master lived in Goochland, was arrested for recruiting in Carterville, Cumberland County. An official there was so impressed by his effectiveness with other "batteaumen," that he organized a patrol following the discovery of the plot, and surveyed the upper waters of the James from Powhatan to Buckingham Counties. The conspiracy also reached in the opposite direction, 70 miles down the peninsula into Gloucester County, where it was organized by another waterman and a preacher. The latter left a note on one occasion which indicates how the organizers attempted to use religious meetings: "all you in gloster must keep still yet — brother X will come and prech a sermont to you soon, and then you may no more about the bissiness." Jacob, the waterman, was a skipper of a small vessel that operated off Ware Neck. In the weeks following the collapse of the conspiracy he was charged with taking refugees from Gloucester into the Southside.

Additional organizers worked among the slaves at the canal project at the Falls of the James River, and at the Coal Pits at Tuckahoe (a few miles above Westham on the upper James). A black post rider, who rode the route between Richmond and Amherst Counties, carried information into the Albemarle piedmont. He contacted slaves at Ross's Iron Works in Goochland and also brought back intelligence from slaves in the neighborhood of Point of Fork. The Fork, about 43 air miles above Richmond, was the site of the state arsenal. According to Governor Monroe, here at the junction of the Rivanna and James Rivers, was the "only place of tolerable security in the Commonwealth." Slaves in this vicinity instructed the postman to inform Gabriel that he should delay his attack until they had taken the arsenal and were proceeding down the river to join him.

In addition to Gabriel and Bowler, three other important recruiters were George Smith, Sam Byrd, Jr., and Woolfolk. Byrd, who like Smith was one of the original organizers, was the son of a free Negro and the slave of a man who allowed him "to hire his own time." Byrd enlisted 37 men at the Hungary Meetinghouse in Deep Run, Henrico County, and "50 odd" in the town of Manchester, across the river from Richmond. At the Young's Spring Meeting, he talked of several hundred recruits from Louisa, Petersburg, and "adjacent counties," and about additional trips to such faraway places as Hanovertown and Charlottesville; the latter is more than 100 miles due west of Richmond.

Ben Woolfolk coordinated the Henrico and Caroline County contingents. His contact in Caroline was a blacksmith and another highly assimilated recruiter who usually did not work on his home quarter. Thornton belonged to Paul Thilman and worked at the Hanover County courthouse. Two weeks before the attack, he and Woolfolk left the blacksmith shop, purchased liquor at Ellis's Tavern — "to treat their men that day" — with money from a "subscription" Gabriel conducted, and moved on to recruit at a "preaching" at Littlepage's Bridge. Following the sermon they assembled with the men on the creek, drank grog, and discussed "the War."

Afterwards back in his shop Thornton told Woolfolk that he had "about 20 or 30 men" from four plantations. Gabriel would make him a "Captain of Company," Woolfolk said; but Thornton replied, "he was a General and was to go under the name of Colo. Taylor on this occasion & would make his men obey him." Asked if he needed swords, Thornton stated he would arm his own men. Woolfolk observed that the organizers were "at a loss how to make Cartridges"; and "immediately," the blacksmith made one and "gave it to him as a Sample." Thornton, a proud and competent man, was the one recruiter who did not find it necessary to exaggerate his resources in men and materiel. But as was so often the case with enlistees, and some of the leading recruiters as well, he appeared only once in the documents and the chronology of events and never again. Woolfolk summarized his Caroline County experience for the trial judges by observing: "He left the shop & knows nothing more of Thornton."

"I Could Kill a White Man as Free as Eat"

The accounts of the recruitment procedure reveal the conspiracy's meaning for most slaves, and indicate how the first group lost the initiative to Gabriel and his brothers — Martin, a preacher, and Solomon, a blacksmith. Recruitment usually followed a pattern. The organizer contacted a man in a small group of blacks, and in words like these asked, "Was he willing to fight the white people for his freedom?" The enlistee often responded by declaring his hatred for whites and willingness to kill them without compassion, by sharing his views of the insurrection's goals, and by requesting a command position. Sometimes the leader's questions were put in the context of the slave's manhood or toughness. Patrick was asked "if he was a Man?"; Woolfolk told Jacob that he "looked so poor and weakly that he could not kill a man." The response was perhaps predictable. Jacob struck back: "Do not take me by my looks, I could kill a white man as free as eat." Following a Sunday barbecue, Gabriel revealed his plans to his two brothers, who locked hands and exclaimed, "Here are our hands & hearts. We will Wade to our Knees in blood sooner than fail in the attempt." But the leaders were seldom so effusive; and some in the face of certain death were quietly eloquent: "My name is Solomon, and [I] am good, what is of me, for fighting."

Challenges were often made before other men. In one trial a state witness said that when he recruited the defendant he asked him if he were one of George Smith's men.

He said yes, by God I am — He asked him if he thought he could kill White people stoutly; Yes says he by God I can; and I will fight for my freedom as long as I have breath, and that is as much as any man can do.

This enlistee's little boy, standing nearby while "minding" one of their master's children, "gave" his father "offence," for which "he was whipt." When the master's son also cried, the black man turned and said, "If you were big enough you would have my shirt off, but I hope you never will be big enough."

Two members of the rank-and-file have left fuller accounts of their transformation from fugitives to insurrectionists. Gilbert, a sensitive and intense man, held deep and positive feelings for his master; while King, a waitingman, was a deeply embittered man whose hatred for whites was unadulterated.

King's life changed dramatically one July market day in Richmond. While lounging with a group of black men before Francis Vanne's Shop, Woolfolk mentioned that he was "encouraged" by King's "language and deportment." The slave replied, he "never intended, or suffered white people to have much their way with him," and the ritual proceeded in this manner:

Are you a true man?
Pris[one]r: I am true hearted man.
Witn[ess]: Can you keep a *proper*, or *important* secret?
Pris[one]r: Yes
Witn[ess]: The Negroes are about to rise and fight the White people for their freedom.

"They ought to have taken the rebellion into consideration a long time ago," King said. "Yes," he "was ready to join them at any moment," and he would "slay the white people like sheep."

After the conspiracy's discovery, King and another slave entered Mary Martin's Grog Shop, "as the Guards were going out." "In a surly & abrupt style," he demanded a drink on credit. Mary refused, "I trust nobody." So King paid and, turning to his friend who was journeying to visit his wife, said he wished he could do the same. Mary joined in. "Why didn't he visit his wife?" "It was too far," King said, "and the white people ha[ve] turned so comical a man can't go out of his house now but he's taken up to be hanged." He then asked his companion to tell a mutual friend: "We are all alive as yet, looking hard at the bacon, but can't get at it, 'as we are doing what we can.' 'What we can't do with our Guns, we will do with Bayonets.' " Placing his finger to his forehead, King concluded, "Nobody knows what is here yet." Mary indulged the court further: "She had no bacon in her shop — nor had they any that she saw." Even though his master petitioned for a pardon, King was condemned and executed on October 3.

Few conspirators outside the small leadership clique were as active in promoting the rebellion as William Young's Gilbert. But in his eagerness to get at whites, he encountered a number of petty, frustrating situations. At the Young's Spring Meeting when Martin vowed "to turn out & fight with his stick," Gilbert replied, "He was ready with his pistol, but it was in need of Repair." When approached by Gabriel and asked if he had a sword, Gilbert replied that his Master had one hanging up in the house, which he would get and make himself a belt for it." He also depended on the use of his master's horse; but, on the day before the rebellion, he expressed "regret . . . that their master was up the country" so that he would have to "take the Bald [horse]." There were larger disappointments compounded by the slave's feelings about himself and his owner. During the conversation about the sword, he "asked to be made a Captain," but Gabriel refused, "saying he stuttered too much to give the word of Command." Later Gilbert also said that his "Master and Mistress should be put to death, but by the men under him (as he could not do it himself) because they raised him."

"The Main Spring and Chief Mover"

Gilbert first enlisted with George Smith, who seemed unable to distinguish between a plan and its execution. In fact Smith's recruitment of men in itself indicated that his group was moving too slowly, indecisively, and ceremoniously. So Gilbert joined Gabriel, because, as he later testified, he realized that Gabriel "would carry the business into execution."

This explanation focuses sharply on the style of Gabriel's leadership. More than any other organizer he sensed the narcotic and self-justifying effects of revolutionary rhetoric and organization. Because he was able to make decisions, delegate responsibilities, and pursue routine tasks to their completion in order to avert the strong possibility of disaster, the rebellion came to be his. And it bore his own quietly methodical, businesslike character. But Gabriel cannot be characterized like Woolfolk and Bowler, because his most essential qualities remain hidden and unrecoverable in the manuscripts. Although he is referred to in many depositions, he refused to confess when captured. Gabriel was a powerful force pushing the conspiracy toward fruition, a man imbued not so much with messianic fervor as with a sense of what had to be done. The whites also recognized his unusual abilities; a county justice, using an especially appropriate mechanical metaphor, noted that Gabriel was "the Main Spring and Chief Mover."

Thus the direction of the rebellion shifted to Prosser's blacksmith shop, where Gabriel and his brothers gave form and substance to the notion of revolution. During the early summer months the conspiracy matured under their direction. In the second week of August, William Young left his plantation for a fortnight, and the insurrectionists returned there, ostensibly to bury a Negro child.

"I Can No Longer Bear What [I Have] Borne"

Saturday afternoon, August 10, the mourners drifted back from the black infant's grave. Gabriel, who often used religious gatherings for his own political purposes, invited the slaves to drink grog with him on the banks of the spring. Understanding that he must build a following among the country people, secrecy was ignored. He asked those assembled who wished to join him to stand and those who did not to sit. He and Bowler moved among the men, promoting the war and enlisting fighters. Unsatisfied with this cooperative arrangement, Bowler asked rhetorically what Gabriel would do for war materiel, and before Gabriel replied, Bowler rushed on and asked those "who have agreed to engage in the Insurrection to give him their Voice for General." "The votes [were] taken," and "Gabriel [had] by far the greater number." Although he had miscalculated Gabriel's hold on the slaves, Bowler was made second in command, a "Captain of Lighthorse."

Following the election they debated the critical issue of when to attack. Although the vernacular was religious, the deliberations were practical and realistic. Some, including a few leaders, were apprehensive. While recruiting in the countryside, George Smith came to understand the plantation slave's dual nature: his bitter hatred for whites and his inability to do much about it. So Smith argued that they defer "the business some time longer." But Gabriel replied, "The Summer was About over, & he wished them to enter upon the business before the winter got too cold." At this crucial moment, with the decision in the balance, he suggested that "the Subject should be refered" to his brother Martin, the preacher, who stepped forward and intoned, "There was this expression in the Bible that delays breed danger." But Martin quickly turned from Scriptural sanction to more rational, secular considerations and argued that the time for revolution was very near: the country was at peace, the soldiers were discharged, their arms "all put away," and "there were no patrols in the Country." He paused, then crossing what for many was an insurmountable barrier, Martin spoke from within. "I can no longer bear what [I have] borne." The proceedings were open, and the silence was broken by "others who spoke to the company" and said that Woolfolk had "something to say." Woolfolk also used the Bible, but to loosen the spectre of defeat. "He had heard in the days of old, when the Israelites were in Servitude to King Pharaoh, they were taken from him by the power of God — & were carried away by Moses. . . . But I can see nothing of that kind in these days." Martin quickly replied, "Their cause was similar to [the] Israelites'," but he had read in his Bible "where God Says, if we worship him, we should have peace in all our land," and "five of you shall conquer an hundred & a hundred a thousand of our enemies." At this point the preacher held the floor and made the most important decision. "After this they went into consultation upon the time they should execute the plan. Martin spoke & appointed for them to meet in three weeks which was to be a Saturday night (August

30)." With this achieved, Bowler and Gabriel withdrew into "secret conversations," which were "interrupted" by the "appearance" of Young's overseer. The conspirators dispersed after agreeing to meet in front of Moore's Schoolhouse the following Sunday (while their masters met within the schoolhouse), "where a final Conclusion on the business would take place."

The conspiracy had peaked at the Young's Spring meeting. In the few weeks before the attack a certain indefinable but no less real revolutionary élan was dissipated; if sustained, it might have carried the rank-and-file from words to deeds. During the meeting itself there were clear signs of a potentially disastrous disunity: Woolfolk's comment about the unfulfilled search for a Moses; George Smith's desire to postpone the rebellion; and the recruiters' deceptive responses to questions about the numbers they had actually enlisted.

The recruiters' exaggerated reports conveyed both the enlistee's fervent promise, made while in company with his friends, and the recruiter's belief that the command he received would be proportionate to the numbers of enlistees he claimed. When asked to produce their lists, the organizers often couched their responses in vague allusions to the "warehouse boys," the "boys across the river," or the "boys in town." Sam Byrd was asked for his record at the Young's Spring meeting, and he said, while he did not have his list "about him," he "supposed he had about five hundred, who were to be assembled by him and given up to Gabriel on the Night [of] the Attack." Some sensed what was going on. Gilbert asked a Richmond Free Negro, Matt Scott, who said he had a hundred men, for his list. "Some other time," Scott answered; and, Gilbert testified, he "never did see the list."

The recruiters' dangerously misleading estimates of men and materiel were further distorted by the leaders — especially when they addressed groups of slaves in the countryside. In one instance, Gabriel himself (while displaying two bullet molds which he said he had worn out producing several pecks of shot) proclaimed that he "had nearly 10,000 men: 1000 in Richmond, about 600 in Caroline Country and nearly 500 at the Tuckahoe Coal Pits, besides others at different places." Significantly, estimates of the number prepared to fight diminished as the point of departure approached. Gabriel's was made three weeks before the attack, while addressing the gathering at Young's Spring. A week later, August 20, a slave asked Solomon how many would follow them: the answer was 3000; and nine days later, Gabriel's wife, Nanny, told a black man "that 1000 Men were to meet her husband near Prosser's Tavern the ensuing Night."

But Gabriel understood what was and was not happening with regard to recruitment in the countryside. He only talked of 10,000 men before gatherings of slaves of all kinds; in the privacy of Prosser's blacksmith shop, he carefully assessed his limited resources and planned accordingly. In its tactical dimensions his rebellion was a coup that he hoped would inspire insurrection: a small guerrilla force of about 200 men would enter Richmond at midnight and thoroughly terrorize the city, initially by burning its warehouse district, killing indiscriminately, capturing stores of arms, and taking the Governor as a hostage.

The Governor, James Monroe, also understood the real nature of the rebellion.

He referred to it as an "experiment," a "project," undertaken by "bold adventurers," who relied on a "successful . . . first effort," rather than a "very extensive preconcerted combination." Against this background, the nature of the slaves' exaggerated discussions in recruitment is more understandable. The organizers, the "bold adventurers," sought to build a viable following among the country people, who they hoped would follow up their initial attack. Thus Gabriel's strategy: he recognized that unless he struck suddenly, sensationally, and decisively — presenting slaves as well as free men with a *fait accompli* — there would be no mass uprising.

Gabriel's tactics, which were needlessly complicated, were not as astute as his strategy. Even though the city was the key to his plan, it was decided that the conspirators would rendezvous six miles out in the countryside. Once assembled they would enter Richmond in three wings (two would be unarmed) from the north and south. One group would fire the wooden buildings in Rocketts, the warehouse district, in order to draw off the townsmen from the residential areas; the others, commanded by Gabriel, would capture the capitol buildings, the store of arms in the Penitentiary, and the Governor. When the whites returned from the fires, tired and confused, the insurgents would close with them. If successful, if the "White people agreed to their freedom," Gabriel would raise a white flag in order to notify "their brothers" outside the city, who would presumably rise up and join the fortified insurrectionists.

There were back-up plans based on the slaves' knowledge that the whites were especially vulnerable in their towns. Gabriel said that if they "sustained any considerable loss," they would "bend their course" for either of two small towns, Hanovertown or Yorktown. At this point their plans trailed off into a vague notion of attempting to "form a junction" with some slaves who "they understood from Mr. Gregory's overseer were in rebellion in some quarter of the country."

The question of who was to direct the initial military operations also portended disaster. Slaves knew little of arms and less of tactical leadership. When asked by his brother whether or not Jack Bowler knew "anything about carrying on war," Gabriel replied negatively. Who would he "employ?" Solomon continued. A Frenchman from Caroline County, "who was at the Siege of Yorktown," Gabriel said, "was to meet him at the Brook." The Frenchman was to be "Commander & manager the first day"; but "after exercising the Soldiers," following the attack, his "command was to be resigned to Gabriel." This Frenchman was allegedly Charles Quersey, who three or four years prior to the conspiracy had lived at Francis Corbin's in Caroline. William Young's Gilbert credited Quersey with initiating the rebellion: he "frequently advised the negroes to rise & kill the White people, and said he would help them & shew them how to fight." Gilbert had not seen him "since, but is inform'd by several Negroes, that he has been very active in encouraging the Negroes in this late Business." Nineteenth-century pre-industrial folk fighting desperate anticolonial struggles against overwhelmingly powerful Europeans often had similar views: the nationals of a European power hostile to the mother country would miraculously appear and fight on their side. "They had understood,"

Woolfolk testified, "that the French were at war with this Country — for the money which was due them & that an army was landed at South Key which they hoped would assist them."

Sound in strategy but bogged down by confusing tactics, imperiled by a lack of men and military leadership, the conspiracy moved into its final days. At noon on the day of the attack, Saturday, August 30, it began to rain. By mid-evening the thunderstorm had swelled streams and washed out roads and bridges; communication, movements, and morale collapsed. The whites later repeatedly referred to this great storm as "Providential."

Although it is a moot point how many men would have met at Prosser's at midnight, August 30, no one rendezvoused either Saturday or the following night, when the attack was rescheduled. In the meantime, security was suddenly broken. For months hundreds of slaves, including women and children, maintained secrecy while listening to the discussions and pondering their places in the new scheme of things. By Saturday morning, however, at least three slaves had informed their masters that the conspiracy was going to become reality. Monroe dispatched two troops-of-horse which swept back and forth through the area of the rendezvous. But they found nothing, because the leaders had postponed the attack; one man who came to the Prosser plantation that stormy night was told by Gabriel to return the next evening. Another slave informed (she said that three or four hundred, "some from Town & some from the Country" would meet), but again the troop commanders' reports were negative. Thus Monroe noted, "I was on the point of concluding there was no foundation for the alarm." And even when he came to a partial understanding of what he was confronting, his deployment of men in the capital indicated the Governor's serious doubts about the extent of the conspirators' success among plantation Negroes.

In the aftermath, the state proceeded cautiously and confidently while making arrests, using informers and conducting the trials. Within a few days twenty slaves were captured in Henrico and Caroline Counties. Thereafter arrests continued more slowly. On September 15, Monroe wrote Jefferson that ten slaves had been executed and "at least" twenty would be condemned and "perhaps forty." The former estimate is closer to the total number executed; but the exact number of convictions is unknown because the records of payments to the slaves' masters are incomplete. At least twelve slaves were acquitted, one of whom was Sam Byrd's free father, who was accused of recruiting in Hanovertown. Another seven conspirators were pardoned.

"The Business Only Required a Beginning"

For Gabriel the final scene comprised many of the elements that so often made slavery a tragic and crazy reality for even the most talented and resourceful slaves.

In his last moments of real freedom, he was aided by a white and betrayed by a black man.

Richardson Taylor, who tried to carry Gabriel to safety, was the master of the schooner *Mary* and an embodiment of the fiercely contradictory values of his postwar society. Taylor was a "family man," an ex-overseer, a ship captain with a crew of slaves, and an antislavery Methodist. Although he later feigned innocence by virtue of his ignorance of the matter, Taylor knew about Gabriel. Before he weighed anchor in Richmond and dropped down the James for Norfolk, several insurrrectionists were tried and executed. Late Saturday night, September 17, the *Mary* conveniently ran onto Ward's Reach, four miles below the capital. The following morning Gabriel ran from a patch of woods, crossed the sand bar, and, after tossing his bayonet into the water, was taken aboard. Taylor later claimed that he was "unwell" during this episode; when he awoke the ship was underway. Coming on deck he questioned his strange passenger, who said he was a free Negro, Daniel, who unfortunately had left his manumission papers ashore. While Taylor let the matter drop, his slave crewmen, Isham and Billy, insisted that the man was Gabriel; and, "it was their opinion that he was the person (for whom) the reward was offer[e]d."

The *Mary* was eleven days in passage. Taylor overlooked numerous opportunities to put ashore and either inquire or dispose of his strange passenger. When he was finally boarded by an official in Norfolk, he said nothing about Gabriel. But Isham, who later testified that he was to be freed if he converted to Methodism, brought the officials back to the ship. They were amazed: "Capt. Taylor is an old inhabitant been an overseer & must have known that neither free blacks nor slaves could travel in this Country without papers." This time Gabriel left in chains; and, although he once mentioned he would talk about the rebellion — but only to Monroe — he remained silent while he awaited execution.

In the weeks following the trials, there was a series of small, insurrectionary actions throughout the state. In November, Paul Thilman, the owner of the Caroline County blacksmith, Thornton, reported that the Negroes "in the neighbourhood" of the Hanover County courthouse had been "very riotous & ungovernable" on a Thursday and Friday. On Saturday they broke into a jail and set free two insurrectionists who were handcuffed and chained to the floor. Once free, the prisoners assaulted the guard, "knocked him down stamped [on] him" and ran off. "A great number of Negroes were present & pretended" to pursue them. Thilman felt that the jail break was well planned; for "a great number" of slaves had visited the prisoners throughout the week "under the pretence of a preaching." He reported an additional "incident" in Hanover which further indicated that the "concert" between that county's slaves and those in Caroline was still intact. Mr. Paul Woolfolk, "going down his plantation," fell in with two slaves armed with "bayonets." Woolfolk, who was armed with an axe, "threaten[ed] them with an assault" if they did not surrender. The conspirators, equal to the occasion, told him "to come on, they were ready for him — that they would go where they pleased." They did, and were last reported crossing Charles Carter's plantation.

But the slaves' unusually open and violent activities were uncoordinated. In the grim days following the conspiracy's discovery, it became clearly evident that rebellion waited on Gabriel and his few "bold adventurers." In court the following testimony was typical: "all the negroes in Petersburg were to join him [Gabriel] after he had commenced the insurrection"; and "as soon as the boys on this side made a *brake,* the boys from Manchester would come over and join them." On the weekend following the storm, about one-hundred-and-fifty slaves actually gathered at Whitlock's Mill outside Norfolk. "They never left this neighborhood until the Tuesday after it was known that the Richmond plan had failed," reported one planter. When a number of "mulattoes, negroes, & some whites, whose connections were with the negroes," were examined, they said that the people at the mill were "to do what those of Richmond were about to do." Nor did the slaves' expectations readily subside. Three months later one Benjamin DuVal wrote Monroe that he had overheard a "parcel" of Richmond Negroes talking about the "Norfolk Cowards." "Cowards & Liberty," were "several times expressed conjoined with other words that I could not distinctly hear." And one Negro said "that there never was or would be a better time than the present" and observed "that the business only required a beginning.

An old road runs out past the Gloucester County Court House to Ware's Neck. One hundred and seventy years ago one of Gabriel's recruiters hurriedly shoved a note into the neck of a bottle which he dropped alongside that road. It concerned Jacob, the black skipper who carried refugees into the Southside after the conspiracy was uncovered.

September 20: 1800

dear frind

Tel jacob at john Williams johny is taken up and wil be hanged i is afraide so all you in gloster must keep still yet brother X will come and prech a sermont to you soon, and then you may no more about the bissiness. i must be killed if the white peple catch me and carry me to richmon

i am your tru frind
A. W.

In the bitter aftermath of the rebellion that did not happen; running away was once again the only alternative for slaves who refused to accept slavery. Even though insurrection was in the air, and "only required a beginning," the slaves "looked at the bacon" but "couldn't get at it."

A Society "Ill at Ease"

"It is always the individual that really thinks and acts and dreams and revolts," wrote Edward Sapir many years ago. Although the meaning of Gabriel's Insurrection lies in its narration, in its tragic and personal dimension, a discussion of the most strategic preconditions for rebellion in 1800 completes our view of the revolutionary situation. There are essentially four ways of examining the conspiracy's setting and what accounted for its failure: (1) the nature of the insurrectionists' tasks; (2) their understanding of the values of the Revolutionary era; (3) their views of religious revivalism; and (4) the relationship between acculturation levels and patterns of slave behavior in late eighteenth-century Virginia.

Depositions and lists supplied by informers offer a fairly complete picture of the conspirators' place and function in society. These men were unified by common work experiences. While their routines cut across several categories — semi-skilled and skilled, routine and artistic — they were all highly mobile men and thus unusually familiar with the society outside the plantation's confines. Several were from coal mines, iron foundries, and rope works — industries whose growth in scale and number was accelerated by the Revolutionary War — or from such new industries as the Public Canal Works. Privileged domestics, who have not fared too well in studies of American Negro slavery, were as well represented as any other group: Robin and Charles, who were waiters at the Eagle Tavern and Priddy's Ordinary; some janitors and custodians who worked in the capitol buildings and the Penitentiary; as well as the waitingmen, King and John Mayo's George. Blacksmiths from Goochland, Caroline, and Henrico Counties, the only type of highly esteemed draftsmen represented, played crucial roles as recruiters. Several warehousemen were also implicated. Others worked at assignments which required extensive travel; they included several boatmen (from the upper waters of the James between Powhatan and Buckingham Counties), and the postman who rode a route between Richmond and Charlottesville. These men were more independent than all the other conspirators, for they only rarely worked in the company of whites.

Most conspirators, in fact, were more autonomous than the slaves they would lead. They had a life of their own, and their masters are conspicuously absent from the lengthy and detailed depositions. The only whites who participated in any meaningful way in their planning, moreover, were those whom the conspirators could use — Methodists, petty merchants, and tavern keepers. Several conspirators were owned by women; at least three came from estates in probate. Several who were hired out or allowed to hire their own time were also at least a step or two removed from their masters. In this period of economic readjustment and diversification, allowing a slave to hire his own time was an illegal but highly popular and profitable practice. And some were so far removed from their masters that their provenance was difficult to determine. One confused official described William

Young's Gilbert in the following way: "At the time the Fire took place in Mr. Percells, he was then living with John Young in Caroline County." And Brutus, "alias Julius," who belonged to one William Anderson, was hired to a prominent Richmond physician, Dr. William Foushee, when he ran off and joined the rebellion.

These fugitives, like John Mayo's runaway George, were men who possessed the requisite guile, fluent English, and occupational skills for passing as free men. By the end of the century a significant change had taken place in the revolutionary awareness of men like this who had previously viewed slavery as an individual problem and resisted it as fugitives: these men and this change, in fact, are the key to the relationship between the conspiracy's social and personal dimensions. Writing in 1801 about runaways who became insurrectionists, St. George Tucker, aristocrat and lawyer, analyzed for members of the state legislature the conspiracy's preconditions. Comparing the slaves' reactions to the Royal Governor's Emancipation Proclamation in 1775 and to Gabriel, he discussed their exceptionally rapid material and spiritual development in the "few short years" following the War. He attributed their new outlook to the growth of towns, trades, and a complementary increase in the extent of literacy among slaves. More opportunities for work in commercial areas brought about a "prodigious change" in the skilled slaves' outlook, a change Tucker characterized as the "love of freedom," and that "evolving spirit we fear." While only a few runaways — a "few solitary individuals" — joined the British in 1775, the insurrectionists of 1800 organized extensively to "assert their claims," while rest[ing] their safety on success alone." The difference between the two rebellions, Tucker argued, was basically ideological: in 1775 slaves "fought [for] freedom merely as a good; now they also claim it as a right."

Thus in the closing years of the century, revolutionary conflict and ideology were resolved for most free men, but not for black men, especially if they were artisans. Between 1775 and 1800, a type of slave who was literate, skilled, mobile, and working in a commercial environment accepted the fact that regardless of his comparatively privileged position, and the whites' efforts to ameliorate slavery, the institution would survive and grow. Artisans had become sufficiently marginal to believe that the values and "rights" of the Revolutionary era were theirs also and that they were sufficiently resourceful and strategically placed to do something about their situation with the aid of other men. Nonetheless, their expanded revolutionary consciousness was still focused by their traditional and relatively advantaged positions. So, to the extent that they were motivated by ideas, these ideas established definite boundaries for their revolutionary action.

The insurrectionists' goals were essentially political. While using the rhetoric of their generation to clearly distinguish between their oppressors and slavery's victims, white as well as black, they displayed a keen sense of their own time and place. One man testified that he wanted "to fight for his Country," and another said they were to "subdue the whole of the Country where Slavery was permitted but no further." "As far as I understand all the whites were to be massacred, except the Quakers, the Methodists & Frenchmen," Woolfolk testified, and "they were to be spared on account as they conceived of their being friendly to liberty." Prosser's Ben, an eighteen-year-old who worked beside Gabriel in the blacksmith shop, mentioned that "whites were to [be] murdered & killed indiscriminately excepting French Men, none of whome were to be touched." And another said simply, they "intended to spare all poor white women who had no slaves." The continual discussions of who was to be spared or killed, as well as the occasionally cathartic posturing that characterized the recruitment process, seldom impaired the participants' expression of their clear understanding of the leading principles of the day.

The organizers' discussions regarding Richmond are even more informative of both the origin and political character of their revolutionary style. These rational and calculating men were neither self-indulgent nor self-destructive; for at times, it seemed, they wanted a political settlement, not a reformation. Gabriel once said that all townsmen except those who agreed to fight with them would be killed. His brother remarked in passing that they were to possess themselves of the whites' property; George Smith asked that they preserve the brick storehouses in Rocketts "for their own use." Recall their strategy: the insurgents would fortify the city, take the Governor hostage, and then — it is assumed — they would negotiate. At this point, Gabriel again set the tone. When the capital was secured, "on the day it should be agreed to," he "would dine and drink with the merchants of the City."

Although it is possible only to outline here a hypothesis I have developed more thoroughly elsewhere, it is useful to view the occupational and ideological values separating organizers from those they had to recruit as basically a function of their comparatively more thorough assimilation. The slaves' awareness of their profound cultural differences was sharpened by the dramatic quality of religious life at the end of the century. The country people, reluctant and suspicious, came out of the quarters and gathered in the large and exciting revivals of the Great Awakening. Seeking spiritual assistance, they were confronted by Gabriel and his men, who used the meetings to disguise both their real intentions and their organizational structure and to recruit men and discuss tactics. The high point of the revivals was the exhortation which, if it had been used by Gabriel, could have been the catalyst for changing religious fervor and concern for the here-after into revolutionary action in the here-and-now. But this never happened. The leaders and their potential followers were faithful in different ways. The conspiracy was comprised of autonomous men confronting religious men. Because of the nature of its leader and the rational, political character of its goals, Gabriel's Rebellion never became a viable part of the great religious revivals.

Because religious and eschatological elements often generate the large-scale rebellions of pre-industrial folk, perhaps it was not merely coincidental that one leader looked beyond the country people's fundamentalism to an even more ancient heritage, which leavened their Christianity. For some, like the leader George Smith, Africa was still a very meaningful part of their lives. Smith, who was closer to the soil and harvest cycles than any other organizer, once proposed that he hire his own time, travel down country to what he called the "pipeing tree," and enlist the "Outlandish people"; for they were "supposed to deal with Witches and Wizards, and thus [would be] useful in Armies to tell when any calamity was about to befall them." Whether or not Smith later talked about bullets turning to water is an intriguing conjecture; but he did announce to the gathering at Young's Spring that when he finished plowing his master's cornfield, he would make as many cross-bows "as he could." Although there was no more said about wizards, cross-bows and Africa, Smith in his own way called attention to the one means — charisma — by which the slaves could have transcended their significant cultural and occupational differences. But his proposal (as well as Woolfolk's unfulfilled search for a Moses) calls attention to the relationship between acculturation levels and religious beliefs and practices on the one hand and styles of rebelliousness on the other. Here is the source of Gabriel's failure; at a time when revivalism was a vital force among plantation slaves, those who would lead based their appeals in political and secular terms. Unlike Nat Turner's magnificent Old Testament visions, which transfigured him and sustained his movement, Gabriel's Rebellion, lacking a sacred dimension, was without a Moses, and thus without a following.

Preliminary research indicates that the acculturative experience, a hitherto neglected dimension of slavery, may also enrich our understanding of the other major insurrections about which the slaves have provided ample testimony. The cultural differences among slaves — so evident and divisive in the 1800 rebellion — were also manifested in the religious dimensions of the insurrections of Denmark Vesey (Charleston, South Carolina, 1822) and Nat Turner (Southampton County, Virginia, 1831).

Religion and magic sustained Nat Turner's Rebellion. Executed by comparatively unskilled, immobile, plantation slaves in an economically backward area, this insurrection was neither as politically coherent nor as extensive as Gabriel's. Turner, who was not a preacher in the conventional sense but a seer and a holy man, also politicized his men by means of dream interpretations and feats of fortune telling and numerology. In this instance, too, an astrological event (an eclipse of the sun) made a tremendous impact on the black country folk; they saw it as a favorable sign. Denmark Vesey, the third great insurrectionist, stands midway between Gabriel and Turner. While he normallly based his appeals on political grounds, he recognized the connecton between religious sanctions and rebellion from below. On a few special occasions he used sermons based on the Bible; he also delegated to Gullah Jack, a native African and "doctor," the responsibility of forming the rural blacks of the low country's sea islands into "African legions." But, like Gabriel, he failed because his rebellion was urban-based and restricted to artisans, shopkeepers, and free Negroes. Only Nat Turner, who charged his plan with supernatural signs and sacred, poetic language that inspired action, was able to transcend the worlds of the plantation and the city. Only Turner led a sustained insurrection.

But Gabriel's men were ensnared in an earlier and different era. Although these artisans by 1800 had become so much more numerous, strategically placed, and imbued with an ideology supporting collective action, they were still isolated — cut off not only from their own people, but from the new economic realities of the ante-bellum period. There is, then, in their conspiracy a note of cultural despair. Since the South was again moving away from manufacturing and economic diversification, the occupational strata and milieu which produced this type of slave were rapidly becoming anachronistic. From this threat to their way of life came this group's despair. Isaac declared "if the [insurrection] was not soon, he would run off, as he was determined not to serve a white man [for] another year," and Martin said he could no longer bear what he had borne. In the case of a third, the transformation from slave to free man was expressed forthrightly as "I will kill or be killed." And Solomon, one of the few mulattoes in the conspiracy, joined and died even though he was to be legally free at age 31.

But where were the other slaves? The reality of slavery in post-war Virginia was radically different for leaders and followers. An elite initiated, planned, and dominated Gabriel's Rebellion. In the four months before the insurrection, they lived and were sustained by it; they knew one another well. Living with death, they accepted it. Slowly and profoundly, freedom, revolution, and death came to be a large part of their lives. Meanwhile, the rank-and-file simply raised their hands at meetings; a few personalized their commitment by volunteering for specific responsibilities and acquiring weapons. Enlisting in the most inauthentic manner, they did not share the leaders' distinctive revolutionary awareness. Thus their commitment was fragile at best; in the end, Gabriel and his men stood alone.

Notes

[1] A shorter version of this essay, which did not deal with the relationship between religion, acculturation levels, and slave resistance, was read at the Wayne State Convocation (May 1969), "The Black Man in America: 350 Years, 1619–1969," and published in Peter I. Rose, ed., *Americans from Africa*, 2 vols. (New York, 1970), II, 53–74; it is also the basis for the concluding chapter of my book *Africans and English Colonists in Eighteenth-Century Virginia: The Colonial Setting for American Negro Slavery* (Oxford University Press, forthcoming).

[2] Unless otherwise indicated, sources for this paper are the Executive Papers (September–December 1800) in the Virginia State Library (Richmond). These two boxes contain approximately 105 items marked "Negro Insurrection 1800," including the following types of documents: letters from officials and ranking state politicians and military men to Governor James Monroe; "certificates from the Examining Magistrates (the Justices of Henrico and Caroline Counties)," who recorded the conspirators' depositions; resolutions concerning the conspiracy from the Richmond, Williamsburg, and Petersburg Common Halls; "Informations" taken from slave informers and transcribed by clerks of the court; court transcripts and depositions submitted as evidence, including the testimony of the most important informers, Paul Grayham's Ben Woolfolk, Thomas H. Prosser's Solomon and Ben, and William Young's Gilbert; and many bits and pieces of undated and unendorsed documents, including some important lists of suspects used by officials while making arrests.

About two-thirds of this material is reprinted in Henry W. Flournoy, ed., *Calendar of Virginia State Papers and Other Manuscripts Preserved in the Capital at Richmond,* 11 vols. (Richmond, Va., 1875–1893), IX. Some depositions are also reprinted in the *Richmond Recorder,* April 13, 1803 ("Documents Respecting the Insurrection of the Slaves"), Virginia State Library microfilm. All of the major correspondence and trial transcripts are in Governor Monroe's copybook, Executive Communications, September-December 1800, Virginia State Library. John Mayo's advertisement for the fugitive and conspirator, George, is in the *Virginia Gazette and General Advertizer,* February 7, 1800; and St. George Tucker's *Letter to a Member of the General Assembly* (Richmond, 1801) is in the Virginia State Library microfilm collection.

³ *The Evidence.* The slaves were imprisoned separately; and, although about four of the accused were pardoned, only a small number were spared because they confessed. The following endorsements of depositions indicate that the evidence was handled in a careful and critical manner: "The Witness was at Mr. Young's on the night spoken of by Prosser's Ben (whose testimony is Confirmed by him in every Part)"; "He confirms Verbatem Prosser's Ben's Testimony." When the clerks or justices knowingly imposed themselves between what was said and what they heard, they usually made a note of it: "This statement is made with the aid of some notes, but principally from recollection; minute circumstance is detailed in it, they feel assured that no material circumstance is omitted" (from the trial of William Young's Gilbert).

Resistance to Slavery

George M. Fredrickson
Christopher Lasch

The issues involved in the study of "resistance" to slavery are badly in need of clarification. The problem, one would suppose, is not whether the plantation slave was happy with his lot but whether he actively resisted it. But even this initial clarification does not come easily. Too many writers have assumed that the problem of resistance consists mainly of deciding whether slaves were docile or discontented and whether their masters were cruel or kind. In this respect and in others, as Stanley Elkins noted several years ago, the discussion of slavery has locked itself into the terms of an old debate.[1] The proslavery stereotype of the contented slave, which was taken over without much conceptual refinement by U.B. Phillips and others, has been attacked by recent historians in language much the same as that employed by the abolitionists more than a hundred years ago, according to which slaves hated bondage and longed to be free. "That they had no understanding of freedom," Kenneth Stampp argues, ". . . is hard to believe." A few pages later, and without any intervening evidence, Stampp progresses from this cautious thought to a fullblown statement of the case for "resistance." "Slave resistance, whether bold and persistent or mild and sporadic, created for all slaveholders a serious problem of discipline." He concludes, in a burst of rhetoric, that "the record of slave resistance forms a chapter in the story of the endless struggle to give dignity to human life."[2]

It should be apparent that the traditional terms of reference, on either side of the dispute, are not sufficiently precise to serve as instruments of analysis. One of the faults of Phillips' work is his consistent failure to distinguish between cruelty and coercion. By compiling instances of the kindness and benevolence of masters, Phillips proved to his own satisfaction that slavery was a mild and permissive institution, the primary function of which was not so much to produce a marketable surplus as to ease the accommodation of the lower race into the culture of the higher. The critics of Phillips have tried to meet him on his own ground. Where he compiled lists of indulgences and benefactions, they have assembled lists of atrocities. Both methods suffer from the same defect: they attempt to solve a conceptual problem — what did slavery do to the slave — by accumulating quantitative evidence. Both

George M. Frederickson and Christopher Lasch, "Resistance to Slavery," *Civil War History*, XIII (December 1967), pp. 315–29. Reprinted with permission of the publisher.

methods assert that plantations conformed to one of two patterns, terror or indulgence, and then seek to prove these assertions by accumulating evidence from plantation diaries, manuals of discipline, letters and other traditional sources for the study of slavery. But for every instance of physical cruelty on the one side an enterprising historian can find an instance of indulgence on the other. The only conclusion that one can legitimately draw from this debate is that great variations in treatment existed from plantation to plantation. (But as we shall see, this conclusion, barren in itself, can be made to yield important results if one knows how to use it.)

Even if we could make valid generalizations about the severity of the regime, these statements would not automatically answer the question of whether or not widespread resistance took place. If we are to accept the testimony of Frederick Douglass, resistance was more likely to result from indulgence and rising expectations than from brutalizing severity.[3] A recent study of the geographical distribution of authentic slave revolts shows that most of them occurred in cities and in areas of slavebreeding and diversified agriculture, where, according to all accounts, the regime was more indulgent than in the productive plantation districts of the Cotton Kingdom.[4] Open resistance cannot be inferred from the extreme physical cruelty of the slave system, even if the system's cruelty could be demonstrated statistically.

II

There is the further question of what constitutes resistance. When Kenneth Stampp uses the term he means much more than open and flagrant defiance of the system. To him resistance is all noncooperation on the part of the slaves. And it cannot be denied that the annals of slavery abound in examples of this kind of behavior. Slaves avoided work by pretending to be sick or by inventing a hundred other plausible pretexts. They worked so inefficiently as to give rise to the suspicion that they were deliberately sabotaging the crop. They stole from their masters without compunction, a fact which gave rise to the complaint that slaves had no moral sense, but which is better interpreted as evidence of a double standard — cheating the master while dealing honorably with other slaves. Nor was this all. Their grievances or frustrations led at times to the willful destruction of the master's property by destroying tools, mistreating animals, and setting fire to plantation buildings. Less frequently, they took the ultimate step of violent attack on the master himself. Perhaps the most common form of obvious noncooperation was running away; every large plantation had its share of fugitives.[5]

The question which inevitably arises, as Stampp piles up incident after incident in order to show that slaves were "a troublesome property," is whether this pattern of noncooperation constitutes resistance. Resistance is a political concept. Political activity, in the strictest sense, is organized collective action which aims at affecting the distribution of power in a community; more broadly, it might be said to consist of any activity, either of individuals or of groups, which is designed to create a consciousness of collective interest, such consciousness being the prerequisite for effective action in the realm of power. Organized resistance is of course only one form of political action. Others include interest-group politics; coalitions of interest groups organized as factions or parties; reform movements; or, at an international level, diplomacy and war. In total institutions, however, conventional politics are necessarily nonexistent.[6] Politics, if they exist at all, must take the form of resistance: collective action designed to subvert the system, to facilitate and regularize escape from it; or, at the very least, to force important changes in it.

Among despised and downtrodden people in general, the most rudimentary form of political action is violence; sporadic and usually short-lived outbursts of destruction, based on a common sense of outrage and sometimes inspired by a millennialistic ideology. Peasant revolts, all over the world, have usually conformed to this type.[7] In total institutions, prison riots are perhaps the nearest equivalent. In American slavery, the few documented slave rebellions fall into the same pattern.[8] What makes these upheavals political at all is that they rest on some sense, however primitive, of collective victimization. They require, moreover, at least a minimum of organization and planning. What makes them rudimentary is that they do not aim so much at changing the balance of power as at giving expression on the one hand to apocalyptic visions of retribution, and on the other to an immediate thirst for vengeance directed more at particular individuals than at larger systems of authority. In the one case, the sense of grievance finds an outlet in indiscriminate violence (as against Jews); in the other, it attaches itself to a particular embodiment of authority (as in prisons, where a specific departure from established routine may set off a strike or riot demanding the authority's dismissal and a return to the previous regime). But in neither case does collective action rest on a realistic perception of the institutional structure as a whole and the collective interest of its victims in subverting it. That explains why such outbreaks of violence tend to subside very quickly, leaving the exploitive structure intact. Underground resistance to the Nazis in western Europe, on the other hand, precisely because it expressed itself in an organized underground instead of in futile outbreaks of indiscriminate violence, had a continuous existence which testifies to the highly political character of its objectives.

It is easy to show that Negro slaves did not always cooperate with the system of slavery. It is another matter to prove that noncooperation amounted to political resistance. Malingering may have reflected no more than a disinclination to work, especially when the rewards were so meager. Likewise, what is taken for sabotage may have originated in apathy and indifference. Acts of violence are subject to varying interpretations. If there is something undeniably political about an organized, premeditated rebellion, an isolated act of violence could arise from a purely personal grievance. Even the motive of flight is obscure: was it an impulse, prompted by some special and immediate affront, or was it desertion, a sort of separate peace? These acts in themselves tell us very little. We begin to understand them only when we understand the conceptual distinction between resistance and noncooperation; and even then, we still feel the need of a more general set of conceptions, derived from recorded experience, to which slavery — an unrecorded experience, except from the masters' point of view — can be compared; some general model which will enable us to grasp imaginatively the system as a whole.

III

Only the testimony of the slaves could tell us, once and for all, whether slaves resisted slavery. In the absence of their testimony, it is tempting to resort to analogies. Indeed it is almost impossible to avoid them. Those who condemn analogies, pretending to argue from the documentary evidence alone, delude themselves. Resistance to slavery cannot be established (any more than any other general conception of the institution can be established) without making an implicit analogy between Negro slavery and the struggles of free men, in our own time, "to give dignity to human life" by resisting oppression. The question, in the case of slavery, is not whether historians should argue from analogy but whether they are willing to make their analogies explicit.

Stanley Elkins compares slavery to the Nazi concentration camps and concludes that the effect of slavery was to break down the slave's adult personality and to reduce him to a state of infantile dependence, comparable to the condition observed by survivors of the concentration camps. In evaluating this particular analogy, we are entitled to ask how well it explains what we actually know about slavery. In one respect, it explains too much. It explains the fact that there were no slave rebellions in the United States comparable to those which took place in Latin America, but it also rules out the possibility of noncooperation. Elkins' analogy suggests a state of internalized dependency that does not fit the facts of widespread intransigence, insubordination, and mischief-making. Stampp may not adequately explain this pattern of behavior, but he convinces us that it existed. Elkins is open to criticism on empirical grounds for failing to take into account a vast amount of evidence that does not fit his theory of slave behavior. Many of Elkins' critics, however, have not concerned themselves with the substance of his analogy. Raising neither empirical nor theoretical objections against it, they have seized on its mere existence as a means of discrediting Elkins' work. He should rather be congratulated for having made the analogy explicit, thereby introducing into the study of slavery the kinds of questions that modern studies of total institutions have dealt with far more systematically than conventional studies of slavery.

Elkins was careful to emphasize the limits of the comparison. He did not argue that the plantation resembled a concentration camp with respect to intentions or motives; "even 'cruelty,'" he added, "was not indispensable as an item in my equation." His "essentially limited purpose" in bringing the two institutions together was to show the psychological effects of closed systems of control; and the objections to the analogy may after all derive not from the analogy itself but from a tendency, among Elkins' critics, to take it too literally. As Elkins observes, the "very vividness and particularity [of analogies] are coercive: they are almost too concrete. One's impulse is thus to reach for extremes. The thing is either taken whole hog . . . ; or it is rejected out of hand on the ground that not all of the parts fit." It is precisely because all the parts don't fit that an analogy is an analogy rather than a literal correspondence, and it ought to be enough, therefore, if just one of the parts demonstrably fits.[9]

The real objection to Elkins' analogy is not that analogies in themselves are pernicious but that there is no compelling theoretical reason, in this case, to stop with one. The concentration camp is only one of many total institutions with which slavery might have been compared; a total institution being defined, in Erving Goffman's words, as "a place of residence and work where a large number of like-situated individuals, cut off from the wider society for an appreciable period of time, together lead an enclosed, formally administered round of life."[10] An excellent example — the one, indeed, that springs immediately to mind — is the prison, "providing," Goffman says, that "we appreciate that what is prison-like about prisons is found in institutions whose members have broken no laws."[11] In several respects, prisons, especially penitentiaries, are more analogous to plantation slavery than concentration camps. Prisons are not, like the concentration camps, designed as experiments in deliberate dehumanization, although they often have dehumanizing effects; in this respect the motive behind the system more nearly approximates that of slavery than of the concentration camp. More important, the problem of control is more nearly analogous. The disproportion between the authority of the guards and the impotence of the inmates is not absolute, as it was at Dachau and Buchenwald, but subject, as it seems to have been under slavery, to a number of variables — the temperament of the guard or master, the composition of the prisoners or slaves, the immediate history of the institutions involved.

Prison officials, like slaveowners and overseers, face a constant problem of noncooperation. "Far from being omnipotent rulers who have crushed all signs of rebellion against their regime, the custodians are engaged in a continuous struggle to maintain order — and it is a struggle in which the custodians frequently fail."[12] This situation occurs, according to the sociologist Gresham Sykes, because although the custodians enjoy an absolute monopoly of the means of violence, their enormous power does not rest on authority; that is, on "a rightful or legitimate effort to exercise control," which inspires in the governed an internalized sense of obligation to obey. In the absence of a sense of duty among the prisoners, the guards have to rely on a system of rewards, incentives, punishments, and coercion. But none of these methods can be carried too far without reaching dangerous extremes of laxity or demoralization. As in most total institutions — the concentration camp being a conspicuous exception — rigid standards of discipline tend to give way before the need to keep things running smoothly without undue effort on the part of the custodians. An absolute monopoly of violence can be used to achieve a state of total terror, but it cannot persuade men to work at their jobs or move "more than 1,200 inmates through the mess hall in a routine and orderly fashion."[13] The result, in the maximum-security prison, is a system of compromises, an uneasy give-and-take which gives prisoners a limited leverage within the system. To the extent that this adjustment limits the power of the guards, a corruption of authority takes place.[14]

Plantation literature produces numerous parallels. We can read the masters' incessant and heartfelt complaints about the laziness, the inefficiency, and the intractibility of slaves; the difficulty of getting them to work; the difficulty of enlisting their cooperation in any activity that had to be sustained over a period of time. We can read about the system of rewards and punishments, spelled out by the master in such detail, the significance of which, we can now see, was that it had had to be resorted to precisely in the degree to which a sense of internalized obedience had failed. We see the same limitation of terror and physical coercion as has been observed in the prison; for even less than the prison authorities could the planter tolerate the demoralization resulting from an excess of violence. We can even see the same "corruption of authority" in the fact that illicit slave behavior, especially minor theft, was often tolerated by the masters in order to avoid unnecessary friction.

One of the most curious features of the "society of captives," as described by Sykes is this: that while most of the prisoners recognize the legitimacy of their imprisonment and the controls to which they are subjected, they lack any internalized sense of obligation to obey them. "The bond between recognition of the legitimacy of control and the sense of duty has been torn apart."[15] This fact about prisons makes it possible to understand a puzzling feature of the contemporary literature on slavery, which neither the model of submission nor that of resistance explains — the curious contradiction between the difficulty of discipline and the slaves' professed devotion to their masters. Those who argue that the slaves resisted slavery have to explain away their devotion as pure hypocrisy. But it is possible to accept it as sincere without endorsing the opposite view — even in the sophisticated form in which it has been cast by Stanley Elkins — that slaves were children. The sociology of total institutions provides a theory with which to reconcile the contradiction. "The custodial institution," Sykes argues, "is valuable for a theory of human behavior because it makes us realize that men need not be motivated to conform to a regime which they define as rightful."[16] It is theoretically possible, in short, that slaves could have accepted the legitimacy of their masters' authority without feeling any sense of obligation to obey it. The evidence of the masters themselves makes this conclusion seem not only possible but highly probable. Logic, moreover, supports this view. For how could a system that rigorously defined the Negro slave not merely as an inferior but as an alien, a separate order of being, inspire him with the sense of belonging on which internalized obedience necessarily has to rest?

IV

It might be argued, however, that slaves developed a sense of obedience by default, having had no taste of life outside slavery which would have made them dissatisfied, by contrast, with their treatment as slaves. It might be argued that the convict's dissatisfaction with prison conditions and the insubordination that results derives from his sense of the outside world and the satisfactions it normally provides; and that such a perspective must have been lacking on the plantation. Elkins, in denying the possibility of any sort of accommodation to slavery short of the complete assimilation of the master's authority by the slave, contends that a consciously defensive posture could not exist, given the total authority of the master and the lack of "alternative forces for moral and psychological orientation."[17] This objection loses its force, however, if it can be shown that the slave did in fact have chances to develop independent standards of personal satisfaction and fair treatment within the system of slavery itself. Such standards would have made possible a hedonistic strategy of accommodation, and in cases where such a strategy failed, strong feelings of personal grievance.

It is true that the plantation sealed itself off from the world, depriving the slave of nearly every influence that would have lifted him out of himself into a larger awareness of slavery as an oppressive social system which, by its very nature, denied him normal satisfaction. In order to understand why slaves did not, as Elkins suggests, become totally submissive and ready to accept any form of cruelty and humiliation, it is necessary to focus on an aspect of slavery which has been almost totally ignored in discussion of slave personality. The typical slave, although born into slavery, was not likely to spend his entire life, or indeed any considerable part of it, under a single regime. The slave child could anticipate many changes of situation. It would appear likely, from what we know of the extent of the slave trade, that most slaves changed hands at least once in their lives; slave narratives and recollections suggest that it was not at all uncommon for a single slave to belong to several masters in the course of his lifetime of servitude. In addition, the prevalence of slave-hiring, especially in the upper South, meant that many slaves experienced a temporary change of regime. Even if a slave remained on the same plantation, things could change drastically, as the result of death and the accession of an heir, or from a change of overseer (especially significant in cases of absentee ownership).[18] Given the wide variation in standards of treatment and management techniques — a variation which, we suggested earlier, seems the one inescapable conclusion to be drawn from the traditional scholarship on the management of slaves — we are left with a situation that must have had important psychological implications. An individual slave might — like Harriet Beecher Stowe's Uncle Tom — experience slavery both at its mildest and at its harshest. He might be sold from an indulgent master to a cruel one or vice versa. He might go from a farm where he maintained a close and intimate relationship with his master to a huge impersonal "factory in the fields," where his actual master would be only a dim presence. These changes in situation led many slaves to develop standards of their own about how they ought to be treated and even to diffuse these standards among the stationary slave population. By comparing his less onerous lot under a previous master to his present hard one, a slave could develop a real sense of grievance and communicate it to others.[19] Similarly, slaves were quick to take advantage of any new leniency or laxity in control.[20] Hence it is quite possible to account for widespread noncooperation among slaves as resulting from a rudimentary sense of justice acquired entirely within the system of slavery itself. These standards would have served the same function as the standards convicts bring from the outside world into the prison. At the same time it is necessary to insist once again that they give rise to a pattern of intransigence which is hedonistic rather than political, accommodationist rather than revolutionary.

If this picture of slave motivation is less morally sublime than contemporary liberals and radicals would like, it should not be construed as constituting, in any sense, a moral judgment on the Negro slave. Sporadic noncooperation within a broad framework of accommodation was the natural and inevitable response to plantation slavery. It should go without saying that white men born into the same system would have acted in the same way. Indeed, this is the way they have been observed to act in modern situations analogous to slavery. In total institutions, the conditions for sustained resistance are generally wanting — a fact that is insufficiently appreciated by those armchair moralists who like to make judgments at a safe distance about the possibilities of resistance to totalitarianism. Rebellions and mutinies "seem to be the exception," Erving Goffman observes, "not the rule." Group loyalty is very tenuous, even though "the expectation that group loyalty should prevail forms part of the inmate culture and underlies the hostility accorded to those who break inmate solidarity."[21]

Instead of banding together, inmates of total institutions typically pursue various personal strategies of accommodation. Goffman describes four lines of adaptation, but it is important to note that although these are analytically distinguishable, "the same inmate will employ different personal lines of adaptation at different phases in his moral career and may even alternate among different tacks at the same time." "Situational withdrawal," a fatalistic apathy, is the condition into which many inmates of concentration camps rapidly descended, with disastrous psychic consequences to themselves; it undoubtedly took its toll among slaves newly arrived from Africa during the colonial period. "Colonization," which in some cases can be regarded as another type of institutional neurosis, rests on a conscious decision that life in the institution is preferable to life in the outside world. Colonization, in turn, must be distinguished from "conversion," the inmate's internalization of the view of himself held by those in power. In Negro slavery, this is the "Sambo" role and is accompanied, as in the concentration camp, by an infantile sense of dependence. Colonization, on the other hand, would apply to the very small number of slaves who agreed to reenslavement after a period as free Negroes.[22]

The fourth type of accommodation is "intransigence," which should not be confused with resistance. The latter presupposes a sense of solidarity and an underground organization of inmates. Intransigence is a personal strategy of survival, and although it can sometimes help to sustain a high morale, it can just as easily lead to futile and even self-destructive acts of defiance. In slavery, there was a substantial minority who were written off by their masters as chronic troublemakers, "bad niggers," and an even larger group who indulged in occasional insubordination. It is precisely the pervasiveness of "intransigence" that made slaves, like convicts, so difficult to manage, leading to the corruption of authority analyzed above. But as we have already tried to show, there is nothing about intransigence that precludes a partial acceptance of the values of the institution. In fact, Goffman observes that the most defiant of inmates are paradoxically those who are most completely caught up in the daily round of institutional life. "Sustained rejection of a total institution often requires sustained orientation to its formal organization, and hence, paradoxically, a deep kind of involvement in the establishment."[23] The same immersion in the institutional routine that makes some inmates so easy to manage makes others peculiarly sensitive to disruptions of the routine, jealous of their "rights" under the system. Indeed, periods of intransigence can alternate, in the same person, with colonization, conversion, and even with periods of withdrawal.

The concentration camp was unique among total institutions in confronting the typical prisoner with a choice between situational withdrawal, which meant death, and conversion, which, in the absence of alternatives, came to dominate the personality as a fully internalized role. In other total institutions, however, all four roles can be played to some extent, and "few inmates seem to pursue any one of them very far. In most total institutions most inmates take the tack of what some of them call 'playing it cool.' This involves a somewhat opportunistic combination of secondary adjustments, conversion, colonization, and loyalty to the inmate group, so that the inmate will have a maximum chance, in the particular circumstances, of eventually getting out physically and psychologically undamaged."[24] The slave had no real prospect of "getting out," but unless he was infantilized — a hypothesis that now seems quite untenable — he had a powerful stake in psychic survival. He had every reason to play it cool; and what is more, slavery gave him plenty of opportunities.

But the most compelling consideration in favor of this interpretation of slavery is that the very ways in which slavery differed from other total institutions would have actually reinforced and stabilized the pattern of opportunistic response that we have described. The most obvious objection to an analogy between slavery and the prison, the mental hospital, or any other institution of this kind is that slaves for the most part were born into slavery rather than coming in from the outside as adults; nor did most of them have any hope of getting out. We have answered these objections in various ways, but before leaving the matter we should point out that there is, in fact, a class of people in modern asylums — a minority, to be sure — who spend the better part of their lives in institutions of one kind or another. "Lower class mental hospital patients," for instance, "who have lived all their previous lives in orphanages, reformatories, and jails," are people whose experience in this respect approximates the slave's, especially the slave who served a series of masters. As a result of their continuous confinement, such patients have developed a kind of institutional personality. But they are not, as one might expect, Sambos — genuine converts to the institutional view of themselves. Quite the contrary; these people are the master-opportunists, for whom "no particular scheme of adaptation need be carried very far."[25] They have "perfected their adaptive techniques," experience having taught them a supreme versatility; and they are therefore likely to play it cool with more success than those brought in from the outside and incarcerated for the first time. These are the virtuosos of the system, neither docile nor rebellious, who spend their lives in skillful and somewhat cynical attempts to beat the system at its own game.

V

There is a passage in Frederick Douglass' *Narrative* that suggests how difficult it was even for an ex-slave — an unusually perceptive observer, in this case — to understand his former victimization without resorting to categories derived from experiences quite alien to slavery, categories that reflected the consciousness not of the slaves themselves but, in one way or another, the consciousness of the master-class. Douglass described how eagerly the slaves on Colonel Lloyd's Maryland plantations vied for the privilege of running errands to the Great House Farm, the master's residence and home plantation. The slaves "regarded it as evidence of great confidence reposed in them by the overseers; and it was on this account, as well as a constant desire to be out of the field from under the driver's lash, that they esteemed it a high privilege, one worth careful living for. He was called the smartest and most trusty fellow, who had this honor conferred upon him the most frequently."

Then follows a passage of unusual vividness and poignancy:

The slaves selected to go to the Great House Farm, for the monthly allowance for themselves and their fellow-slaves, were peculiarly enthusiastic. While on their way, they would make the dense old woods, for miles around, reverberate with their wild songs, revealing at once the highest joy and the deepest sadness. . . . They would sometimes sing the most pathetic sentiment in the most rapturous tone, and the most rapturous sentiment in the most pathetic tone. Into all of their songs they would manage to weave something of the Great House Farm. Especially would they do this, when leaving home. they would then sing most exultingly the following words: —

'I am going away to the Great House Farm!
O, yea! O, yea! O!'

This they would sing, as a chorus, to words which to many would seem unmeaning jargon, but which, nevertheless, were full of meaning to themselves. I have sometimes thought that the mere hearing of those songs would do more to impress some minds with the horrible character of slavery, than the reading of whole volumes of philosophy on the subject could do.

But as these passages so clearly show, the "horrible character of slavery" did not lie, as the abolitionists tended to think, in the deprivations to which the slaves were forcibly subjected — deprivations which, resenting, they resisted with whatever means came to hand — but in the degree to which the slaves (even in their "intransigence") inevitably identified themselves with the system that bound and confined them, lending themselves to their own degradation. In vying for favors they "sought as diligently to please their overseers," Douglass says, "as the office-seekers in the political parties seek to please and deceive the people."[26]

Even more revealing are the reflections that follow. "I did not, when a slave, understand the deep meaning of those rude and apparently incoherent songs. I was myself within the circle; so that I neither saw nor heard as those without might see and hear." It was only from without that the slave songs revealed themselves as "the prayer and complaint of souls boiling over with the bitterest anguish" — anguish, it should be noted, which expressed itself disjointedly, "the most pathetic sentiment" being set to "the most rapturous tone." It was only from without that the "dehumanizing character of slavery" showed itself precisely in the slave's incapacity to resist; but this perception, once gained, immediately distorted the reality to which it was applied. Douglass slides imperceptibly from these unforgettable evocations of slavery to an abolitionist polemic. It is a great mistake, he argued, to listen to slaves' songs "as evidence of their contentment and happiness." On the contrary, "slaves sing most when they are most unhappy." Yet the slaves whose "wild songs" he has just described were those who were "peculiarly enthusiastic," by his own account, to be sent to the Great House Farm, and who sang "exultingly" along the way. The ambiguity of the reality begins to fade when seen through the filter of liberal humanitarianism, and whereas the songs revealed "at once the highest joy and the deepest sadness," in Douglass' own words, as an abolitionist he feels it necessary to insist that "crying for joy, and singing for joy, were alike uncommon to me while in the jaws of slavery."[27]

If the abolitionist lens distorted the "horrible character" of slavery, the picture of the docile and apparently contented bondsman was no more faithful to the reality it purported to depict. But this should not surprise us. It is not often that men understand, or even truly see, those whom in charity they would uplift. How much less often do they understand those they exploit?

Notes

[1] Stanley Elkins, *Slavery: A Problem in American Institutional and Intellectual Life* (Chicago, 1959), Ch. I.

[2] Kenneth Stampp, *The Peculiar Institution* (New York, 1956), pp. 88, 91.

[3] Frederick Douglass, *The Narrative of the Life of Frederick Douglass, an American Slave* (Cambridge, 1960), pp. 132–133.

[4] Martin D. de B. Kilson, "Towards Freedom: An Analysis of Slave Revolts in the United States," *Phylon*, XXV (1964), 179–183.

[5] Stampp, *Peculiar Institution*, Ch. III.

[6] Total institutions are distinguished not by the absolute power of the authorities — a definition which, as will become clear, prejudges an important issue — but by the fact that they are self-contained, so that every detail of life is regulated in accordance with the dominant purpose of the institution. Whether that purpose is defined as healing, punishment, forced labor, or (in the case of the concentration camps) terror, all total institutions are set up in such a way as to preclude any form of politics based on consent.

[7] See E. J. Hobsbawm, *Primitive Rebels: Studies in Archaic Forms of Social Movement in the 19th and 20th Centuries* (Manchester, 1959); Norman Cohn, *The Pursuit of the Millennium* (New York, 1957).

[8] Nat Turner's rebellion in 1831, the only significant slave uprising in the period 1820–1860 that got beyond the plotting stage, would seem to be comparable to a millennialist peasants' revolt. Turner was a preacher who, according to his own testimony, received the visitation of a spirit commanding him to "fight against the serpent, for the time was fast approaching when the first should be last and the last should be first." Quoted in Herbert Aptheker, *American Negro Slave Revolts* (New York, 1943), p. 296. See also Aptheker, *Nat Turner's Slave Rebellion* (New York, 1966).

[9] Elkins, *Slavery*, pp. 104, 226.

[10] Erving Goffman, *Asylums: Essays on the Social Situation of Mental Patients and Other Inmates* (Garden City, 1961: Chicago, 1962), p. xiii.

[11] *Ibid.*

[12] Gresham M. Sykes, *The Society of Captives: A Study of a Maximum Security Prison* (Princeton, 1958), p. 42.

[13] *Ibid.*, p. 49.

[14] *Ibid.*, pp. 52–58.

[15] *Ibid.*, p. 46.

[16] *Ibid.*, p. 48.

[17] Elkins, *Slavery*, p. 133n.

[18] Frederic Bancroft, in *Slave Trading in the Old South* (New York, 1959), concludes (pp. 382–406) that more than 700,000 slaves were transported from the upper South to the cotton kingdom in the years 1830–1860, and that most went by way of the slave trade. He also estimates (p. 405) that in the decade 1850–1860 an annual average of approximately 140,000

slaves were sold, interstate or *intra-state*, or hired out by their masters. This meant that one slave in twenty-five changed his *de facto* master in a given year. When we add to these regular exchanges the informal transfers that went on within families, we get some idea of the instability which characterized the slave's situation in an expansive and dynamic agricultural economy. The way slaves were sometimes shuttled about is reflected in several of the slave narratives, especially Frederick Douglass, *Narrative;* Solomon Northrup, *Twelve Years a Slave* (Auburn, Buffalo, and London, 1853); and [Charles Ball] *Fifty Years in Chains: Or the Life of an American Slave* (New York, 1858).

[19] Positive evidence of this development of internal standards and of the vacillation between contentment and dissatisfaction to which it gave rise is as difficult to find as evidence on any other aspect of slave psychology. As we have indicated, adequate records of personal slave response simply do not exist. There is, however, some indication of this process in the slave narratives and recollections. One of the most revealing of the slave narratives is Charles Ball, *Fifty Years in Chains.* Ball's account seems truer than most to the reality of slavery because, unlike most fugitives, he escaped from servitude at an age when it was difficult for him to acquire new habits of thought from his free status and association with abolitionists. Ball recounts the common experience of being sold from the upper South with its relatively mild and permissive regime into the more rigorous plantation slavery farther south. Upon his arrival on a large South Carolina cotton plantation, Ball, who was from Maryland, makes the acquaintance of a slave from northern Virginia who tells him what he can now expect. "He gave me such an account of the suffering of the slaves, on the cotton and indigo plantations — of whom I now regarded myself as one — that I was unable to sleep this night." (pp. 103–104.) Later, he describes himself as "far from the place of my nativity, in a land of strangers, with no one to care for me beyond the care that a master bestows upon his ox . . . ." (p. 115.) The regime is indeed a harsh one, and he feels very dissatisfied, except on Sunday when he is taken up by the general hilarity that prevails in the slave quarters on the holiday. Eventually, however, he experiences a temporary improvement in his situation when he is given to his master's new son-in-law, who seems kindly and permissive. In a remarkable description of slave hedonism, Ball recalls his state of mind. "I now felt assured that all my troubles in this world were ended, and that, in future, I might look forward to a life of happiness and ease, for I did not consider labor any hardship, if I was well provided with good food and clothes, and my other wants properly regarded." (p. 266.) This is too good to last, however; and Ball's new master dies, leaving him in the hands of another man, "of whom, when I considered the part of the country from whence he came, which had always been represented to me as distinguished for the cruelty with which slaves were treated, I had no reason to expect much that was good." (pp. 271–272.) His new master turns out to be much less harsh than anticipated, but the master's wife, a woman with sadistic tendencies, takes a positive dislike to Ball and resents her husband's paternal attitude toward him. When the master dies, Ball recognizes his situation as intolerable and resolves upon flight. (p. 307.) Ball's narrative reveals the way in which a slave could evaluate his changes of condition by standards of comfort and accommodation derived from experience within the system itself. In desperate situations, this evaluation could lead to extreme forms of noncooperation.

Despite the fact that he was recalling his experience after having escaped from slavery and, presumably, after coming under the influence of northern antislavery sentiment, Ball's general attitude remained remarkably accommodationist, at least in respect to slavery at its best. In a revealing passage, he notes that the typical slave lacks a real sense of identity of interest with his master, is jealous of his prerogatives, and steals from him without qualms. Yet, Ball concludes, there "is in fact, a mutual dependence between the master and his slave. The former could not acquire anything without the labor of the latter, and the latter would always remain in poverty without the judgment of the former in directing labor to a definite and profitable result." (p. 219.)

[20] See Stampp, *Peculiar Institution,* pp. 104–108.

[21] Goffman, *Asylums,* pp. 18–19. Cf. Donald Clemmer, *The Prison Community* (New York, 1958), pp. 297–298: "The prisoner's world is an atomized world. . . . There are no definite communal objectives. There is no consensus for a common goal. The inmates' conflict with officialdom and opposition toward society is only slightly greater in degree than conflict

and opposition among themselves. Trickery and dishonesty overshadow sympathy and cooperation. . . . It is a world of 'I,' 'me,' and 'mine,' rather than 'ours,' 'theirs,' and 'his.' " Clemmer adds, p. 293: "Such collective action of protest as does arise, comes out of an immediate situation in which they themselves are involved, and not as protest to an idea."

[22] Colonization, while uncommon among slaves, is frequently encountered in prisons and particularly in mental institutions. The high rate of recidivism among convicts and the frequency with which mental patients are sent back to asylums reflect not simply a relapse into a former sickness which the institution did not cure, but in many cases, a sickness which the institution itself created — an institutional neurosis which has its own peculiar characteristics, the most outstanding of which is the inability to function outside systems of total control.

[23] Goffman, *Asylums*, p. 62.

[24] *Ibid.*, pp. 64–65.

[25] *Ibid.*, pp. 65–66.

[26] Douglass, *Narrative*, pp. 35–37.

[27] *Ibid.*, pp. 37–38.

The General Causes of Jamaican Slave Revolts

H. Orlando Patterson

With the possible exception of Brazil, no other slave society in the New World experienced such continuous and intense servile revolts as Jamaica. During the seventeenth and eighteenth centuries the slaves of Barbados and the Leeward Islands were remarkably docile compared with those of Jamaica, only two mild disturbances taking place in all the latter islands during this time.[1] Aptheker "found records of approximately 250 revolts and conspiracies in the history of American Negro slavery."[2] But his definition of a revolt was rather liberal[3] and in any case, when these 250 cases are spread over the much greater slave population of America and over the much longer period of slavery there, the Jamaican record is far more impressive. In addition, the scale of the average Jamaican revolt was far greater and more dangerous than that of the average American. The most serious revolt in the latter country — that of Nat Turner — involved only 70 slaves. The average number of slaves in the Jamaica revolts of the seventeenth and eighteenth centuries was approximately 400, and the three most serious revolts of the island — the first Maroon war; the 1760 rebellion; and the 1832 rebellion — each involved over a thousand slaves.

For this greater spirit of rebellion among the Jamaican slaves compared with those of the other British slave societies of the New World several causes may be given. First, there was the ratio of masters to slaves. On average, there were, during the seventeenth and eighteenth centuries over ten slaves to every white person in the island; and in the nineteenth century, over thirteen slaves to every white.[4] In Barbados, on the other hand, the average ratio during the entire period of slavery was very close to four slaves to one white,[5] and although after 1724 the number of slaves increased greatly in the Leeward Islands, with the exception of Antigua, it was never more than eight Negroes to one white. In the case of the American South we find that of the fourteen slave states only two — South Carolina and Mississippi — had slave populations which slightly outnumbered the whites. In nine

From H. Orlando Patterson, *The Sociology of Slavery* (London: McGibbon & Kee, Ltd., 1967), pp. 273–83. Reprinted by permission of McGibbon & Kee and Associated University Presses, Inc.

of the other states the slave population varied between 1.5 and 33 per cent; and in three, between 44 per cent and 47 per cent of the total population.[6] Thus, of all the British slave societies Jamaica had by far the highest ratio of slaves to whites. A brief comparative analysis is enough to demonstrate a positive correlation between the density of the slave population and the frequency of servile revolts. If we take the most famous of the slave revolts of ancient times — that of the Sicilian revolt of 134–32 B.C. — we find that it was that area of the Roman Empire which had the highest proportion of slaves in the population which broke into rebellion, Sicily being, according to Mommsen, "the chosen land of the plantation system."[7] In the case of the Leeward Islands we find that the only two serious conspiracies took place in Antigua in 1736[8] and Tortola in 1790[9] both of which had the two highest ratios of slaves to whites in their population.[10] And with regard to the United States Aptheker has noted that "areas of dense Negro population, particularly areas showing a recent accession, were very frequently the centers of unrest."[11] It is not unreasonable to conclude therefore, that the greater density of the Jamaican slave population partly accounts for its larger number of slave revolts in comparison with other slave societies of the New World.

The second general cause accounting for the frequency of Jamaican slave revolts is to be found in the ratio between creole and African slaves. Naturally, a slave population which had a higher proportion of slaves who were born freemen and were enslaved only as adults would exhibit a greater tendency to revolt than one in which there was a higher proportion of creoles who were born into the system and socialized in it. It is significant that almost every one of the revolts of the seventeenth and eighteenth centuries was instigated and carried out by African slaves (and their children born in the rebel camps). The agent for Jamaica in England wrote after the 1776 revolt that the planters had been "more particularly alarmed on Account of many of the Creole Negroes being concerned in it, who never were concerned in former rebellions."[12] In an earlier chapter we have estimated the African sector of the slave population in the middle of the eighteenth century at about a half; at the end of the eighteenth century at a little more than a quarter; and in the last decade or so of slavery, at about a little less than a quarter. The reason for the persistence of the African sector was the failure of the slave population to reproduce itself in Jamaica. On the other hand, we may infer from the more successful attempts at reproduction both in Barbados[13] and the United States[14] that the creole slaves formed a much greater proportion of those populations at a much earlier period than they did in Jamaica. This factor, in turn, partly accounts for the greater frequency of slave revolts in Jamaica.

Thirdly, there was the quality of the slaves bought by the Jamaican planters. It is remarkable that almost every one of the serious rebellions during the seventeenth and eighteenth centuries was instigated and carried out mainly by Akan slaves who came from a highly developed militaristic régime, skilled in jungle warfare.[15] Yet a bill to restrain their entry into the island after the 1765 revolt was defeated.[16] It is significant that modern researches on the descendants of the Maroon rebels reveal a marked degree of Akan cultural survivals among them.[17]

A fourth general cause of these revolts lies in the character of the Jamaican whites — their inefficiency (especially in military matters) and general smugness. Goveia explains the absence of any serious slave revolt in the Leewards in terms of the rigid execution of the slave laws which were "expressly designed to make formal organization virtually impossible."[18] Jamaica too, had many severe laws in this respect but they were made useless by the planters' lack of vigilance. The planters' attitude toward slave revolts oscillated between extreme hysteria and unbelievable smugness. Corbett wrote near the middle of the eighteenth century that:

One would imagine that Planters really think that Negroes are not of the same Species with us, but that being of a different Mould and Nature as well as Colour, they were made entirely for our Use, with Instincts proper for that Purpose, having as great a propensity to subjection as we have to command and loving slavery as naturally as we do liberty; and that there is not need for Management, but that of themselves they will most pleasantly to hard labour, hard Usages of all kinds, Cruelties and Injustice at the Caprice of one white man — such one would imagine is the Planter's Way of thinking.[19]

He bemoans the neglect of the slave laws, and on the hysteria of the planters in time of danger he comments: "As no People are more thoughtless of Danger at a Distance, so I must own they are apprehensive of it enough when it is at hand."[20] The vacillation of the planters was particularly marked during the nineteenth century. Between 1800 and 1825 — due largely to the successful slave revolt in the neighboring island of Haiti — the responses and fears of the planters in respect of conspiracies or suspected plots were out of all proportion to what did in fact take place among the slaves which, in the words of the governor, often amounted to little more than "a very active spirit of enquiry which may be naturally accounted for without attributing to them any criminal intentions."[21] On the other hand, by 1831 the planters had, to use Corbett's phrase, relating to the mid-eighteenth century "took T'other Turn and fell quietly flat a-sleep again." The abolition debate was openly discussed by them in front of their slaves without the slightest awareness of the impact it was having on them. One of them, an assemblyman, even went so far as to write that "Our Slave Population have been too long habituated to hear discussed the details of the question of slavery and emancipation, for us to entertain any alarm from their recollections on this subject."[22] And a visitor to the island during the period of the rebellion wrote that:

The greater part of the inhabitants of Jamaica had indeed been lulling themselves into a fancied and fatal security, while, in fact, they were sleeping on a mine; and any one who suspected the probability of an insurrection was looked upon as a timid alarmist (even after the preparatory notes of insubordination had been sounded).[23]

It was in vain that the governor pleaded with them to be more discreet in their denunciation of the abolitionists.[24] One can well understand then, why the masters had no hint of the widespread rebellion that broke out after Christmas 1831 until a few days before it actually began,[25] although the secrecy with which the slaves kept their plans must be borne in mind.

A fifth cause of slave revolts in the island was to be found in the treatment and maintenance of the slaves. A historian of ancient slavery has noted that "in any slave system the slave group has definite rights — not legal, but actual, and sanctioned by custom. These rights the slaves both accept and insist upon;"[26] and he gives this as "the primary cause of the first Sicilian slave revolt."[27] It has already been pointed out in our chapter on the slave laws that the Jamaican slave, like his American and Sicilian counterpart, had certain minimum customary rights which he insisted upon. Without becoming involved in the rather tired controversy as to which area of the New World had the most severe form of slavery — a controversy which Professor Harris, has, not unreasonably, dismissed as "a waste of time"[28] — it may be suggested that there was one feature of Jamaican slave society which may well have encouraged the greater infringement of the minimal customary rights of the slaves. This was the excessive degree of absenteeism which was greater than in any other slave colony in the New World. Pitman makes the cogent observation that the period during which the whites suffered most from the rebels and general desertion from the estates — i.e., between 1730 and 1739 — was that in which the profits from sugar had greatly declined, in which large numbers of whites were leaving the island and those supervising the slaves were making excessive demands on their labor in addition to reducing their supplies of clothing and food.[29]

Another factor explaining the revolts of the island was its geography. The mountainous interior of the country with its intricate, innumerable ravines, naturally concealed mountain passes, precipices and forests, was ideal for guerrilla warfare. In this respect the African slaves, used to the jungle warfare of their own country, had an insurmountable advantage over their British masters. It was their knowledge of the interior country and the guerrilla tactics they evolved[30] in it which more than compensated for the inferiority of the Maroons in arms and numbers against the whites. The latter sought to redress the balance in their favor by importing Mosquito Indians in the 1720's[31] and specially trained Cuban bloodhounds in 1795,[32] but there is no evidence that either of these measures proved of any use. After 1740, however, with the Maroons on the side of the whites, the opportunities offered by the interior of the country were cut off to future rebels.

Finally, between 1770 and 1832, rebellions in Jamaica were caused partly by the impact of certain social, religious, and political forces current at that time, on the slave. The agent for Jamaica in England suggested that the American Revolution may have been partly responsible for the slave revolt of 1776, the first in which the creole slaves played a significant part.[33] And Balcarres, Governor of Jamaica, insisted that the second Maroon war of 1795 was largely instigated by professional revolutionaries from Haiti, France, and the United States.[34] So much did the planters fear the contagious revolutionary spirit of the Haitian Negroes who had successfully revolted against their masters, that an entire regiment of soldiers who had been recruited from among the slaves to augment the troops of an ill-fated attack on Haiti was refused readmittance into the island. They were disbanded in Haiti and "numbers of them joined the enemy."[35]

The abolition movement also played its part in inciting the slaves to revolt. Its influence, however, was due largely to the misinterpretation (sometimes deliberately) by the slaves of the debates they heard among their masters and — in a few cases — read in local or foreign newspapers.[36] Large numbers of slaves who joined the various conspiracies of the nineteenth century were convinced that the King, or some other benefactor abroad, had sent their "free-paper" but that the planters were maliciously keeping it from them. When the slave trade was abolished in 1807 it was generally believed among the slaves that they had been emancipated. Related to the abolition movement were the activities of the missionaries who had begun to preach among the slaves with some effect since the last decade of the eighteenth century. While these preachers strenuously denied ever inciting the slaves to revolt, there can be little doubt that the latter saw in the egalitarian aspects of Christianity part of the justification they needed to rebel against their masters. When a popular preacher left for a short stay in England in 1831 his return was anxiously awaited as it was the general opinion that he would be returning with "the gift" or their "free-paper."[37] Indeed, the rebellion of 1831–32 was dubbed the "Baptist war" by the Negroes.[38]

As in Jamaica, the American Revolution,[39] the Haitian slave revolution,[40] the abolition movement,[41] as well as rumor of the King having sent orders to set them free and debates about emancipation all played their part in inciting the American slaves to revolt. The Haitian revolution — the only completely successful slave revolt in the New World — was directly inspired and made possible by the French Revolution. There are also instances in ancient slavery where rumors regarding their emancipation incited agitation among slaves, for example, the possible disturbances created in Asia Minor by the rumor of the emancipation of the slaves in Pergamum during the First Century B.C.[42]

The final question to be answered is why was it that despite the favorable conditions discussed above, the Jamaican slaves failed to overthrow their masters? The first answer is the divisions within the slave group itself. These were of two types: firstly, that between the African slaves. Due partly to the deliberate policy of the masters, and, more important, to the nature of the supply of slaves, it was the unusual estate which had all, or even the majority of its slaves from one tribal stock. And it would seem that the different tribal groups hated "one another so mortally that some of them would rather die by the Hands of the English than join with other Africans in an Attempt to shake off their yoke."[43] The second major division was that between the creole slaves and the Africans. We have already discussed the animosity which the creoles bore for the Africans, and it is inconceivable that any of them would allow themselves to be led in a rebellion by an African.

A second reason for the slaves' lack of success was, paradoxically, their early successes against the whites. The whites, having been obliged to come to terms with the Maroons in 1739, then proceeded to use them to prevent or subdue further uprisings. It was unfortunate for the slaves that Cudjoe — the rebel chief with whom the first treaty was signed — should have been as obsequious in his relations with the whites as he was, since the position from which he negotiated with them was not weak. Several of his commanding officers disagreed with the treaty to the extent of rebelling against his authority and attempting to incite the slaves on the plantations to revolt.[44]

Finally, there was the military strength of the whites. It is true that the militia was an inefficient body but, however incompetent its members were, they had at least some semblance of up-to-date military training and a more than adequate supply of arms. Against these the relatively primitive African rebels could never hope to win in an open engagement, and when the possibility of compensating for their disadvantage by resorting to guerrilla warfare was cut off, the chances of a successful revolt became very thin. This was, of course, as long as the whites remained united. Thus, if we compare the Jamaican situation with that of Haiti it will be found that the crucial difference lies in the hopeless division of the master class during the course of the successful rebellion in the latter country.[45] The French Revolution created fatal divisions between the loyalists, radical revolutionaries, and bourgeois revolutionaries among the Haitian planter-class, and, what was worse, the political state of the mother country made it impossible for her to assist the planters until it was too late.

Selfish and incompetent though they were, the Jamaican planters always managed at least to present a united front against the rebels and there was never any question of losing the support of the mother country. Thus, when assistance was asked for during the first Maroon war, two regiments of soldiers from Gibraltar were promptly sent to the island, having an immediate impact on those slaves who were not in revolt.[46] Throughout the remainder of the period of slavery there were always at least two regiments stationed on the island. In addition, Jamaica was a frequent port of call for squadrons of the British navy which, on several occasions (not always to the best effect) offered their services in quelling revolts.[47] It is quite possible too, that the terrible reprisal of the whites after they had subdued a rebellion deterred other slaves from rebelling.[48]

This chapter has attempted to explain the reasons for the frequency and intensity of the resistance of the Jamaican slaves to their exploitation, and the reasons why they did not, like their Haitian neighbors, completely succeed. We have seen that most of this resistance came from among that section of them which had already experienced freedom. But in the last days of slavery even the creole slaves, who had never known what it was to be free, began to organize revolts against their masters, and the last and most damaging of all the rebellions remains a living memory of their struggle for something they had never experienced but for which they felt a need sufficiently strong for which to die.

What then, accounts for the presence of this need which seems to survive under conditions which in every way conspire to smother it? Every rebellion, Camus has written, "tacitly invokes a value." This value is something embedded deep in the human soul, a value discovered as soon as a subject begins to reflect on himself[49] through which he inevitably comes to the conclusion that "I *must* become free — that is, that my freedom must be won."[50] In the final analysis it is the discovery of this universal value which justifies and stimulates the most tractable of slaves to rebel. As Camus pointed out: "Rebellion cannot exist without the feeling that somewhere, in some way you are justified. It is in this way that the rebel slave says yes and no at the same time. He affirms that there are limits and also that he suspects — and wishes to preserve — the existence of certain things beyond those limits. He stubbornly insists that there are certain things in him which are worth while . . . and which must be taken into consideration."[51]

Notes

[1] Elsa Goveia, *Slave Society in the British Leeward Islands, 1780–1800*, Unpublished Ph.D. Thesis, University of London, p. 6.

[2] Aptheker, *American Negro Slave Revolts*, p. 162.

[3] *Ibid.*, p. 10, A minimum of ten slaves, etc.

[4] See Chapter 4 on Slave population; also, Pitman, *The Development of the B.W.I.*, pp.373–74.

[5] *Ibid*, pp. 372–73.

[6] K. Stampp, *The Peculiar Institution*, p. 41.

[7] T. Mommsen, *The History of Rome*, vol. III, pp. 306–10; see also W. L. Westermann, *The Slave Systems of Greek and Roman Antiquity*, p. 65.

[8] Pitman, *op. cit.*, pp. 59–60.

[9] Goveia, *op. cit.*, p. 247.

[10] Pitman, *op. cit.*, pp. 379–80, 383.

[11] Aptheker, *op. cit.*, p. 114.

[12] Fuller to Broad of Trade, 27/10/1776: C.O. 138/27.

[13] See Pitman, "Slavery on British West India Plantations in the 18th Century," in *Journal of Negro History*, 11, 584–668. Thus, in 1817 there were 71,777 creole (345 of them from other islands) and only 5,496 African slaves in Barbados. See BPP, Vol. xvi, 1818, p. 111.

[14] Stampp, *op. cit.*, p. 305; the U.S. slave population grew by natural increase at a rate of 23 per cent each decade.

[15] See W. W. Claridge, *A History of the Gold Coast and Ashanti*, vol. 1, pt. 3–4.

[16] Long, *op. cit.*, Bk. 3, p. 470.

[17] J. J. Williams, *The Maroons of Jamaica* (1938).

[18] Goveia, *op. cit.,* p. 245.

[19] Corbett, *Essay Concerning Slavery,* p. 19.

[20] *Ibid.*.

[21] *Report of the Secret C'ttee at Close of Sessions, 1824.*

[22] A. H. Beaumont, "Compensation-Manumission, etc." enclosed in C.O. 137/179.

[23] T. Foulks, *Eighteen Months in Jamaica,* etc. (1833).

[24] Belmore to Board of Trade, 6/8/1831 in C.O. 137/179.

[25] Belmore to Board of Trade, Jan. 6, 1832, C.O. 137/181.

[26] W. L. Westermann, "Slave Maintenance and Slave Revolts," in *Classical Philology,* Vol. 40, 1945, p. 8.

[27] *Ibid.,* p. 9.

[28] Marvin Harris, *Patterns of Race in the Americas,* p. 72.

[29] Pitman, *op. cit.,* 1917, p. 115.

[30] For a description of these tactics, see Dallas, *op. cit.,* vol. I, pp. 39–40.

[31] *Ibid.,* p. 38; also, Lawes to Board of Trade, C.O. 137/13, f. 93.

[32] Edwards, *Proceedings,* pp. IXV–IXXXI; also Dallas, *op. cit.,* vol. II, letters 9–12.

[33] Fuller to Lords, 27/10/1776: C.O. 138/27.

[34] Earl of Balcarres to the Duke of York, 20/5/1795, in *The Maroon War,* p. 7.

[35] Gardner, *op. cit.,* p. 225.

[36] See Evidence of Rev. T. Stewart, "Papers Relating to Rebellion 1832": C.O. 137/181; Evidence of Lieut. Col. Codrington, *ibid.;* Viscount Goderich to Earle of Belmore, *ibid.,* Bleby, *op. cit.,* pp. 138–42.

[37] B. M. Senior, *Jamaica, As it was, As it is, and as it May be* (1835), pp. 183–84.

[38] T. Foulks; *op. cit.,* p. 112.

[39] Aptheker, *op. cit.,* p. 87.

[40] *Ibid.,* pp. 97–100.

[41] *Ibid.,* pp. 79, 81.

[42] Westermann, "Slave Maintenance and Slave Revolts," *op. cit.,* pp. 9–10.

[43] Leslie, *A New History,* p. 311.

[44] See "Cudjoe's Fidelity," C. E. Long Papers, B.M. *op. cit.*

[45] See C. L. R. James, *The Black Jacobins,* pp. 27–61; 174–98.

[46] Hunter to Board of Trade, 13/11/1731: C.O. 137/19.

[47] Hunter to Board of Trade, C.O. 137/20, f. 165; Swanton to Hunter, *ibid.,* f. 184; Extract out of Lieut. Swanton's Journal Rel. to Expedition against the Rebel Negroes, *ibid.,* f. 192–93; Gardner, *op. cit.,* p. 145.

[48] See Review of Rebellions above.

[49] Gabriel Marcel, *The Existential Background of Human Dignity,* p. 87.

[50] *Ibid.*

[51] Albert Camus, *The Rebel,* p. 19.

Suggestions for Further Reading

Additional reading on the "classic debate" over the extent of slave resistance should include Ulrich B. Phillips' *American Negro Slavery* (Baton Rouge, La.: Louisiana State University Press, 1918) and *Life and Labor in the Old South* (Boston: Little, Brown & Company, 1929). Kenneth Stampp's *The Peculiar Institution* (New York: Alfred A. Knopf, 1956) should be read in its entirety. The standard work on ante-bellum slave revolts is Herbert Aptheker, *American Negro Slave Revolts* (New York: Columbia University Press, 1943). Earlier pioneering discussions of slave revolts are Harvey Wish, "American Slave Insurrections before 1861" (reprinted in this volume) and Joseph C. Carroll, *Slave Insurrections in the United States, 1800–1860* (Boston: Chapman & Grimes, Inc., 1938). On the Elkins thesis, one should consult "The Question of Sambo," *The Newberry Library Bulletin* (December 1958), a report of the discussion that followed Elkins' initial presentation of his ideas, and Ann Lane's forthcoming anthology, *The Debate over Slavery: Stanley Elkins and His Critics* (Urbana, Ill.: University of Illinois Press, in press).

In addition to the essays included in Section Four of this volume, the student interested in new approaches to the study of slave resistance should consult several publications of interest. Sterling Stuckey, "Through the Prism of Folk Lore," *Massachusetts Review* IX (Summer 1968), and Bernard Wolfe, "Uncle Remus and the Malevolent Rabbit," *Commentary* (July 1949), illustrate the insights which can be derived from the analysis of folk songs and stories. Other discussions of this theme will be found in Mark Miles Fisher, *Negro Slave Songs in the United States* (Ithaca, N.Y.: Cornell University Press, 1953), and in John Lovell, "The Social Implications of the Negro Spiritual," *Journal of Negro Education* XVIII (October 1939). Contrasting with the widely held view that religion functioned chiefly as a compensatory escape from the harsh realities of slave life, Vincent Harding's "Religion and Resistance among Antebellum Negroes, 1800–1860," in August Meier and Elliott Rudwick, eds., *The Making of Black America* (New York: Atheneum, 1969), is a fresh and provocative examination of the religious motivation that often underlay resistance to slavery. Marion Kilson's "Toward Freedom: An Analysis of Slave Revolts in the United States," *Phylon* XXV (2nd Quarter, 1964), is a suggestive analysis of the distribution of slave revolts in this country and the kind of social environment in which they were most likely to occur. Finally, Winthrop Jordan's *White over Black: American Attitudes toward the Negro, 1550–1812* (Chapel Hill, N.C.: University of North Carolina Press, 1968), makes some illuminating comments regarding the impact of slave revolts on the status of both bondsmen and free blacks.

Recent anthologies which will guide the reader further into the literature of slave resistance and slave society are William F. Cheek, ed., *Black Resistance before the Civil War* (New York: Glencoe Press, 1970); Laura Foner and Eugene Genovese, eds., *Slavery in the New World: A Reader in Comparative Slavery* (Englewood Cliffs, N.J.: Prentice-Hall, 1969); and Allen Weinstein and Frank O. Gatell, *American Negro Slavery: A Modern Reader* (New York: Oxford University Press, 1968).

A Wadsworth Series:
Explorations in the Black Experience

General Editors

John H. Bracey, Jr.
Northern Illinois University

August Meier
Kent State University

Elliott Rudwick
Kent State University

Robert C. Weaver, "The Villain—Racial Covenants"; Robert C. Weaver, "The Role of the Federal Government"; Herman H. Long and Charles S. Johnson, "The Role of Real Estate Organizations"; Loren Miller, "Supreme Court Covenant Decision—An Analysis"; Herbert Hill, "Demographic Change and Racial Ghettos: The Crisis of American Cities"; Roy Reed, "Resegregation: A Problem in the Urban South"

4 The Process of Ghettoization: Internal Pressures

Arnold Rose and Caroline Rose, "The Significance of Group Identification"; W. E. B. Du Bois, "The Social Evolution of the Black South"; Allan H. Spear, "The Institutional Ghetto"; Chicago Commission on Race Relations, "The Matrix of the Black Community"; E. Franklin Frazier, "The Negro's Vested Interest in Segregation"; George A. Nesbitt, "Break Up the Black Ghetto?"; Lewis G. Watts, Howard E. Freeman, Helen M. Hughes, Robert Morris, and Thomas F. Pettigrew, "Social Attractions of the Ghetto"

5 Future Prospects

Karl E. Taeuber and Alma F. Taeuber, "Is the Negro an Immigrant Group?"; H. Paul Friesema, "Black Control of Central Cities: The Hollow Prize"

Suggestions for Further Reading

Black Matriarchy: Myth or Reality?

Introduction

1 The Frazier Thesis

E. Franklin Frazier, "The Negro Family in America"; E. Franklin Frazier, "The Matriarchate"

2 The Question of African Survivals

Melville J. Herskovits, "On West African Influences"

3 The Frazier Thesis Applied

Charles S. Johnson, "The Family in the Plantation South"; Lee Rainwater, "Crucible of Identity: The Negro Lower-Class Family"; Elliot Liebow, "Fathers without Children"

4 The Moynihan Report

Daniel P. Moynihan, "The Negro Family: The Case for National Action"; Hylan Lewis and Elizabeth Herzog, "The Family: Resources for Change"

5 New Approaches

Herbert H. Hyman and John Shelton Reed, " 'Black Matriarchy' Reconsidered: Evidence from Secondary Analysis of Sample Surveys"; Virginia Heyer Young, "Family and Childhood in a Southern Negro Community"

Suggestions for Further Reading

Black Workers and Organized Labor

Introduction

Sidney H. Kessler, "The Organization of Negroes in the Knights of Labor"; Bernard Mandel, "Samuel Gompers and the Negro Workers, 1886–1914"; Paul B. Worthman, "Black Workers and Labor Unions in Birmingham, Alabama, 1897–1904"; William M. Tuttle, Jr., "Labor Conflict and Racial Violence: The Black Worker in Chicago, 1894–1919"; Sterling D. Spero and Abram L. Harris, "The Negro Longshoreman, 1870–1930"; Sterling D. Spero and Abram L. Harris, "The Negro and the IWW"; Brailsford R. Brazeal, "The Brotherhood of Sleeping Car Porters"; Horace R. Cayton and George S. Mitchell, "Blacks and Organized Labor in the Iron and Steel Industry, 1880–1939"; Herbert R. Northrup, "Blacks in the United Automobile Workers Union"; Sumner M. Rosen, "The CIO Era, 1935–1955"; William Kornhauser, "The Negro Union Official: A Study of Sponsorship and Control"; Ray Marshall, "The Negro and the AFL-CIO"

Suggestions for Further Reading

The Black Sociologists: The First Half Century

Introduction

1   Early Pioneers

W. E. B. Du Bois, "The Study of the Negro Problems"; W. E. B. Du Bois, "The Organized Life of Negroes"; George E. Haynes, "Conditions among Negroes in the Cities"

2   In the Robert E. Park Tradition

Charles S. Johnson, "Black Housing in Chicago"; E. Franklin Frazier, "The Pathology of Race Prejudice"; E. Franklin Frazier, "La Bourgeoisie Noire"; Charles S. Johnson, "The Plantation during the Depression"; Bertram W. Doyle, "The Etiquette of Race Relations—Past, Present, and Future"; E. Franklin Frazier, "The Black Matriarchate"; Charles S. Johnson, "Patterns of Negro Segregation"; E. Franklin Frazier, "The New Negro Middle Class"

3   Black Metropolis: Sociological Masterpiece

St. Clair Drake and Horace Cayton, "The Measure of the Man"

Conflict and Competition: Studies in the Recent Black Protest Movement

Introduction

1   Nonviolent Direct Action

Joseph S. Himes, "The Functions of Racial Conflict"; August Meier, "Negro Protest Movements and Organizations"; Lewis M. Killian and Charles U. Smith, "Negro Protest Leaders in a Southern Community"; Ralph H. Hines and James E. Pierce, "Negro Leadership after the Social Crisis: An Analysis of Leadership Changes in Montgomery, Alabama"; Jack L. Walker, "The Functions of Disunity: Negro Leadership in a Southern City"; Gerald A. McWorter and Robert L. Crain, "Subcommunity Gladiatorial Competition: Civil Rights Leadership as a Competitive Process"; August Meier, "On the Role of Martin Luther King"

2   By Any Means Necessary

Inge Powell Bell, "Status Discrepancy and the Radical Rejection of Nonviolence"; Donald von Eschen, Jerome Kirk, and Maurice Pinard, "The Disintegration of the Negro Non-Violent Movement"; Allen J. Matusow, "From Civil Rights to Black Power: The Case of SNCC, 1960–1966"; Joel D. Aberbach and Jack L. Walker, "The Meanings of Black Power: A Comparison of White and Black Interpretations of a Political Slogan"; David O. Sears and T. M. Tomlinson, "Riot Ideology in Los Angeles: A Study of Negro Attitudes"; Robert Blauner, "Internal Colonialism and Ghetto Revolt"; Charles V. Hamilton, "Conflict, Race, and System-Transformation in the United States"

Suggestions for Further Reading